From the
Country

Camden House

A Harrowsmith Anthology

From the Country

Writings About Rural Canada

Edited by Wayne Grady

CAMDEN
•HOUSE•

PUBLISHING

© Copyright 1991 by Camden House Publishing
(a division of Telemedia Publishing Inc.)

For permission to reprint copyrighted
material, acknowledgement is
gratefully made on pages 302-303.

Canadian Cataloguing in Publication Data

Main entry under title:

From the country

ISBN 0-921820-21-6

1. Country life — Canada — Literary collections.
2. Canadian literature (English) — 20th century.*
I. Grady, Wayne.

PS8237.C68F76 1991   C818'.540808'03271
PR9194.52.C68F76 1991   C91-093132-1

For Merilyn

Trade distribution by
Firefly Books
250 Sparks Avenue
Willowdale, Ontario
Canada M2H 2S4

Printed and bound in Canada by
D.W. Friesen & Sons Ltd.
Altona, Manitoba, for
Camden House Publishing
(a division of Telemedia Publishing Inc.)
7 Queen Victoria Road
Camden East, Ontario
K0K 1J0

Cover:
"Porch in Winter" (detail, oil on panel, 15" x 20")
Bruce St. Clair, 1981. Private Collection.
Photo by T.E. Moore, Toronto

Design by
Linda J. Menyes

Colour separations by
Hadwen Graphics Limited, Ottawa, Ontario

Printed on acid-free paper

Contents

Preface

Anyone who reads a fair amount carries around an anthology in his or her head, a mental list of favourite pieces related, at least superficially, by subject or treatment or just plain whimsy — stories or articles that you've wanted to pass along to your friends with the injunction, "Read this." In the 5½ years that I was with *Harrowsmith* magazine, my own internal compendium came more and more to be composed of writings, some fiction, some nonfiction, some by Canadian writers and some by Americans, about rural Canada.

When I set out to turn my list into an actual book, though, I realized two things. First, I'd have to refine the list. It had nature writing on it, for example — wonderful pieces like Roderick Haig Brown's "Place aux Cignes," excerpts from Franklin Russell's *Watchers at the Pond* and Barry Lopez's *Arctic Dreams* — that really belonged in their own anthology. And as a natural consequence of my work at *Harrowsmith,* my list also contained an abundance of farm writing — Carole Giangrande's *Down to Earth* or Gisèle Ireland's *The Farmer Takes a Wife* — that I think gives too political, and therefore dated, a view of rural life. In the end, I chose pieces that were simply about the land and the people. This, for me, was a most unexpected choice and, for that reason alone, seemed the wisest one.

But because it was unexpected, it urged a refinement of what I meant by "rural Canada." Obviously, it didn't mean simply "nonurban Canada," since there are many parts of Canada that are neither urban nor rural — an uninhabited island in the Arctic, for example, or the top of Mount Rundel. It didn't mean "nature Canada" or even "agricultural Canada" either, since there are vast tracts of the country that are neither unspoiled wilderness nor under active cultivation. "Rural" is at once a broader and a narrower description: by defining it simply as "settled Canada," I leave room for writing about miners and fishermen and trappers as well as farmers. "Rural Canada," then, came to mean "populated nonurban Canada."

Narrower and broader. Now that I had a limiting criterion — I would include pieces about nonurban Canada that also had people in them — I was free to come to some kind of conclusion about the relationship between the land itself and the people who live on it. Here, I was in for another surprise. I had expected that the stories would be about how the people shaped the land — how farmers ploughed and cultivated the living prairie, how loggers shaved the mountains or how miners wrestled the northern landscape into an industrial hinterland; what I found instead was that the best writing was more sensitive to the ways in which the land remains implacably itself and, in fact, shapes the people who inhabit it.

When my list was complete, I discovered it held still more surprises. Many of the archetypes of rural Canada — that is, my own preconceptions — were there, but there were also some new insights. I expected a story from rural Nova Scotia to be about fishing and one from British Columbia to be about lumbermen and trappers. And to some extent, I was right: Edna Staebler's *Cape Breton Harbour* is about the fishermen of Neil's Harbour. There is also a short story, however, about Nova Scotia miners (Alistair MacLeod's "The Closing Down of Summer"). Similarly, there are lumbermen and miners in Edward Hoagland's *Notes From the Century Before*. But there are fishermen in British Columbia too, as Edith Iglauer's *Fishing With John* so beautifully attests. And everyone knows that Quebec is French and Ontario is English; but George Johnston's "Bee Seasons" is an English Quebecker's poetic musing on the vicissitudes of rural life, while Maurice Henrie's *La chambre à mourir* expresses the no less poetic reflections of a Franco-Ontarian. Such jolts to our prejudices about rural Canada abound in this collection and were part of the delight in putting it together.

So what does it all add up to? I think I have noticed several things that distinguish my list from other anthologies dealing with the land. Most of the others are American, for one thing, and deal almost exclusively with nature writing; Daniel Halpern's *On Nature: Nature, Landscape and Natural History,* Stephen Trimble's *Words From the Land: Encounters With Natural History Writing* and Russell Martin and Marc Barasch's *Writers of the Purple Sage* are all excellent collections and in part inspired me to compile my own. There is a Canadian anthology — *Marked by the Wild,* edited by Bruce Litteljohn and Jon Pearce — but it is wildly out of date (it was published in 1973) and contains such a disparate wealth of material — poems, short stories, diary excerpts, historical texts — that the overall effect is difficult to pin down. My list, I think, although it includes American and Canadian writers, fiction and nonfiction, still provides a more unified vision of the Canadian landscape and a more vivid and immediate impression of the people who populate it.

One final surprise: almost all the pieces I ended up choosing were written by people who are not native to the area they are writing about. In the American anthologies, most of the writers were born and raised in the regions they study. Most of the writers in this collection are either exiles or travellers, people who are perennially passing through, and the perceptions they bring to the landscapes they visit are the sharp observations of those for whom alertness and sensitivity are tools of survival as well as windows onto a new kind of world. I think this phenomenon — writers from one part of the country writing about a different part of the country — reflects a sense I have that Canadians are vitally interested in and aware of the geographical complexities involved in just being Canadian. In a recent issue of *Harper's* magazine, Barry Lopez delineated a contradiction in the American conception of geography: "The land itself," he wrote, "vast and differentiated, defies the notion of a national geography. Yet Americans are daily presented with, and have become accustomed to talking about, a homogenized national geography, one that seems to operate independently of the land." I don't think Canadians suffer from this paradox. I don't think Canada, vast and differentiated though it certainly is, defies the notion of a unified national entity, and I think that that is partly because Canadians are endlessly interested in and informing themselves about what is going on in the next town, the next province, the next region. I think that helps to explain the success of the CBC, our alarm at the death of VIA Rail and the fact that Canadian writers tend to write books of linked short stories at least as often as they write novels.

Finally, I hope this anthology—a vastly differentiated collection of joyfully disparate and autonomous components that together make up a single vision of the rural landscape—accurately reflects the reality of Canada itself.

—Wayne Grady

John Steffler
from

The Grey Islands

This man waiting there! The thing I can't get out of my mind. The last thing Leonard mentioned. Practically tossed it in the window as I drove off, like it hardly mattered at all. *A madman is living alone out there.* The one inhabitant left. Holding out in the ruined town. Holding the whole island in his head. Thinking it into reality, every stick, every bird. And God knows what else. What will he do when I step into his thoughts?

Cow Head. The sign briefly points, a small road branching winding among dunes, and I want to follow it, imagining long-legged piers, sand spits trailing houses into the sea, but the pavement unrolls smoothly, pulling me north, motion itself a tunnel, a spell, and I miss the turn, my chance of seeing Cow Head the way so many chances beckon flickering past, the streams, the little graveyards fenced with sticks and, high on a gravel beach, a man spreading nets, his single boat perched on a spruce pole ramp, and I want to talk to him, follow into his words, find him alone at dawn launching himself off the Earth's edge, I could do it, stop *here,* let this be the spot it starts, rock, sea opening to whatever they really hold, but I don't, he's gone and I'm still zooming on, the car packed with bedding, boots, maps and the camera ready for use, I take the hills and valleys in a swoop as though the force it took to tear me away from home has not yet spent itself, and I just grip the wheel and go.

This damn guy gets in the way of everything!
Just before setting out, my mind full of that pure island — me rising strong and clear-edged, carving my habits out of the uncut days — I called on Leonard Quinton to say good-bye. It was then, remembering one last bit of advice, he said, "Oh. There might be a man still out on the island. Carm Denny's his name. But don't let him worry you. He's sure to be more afraid of you than you are of him. He'll run and hide if you try to call on him."

And I heard in a daze about Carm Denny's struggles with little folk, listening devices, fire. His charms and offerings and armaments. His notions and visions. And visions! I'm getting visions too! Visions of me trying to meditate on the tide knowing this froth-jawed fighter of devils and Martians is scanning my every move through the sights of a gun. Visions of two gaunt men stalking one another boulder by boulder over the island hills.

Visions! Visions!

Parsons Pond. Low buildings. Take-outs, confectioneries hiked up on stilts next to the shoulder. Girls on the highway three abreast, eating plates of chips. Two-hundred-pounders. Sausaged into their jeans. I wave and give them a wide berth. People always strolling right on the pavement here. Bored and playing chicken with the passing cars. Hunting bold proposals, long rides. And why should cars have the only pavement to themselves? All the rest of the place puddles, potholes and broken rock. And the road is where people have always walked. A guy in a car no more important than someone in rubber boots. I like this. Blocking the highway while you chat with a couple of friends.

Two rock paws, a wharf to the left and a gravel beach between, the cabin crouching there 10 feet from the shore. A white door and a stoop facing the waves. Long grass ducking, galloping up a hill.

A thick pitted padlock is held to the door with spikes. Splinters and holes up and down where it's been ripped out and hammered back. A contest. Keepers and takers. Owners and travellers. Out here, the law is the other way. The right to shelter takes first place.

Stove, table, two metal bunks. Mattresses once used in bayonet practice probably. Yellow linoleum nailed to the table top, dirt deep in the cracks and gashes. Chain oil, blood, rust, fat, scrawled in like a diary. All the guys gutting their ducks and fish here, cleaning their guns, stripping their engines down, hands dripping black spreading bolts and bearings among the plates of beans.

Feathers turn and lift in the corners when you walk. Back of the stove mush-bottomed boxes, plastic bags bloated with rot, shrunk potatoes gone into sprouts, liquid carrots, cabbages yellow, burst.

Men coming out here at the end of their calculations and budgets and fights and fantasies. Building into crude space. A good time hacking and arsing out at the farthest edge. No home. No sofas. No wives. High boots, hunting knives and booze and not getting washed. Then, the time used up or unable to stand it another day, laughing and boasting, they run to their boats or planes, dropping what nobody owns. And half what they brought. Cupboard crammed with stale pancake mix, margarine, sugar, salt. Salt, for godsake! Like me, everybody brings salt. Nobody takes it away.

Nels didn't like bringing his boat up to the wharf here. Too many rocks around. He steered with his body half out the window, fussing and muttering to himself, me watching the other side ready to shout. He saw me ashore, and then we shook hands, and he jumped back on board. "You're the boss here now," he called over the diesel's racket, and he eased his boat back out.

Some of the stories he told. Amazing things.

Nels

It was late in the fall of the year. We was bringin' the mail from Harbour Deep, young Michael Thoms and me, and we put into Hooping Harbour for the night on account of weather. The fishin' families was gone by that time, and there wasn't a soul in the place. Only the old houses back of the cove. You could just pick them out through the blowin' snow. Black holes where the doors and windows used to be.

I remember it gettin' dark around 3 o'clock that day. The fiercest kind of storm out of the nor'east but comin' down over the land there, so we was set pretty comfortable off the lee shore and tied close to the wharf.

We had the lamp lit and was boilin' the kettle for tea, neither of us sayin' much. We was glad to be below, was all. And I was listenin' to the wind, thinkin' she might shift and we'd have to get the boat farther out, when all of a sudden, there was a *clomp-clomp* up on the deck. And the boat tilted and rose again. The hair on the back of my neck stood up stiff as a brush. Somebody had stepped aboard.

I looked at Michael, and his face was white as a sheet. "It must be a big man," he whispers to me, "the way she went down under his feet."

We waited, right still in our seats, but all we could hear was the wind and the water breakin' across the cove. "Hey!" I shouted. "Who's there?" There wasn't a sound up top. I shouted again, "Hey! Who's out there?"

Nothin'. Not a noise.

We sat for the longest time scarcely takin' a breath. And then there came the sound — right faint at first — of someone touchin' the hatch, someone lightly rattlin' the latch, scratchin' the wood with his nails, quietly, quietly. And then louder and louder. I jumped up, grabbed a guttin' knife and threw the hatch back ready for anythin'. Snow and cold wind come pourin' over me, and a cat, an ugly grey cat, jumped down on the table where we had our plates of food.

I'd never seen such an ugly animal before, like somethin' dead that was up walkin' around. Starved, I guess it was. Left behind by some fishermen at the season's end. Its hair matted flat, more like felt than fur, and its head too big for it — round as a ball — with its yellow eyes poppin' out. But the way it moved, that was the worst thing about it. Right stiff it was, and awkward, like there was machinery under its hide instead of bones.

And yet it wasn't slow. I found *that* when I tried to grab it. Stiff as rusty shears, but steady b'y, and desperate not to get caught. I went after it under the table, back of the stove, over the bunks and finally cornered it on some rope up in the bow of the boat. It didn't scratch or hiss or nothin' when I picked it up. It just went on movin' its legs like it was wound up with a key. And the strange thing was, it didn't feel skinny at all. It felt thick and heavy like it was made of wood inside. And it wasn't warm. But cold. Cold as mud.

It made me right sick to my stomach, that thing. Just the feel of it. I hove it overboard the minute I got my head clear of the hatch.

We cast off then and anchored about 50 feet out. Neither of us slept a wink that night.

For the past two days, a longliner has been anchored out in the bay. A cloud of gulls twisting over it shows when the men are gutting their catch. After dark, they run a generator and have a light on deck. The sound of the generator stops, and the light goes out at about 9:30 or 10:00.

Every once in a while during the day, I hear the sudden whine of their speedboat or the deeper beat of their skiff's engine, and I can't help myself: I go to the window or drop what I'm doing to look their way, thinking they might be coming here. But they never are. They zip up the bay somewhere else or out into open water.

When I first got here, I was afraid I'd never be left alone, that having the island's only wharf out front and a spring up behind would mean I'd be on the main track of everyone passing through this part of the world and that there'd always be people camped around or wanting to share the cabin. But since the first day, I haven't seen a soul.

It's as though everyone cleared out or pulled back the minute I arrived. Whether they did this out of considerateness or shyness or hostility is hard to tell.

Nels

There was my great-uncle Aaron Shale, one of the biggest fish-killers on the coast and a right hard man. The way a lot of 'em used to be.

He'd be out with his boy Clement — that woulda been my Uncle Clement — they'd be fishin' with handlines together, and he expected the boy to jig just as many fish as he did, and as big too. He'd take a thick stick out in the boat with him, and if *he* jigged a fish and the boy didn't, he'd give the boy a wallop with the stick. And not lightly neither, I can tell ya. Or if *he* jigged a big fish and the boy only come up with a small one, he'd hit him for that. Oh, yes, sir! Catchin' big fish was the sorta thing ya could do if ya had a mind to, accordin' to Aaron Shale.

And by and by, the boy learned too. For a time there, he could jig fish right alongside his old man.

Under everything, I'm often vaguely anxious, uneasy in the middle of my actions here. So many things strange to me. The tide, for example. It constantly changes the terrain in the low shoreland east of the cabin, and I'm always a bit afraid of getting stranded there.

Paths appear and become submerged. Little knolls that I cross on foot at one time of the day, and fix in my memory as landmarks, at another time of the day have turned to islands.

At low tide, the sea is bordered by natural meadows. The incoming tide slides up into these grassy fields — a beautiful lush sight — but tricky as far as walking is concerned. It's often impossible to know before stepping forward into the tall grass whether my foot will find solid earth or water below the leaves — and if there is water, how deep it will be.

Nels

From the month of June to the month of October, Aaron Shale never took his oilskins off. He never shifted out of 'em night or day for the whole fishin' season. He was that hard at it. At 11:00 or 12:00 at night, he'd come up from his boats and stores, lie down just like he was and get up again at 3:00 in the mornin' to pull his traps.

Nothin' got in *his* way, my son.

And he *drove* his family and them he had hired on, drove 'em just like he drove hisself. Never a minute's rest as long as the fish was runnin'. He wouldn't so much as allow 'em to *speak* unless it had to do with the fish or the traps or what they needed to do. And he never opened his mouth hisself except to give orders, never even spoke to his wife for weeks on end. He'd come in dinnertime — and his food had to be ready, ready and waitin'; she'd watch till he left the wharf and get it all laid out hot before he opened the door — he'd walk across to his chair, sit down, eat and walk out again without sayin' a word, without even lookin' at her while she stood there beside the stove.

The year his boy Clement died, the fish was some thick. They was bringin' in three, four skiff-loads a day. And Aaron wouldn't take the time to put his son in the ground. He ordered the others to salt the boy, just like a fish, and he kept him like that out on his stage till the end of the season. Then they buried him. When the fish was done.

This morning, two fishermen came ashore to get drinking water from the spring. I stepped outside to meet them, and they set their tall buckets down, willing to chat. Cyril Wellon, the skipper, a short thick man with spattered spectacles, was full of talk. His younger brother, Ambrose, nodded and grinned. I invited them in for tea, and they shifted and shuffled a bit, caught in the midst of the day's work, I suppose, threatened with hospitality. As they came in the door, they ducked and smoothed their hair and seemed to think of their dirty hands and rubber clothes, as though expecting something fancy or foreign. Lace doilies, perhaps. China cups. The sight of the tools and decoys put them at ease — the cabin no different from their boat, really — and they took a good look around, praising the cozy nook I had for myself.

They wanted to know what I was doing, of course, and I asked about their work — three cod traps in the island's coves — and about catches, the price of fish, the number of trips they make. They drank one mug of tea each, then had to go, their brothers on the ship no doubt wondering where they'd gotten to.

Cyril and Ambrose were by again today and gave me a "small" codfish — small enough to feed a small family. They had to get back, they said, so we stood outside in the light rain and gazed at the bay, curtains of drizzle drifting out of the south, everything soft and still. I asked if they'd known Carm at all or any other people who used to live here. "Carm? Oh, yes, I know Carm," Cyril said, without even grinning or showing any surprise that I should ask. "I knew most of the folks one time. I was born over there," he said, pointing across the harbour. "Lived there till I was 26. Third from the church. Place isn't standing now." Nor is the church, I noticed. Always people pointing to where they lived, seeing elaborate structures I can't see. Just grass and rock looking secretive. Everything you do swallowed so fast here. Everything taken away. I wonder, does that make life seem long? Looking back, your childhood world vanished, no beginning to life, no clear markers to measure by, maybe you'd feel you've always been here. Or maybe you'd feel you've never been anywhere.

But these people don't measure by what you see. They carry the world around in their heads. All this rock and water is only a backdrop. Like a felt board to which they attach the cutout figures in their minds.

Baked the cod on a large griddle. Been eating it all night. Big curved flakes of meat, packed in like feathers, as Elizabeth Bishop says. Enough here for two days if it keeps.

Carm

The warm spring is what done it. Snow all gone from around the house in April month, flies thick on the windows sooner than I'd ever seen before, and this one day, I kept getting a queer smell. Garbage and stuff I'd heaved outside, I figured, going bad in the sun. I noticed the smell most right in the house, and that should of gave me a clue, but I was busy with this and that and didn't think much of it. That night, I couldn't sleep, the stink was so fierce. And all at once, I remembered. *The ducks!* The dozen or so ducks I still had, skinned and cleaned from the ones I got in the winter. I had them froze out in the pantry in a big wooden tub. At least, they *used* to be froze. That damn south wind. So I lit a candle and went to the pantry and lifted the lid of the tub, and the stink that came out of there belted me like a loose boom, and there was a white flash at my hand, and the next thing I knew, I was down on my arse on the kitchen floor with a dozen skinned ducks zipping around the room with long blue flames shooting out of their hind ends.

I thought I was seeing stars until one of them whooshed by so close it burnt away half my hair. They were smacking the walls and falling and taking off again like balloons when you blow them up and let them go. I saw one shoot under the daybed, and two or three stopped on the ceiling, spinning round and round, and one bust through the window shade, and that peeled up in a skin of flame, and I watched the bird streaking off in a long blue spiral over the island hills like it had come to life again and gotten free. And by now, the curtains were blazing away and the daybed too, and I jumped up and got out of there just in my long underwear.

In an hour, the house was gone. I had to go right down to the shore because of the heat. The walls and roof lifted up with a roar like burning wings, everything inside blinding red, table and chairs, cupboard and stove, everything, every bit standing just like I left it but made of red coal. Glowing. And you could see through it all like glass. Even my coat on the hook was a mesh of red wire.

And then it came down.

Soundless. And I had to fall in the water to keep from being burnt too, and the sparks and spinning bits climbed straight up the sky. All I owned. All my people had ever owned.

Cyril

We was froze in seven months of the year out here. There was no comin' or goin' then, sir. Except for the time Frank Tobin walked over the ice to Englee for the mail. A day out and a day back. Seen it myself. He come in over the tickle there, the mailbag froze right to him. He'd been into the water once or twice, and he lifted his arm and wanted to give a cheer, but his moustache was froze that thick, he couldn't open his mouth. But that was only one man ever done that, and he was lucky, I'd say, with the ice shiftin' and shovin' around out there every day. It *might* be solid across for a couple hours, then it might be a couple miles of rough sea, or maybe you'd drift away on a big pan, or a storm come up and you'd wander off the wrong way. That's 15 miles of the worst kind of ice for half the year. So you was stuck, see. And you wanted things laid up in advance. There was the salt fish you'd made in the summer, and some would order a barrel of salt meat, and there was a scattered rabbit or partridge you'd get in on the height of land, but ducks was the big thing in the winter. Ducks! My son, you'd never see the like of the ducks here in the wintertime. The shoal water out there where it don't freeze is where they come down. In their thousands. And their tens of thousands!

Usually at twilight it'd be. Down and down they'd come, and you'd wonder where in the name of God they was all comin' from. Out of a winter sky like that with nothin' around but ice for so many miles. And as they come down, they'd all be callin' at once. Not quack, quack, quack or whatever you'd think. But callin' together like that, the sound is somethin' you'd never dream could come from a duck. Big and loud as the wind but real high. A bit like a howl and a bit like a scream, and it rises and falls, rises and falls in waves, and it's comin' from everywhere. Not just from the ducks. But from under the ice. From behind you. From over the hills. The whole sky seems to be howlin', howlin'. Closin' in.

The first time I heard it, I was only a youngster then, and it made me cry. Not because I was scared. It just sort of hauled the sobs up out of me. It was the sound of food, for one thing, I guess. But there's more to it than that. Anyway, we'd load up our guns, old muzzle-loaders, and get out on the ice as close to the open water as we could. Then we'd lie flat on our backs and wait for the ducks to come in over us. I'll never forget this one time. It was fierce cold. Thirty below. And a wind comin' down from the nor'west. My father, my uncle, my cousin Eustace and me went out just before nightfall, a good half-mile over the ice, and lay down at the edge of the lead. I'd of been about 17 at the time. Eustace, he was my best chum then, was a year older than me. He'd been ailin' a lot that winter. Coughin' blood. Well, we lay there with the snow driftin' over us and got our guns set. We used to put everythin' into those guns for shot. Nuts, bolts, nails and such. I'd been scoutin' around for somethin' to use in mine that time, and my grampa said to me, look, how'd this be, and he got his gold pocket watch that hadn't worked for a year or more. Salt was into it, he said, no use keepin' the thing around. So he took it apart with a hammer and shears and fed all the little wheels and springs down the muzzle of my gun. Dropped the hands in last and rammed in a bit of brin. That oughta bring you luck, he said.

So I was lyin' there feelin' my body freeze and prayin' I'd soon be able to blow the b'jesus out of a dozen or so ducks, when finally, I heard the howlin', way off first, and they started comin' down out of the dark. The first ducks always come straight down on the open lead, and the ones after them swing round in the air and hold up a bit and then come down on the backs of the ones that are already pitched, and the ones after them do the same. In waves, like. Howlin' and singin' like Judgement Day. It takes a long time for them all to get landed. And those that are still comin' in don't head for the open water at the edge of the lead, they just keep wheelin' round and comin' down in the centre, ducks on ducks on ducks, and the crowd of them spreads out on the water like molasses pourin' out of a jug. When the flock swung round so it was comin' down over us, we all let fly up into them. Four long flames and I said good-bye to my grampa's watch, and all the other ducks went off the open water again, breakin' one another's necks in midair.

Ninety-seven birds we got at the one time. And you take what you get with the one shot,'cause there's no loadin' again with your hands froze. We were up gettin' the ducks into the sacks we'd been lyin' on, and in the dark, I didn't notice at first that Eustace wasn't doin' the same as the rest of us. I went over to him, and he was lyin' there half covered with ducks. He was stone dead. Already nine parts froze. The funny thing was, he'd fired his gun along with the rest of us. The kick of the old bitch must of knocked the last bit of breath out of him.

The coarse grass growing around the cabin draws its life from a layer of black peat three or four inches deep at the most. Below that are stones and pure sand. I cut squares of turf with an old splitting knife, stab, claw the tangled wads free. The smell that rises is raw and sour — faint bog fumes, wet minerals — the end of some slow process having little to do with the history of animals. I tear the clumped roots, examining them. Prod the exposed earth, turning the grains with my knife. No bugs or grubs. Nothing wriggling or digging or scampering. The few worms I find are thin match-sized things, anaemic, nearly white. Not enough to go over a hook.

I look in various places — high spots, wet spots, under moss, under weeds — I lift stones and pieces of wood, all the fisherman's tricks. At one of the fallen houses, I guess where the door would have been and dig, imagining kitchen scraps, dogs, people pissing, serenading the stars, the whole fertile trail of life. But whatever there was to eat here has been eaten long ago, and the worms have starved or moved on. Resettled like everyone else. My only hope is the house most recently used. I straighten my back, take my knife and jar and walk the half-mile to Carm Denny's shack.

And here, before Carm's door, under the first plank I turn: blood-brown worms, fat, quickly contracting like tendons suddenly laid bare. I move fast too, getting most of them.

Bent, I circle the building grubbing and rooting. Every shingle and stick I lift yields bait. Things Carm ate and didn't eat, turned to worms. A kind of organic shadow of the man. A lingering aura of his heat and movements stirring in the sod. The worms feeding under his window at night when he was here, curling and drawing themselves through years of what he had thrown away, sliding into the sound of his humming, his lonely talk, into and out of the warm rectangle of light that lay in the grass.

And I feel a bond with Carm, as though I am touching some extended parts of him, veins that had spread from his body taking root in the land from which he had never divided himself. I move swiftly, borrowing his life, his island's life, feeling it coiling, pulsing under my hands.

Cyril

The last time I saw Carm was end of September a year ago. Last trip out for the season for us. We'd taken our traps up, and I went along over to see how he was set for the winter, tell him we wouldn't be back till spring. Everything fine, he said, lots of fish and flour and whatnot, startin' to haul wood. Garden okay. So we talked a bit, and I said, well, mind the women don't run away with you out here. I liked to rib him about that, since he was always sayin' he'd seen women walkin' around the cove. He chuckled a bit, sort of shy-like the way he did; then he come up close to me, and he says right serious, Cyril, he says, I want to warn you. Don't come ashore here no more. Stay on your boat, and keep her out in the bay. The cliffs, he said, and he pointed to all them big rocks up behind you here, the cliffs are all gonna come crashin' into the harbour any day. And he looked at me that strange, sir, I swear his eyes didn't have no colour in them, no centre to them at all.

Walked to the old settlement and visited three houses I hadn't seen before, ones overlooking French Cove. The ground is high there and the houses large, noble. Statements of grace and ownership. Now, of course, the windows and doors are empty sockets. Great rents gape in the walls, and the sea, sky and rough hills show through. Have eaten through. The way stones wear out shoes and water eats through steel.

Approaching the first house, I sensed what the ghosts of the place were thinking, and I felt foreign, ashamed, standing there with my knapsack and fishing rod and camera. I left my things in the grass and stepped through the doorway into a colourless space. Among fallen ceilings and shelves. Lost life. Labour nothing can call back. The torture of being deserted given form. An abandoned child built these walls with its cries.

But a tough skeleton too. The core of what happened here. Calm talk of people nailing the rafters up. A clapboard shell. Holding their lives in the hurling winter wind.

Steady rain all day and the air still. Sweeping the cabin this morning, I lifted a piece of linoleum and found a trapdoor, the entrance to Carm's root cellar — just a hole in the rock really, neatly packed with peat. All that seemed to be down there at first was mummified potatoes, and then I noticed a biscuit tin set back on a ledge under the cabin floor. Inside the tin was a Bible, and in the Bible a photograph of a girl. I took these up into the light and spent a long time looking at them, wondering why they were there. The girl, seen from the waist up, is standing against a white clapboard wall. She is wearing a kerchief and a dark coat buttoned to the throat. Her hair, where it shows at her forehead and above one shoulder, is black. She is handsome, her face lean, her jaw and cheekbones strong. Her eyes are large and dark by the look of it. But there is no light in her face, no smile, no desire to please. She is not angry, nor is she frightened or withdrawn into herself, but she is guarded all the same. She does not like whoever is looking at her. I would guess she is 18 or 19. There is nothing written on the back.

The red ribbon bookmark and the photo were both at the same place in the Bible: Genesis 32, all about Jacob's travels. I thought about keeping the Bible up to read but finally decided to put it back where I found it, the tin tightly shut and the photo inside.

Carm

I wasn't always alone, like people think. The year after my mother died, a boat coming late from the Labrador called in here. Had lost its fresh water in a gale and needed to make repairs, so they anchored in the bay and they used my wharf, and twice they had supper with me. There was a girl among them, had been all summer making fish on the Labrador, and I took a liking to her. She was straight and beautiful, and I knew she liked my place by the way she stood at the window, the way she touched the lamp, the chair, and I said to her right out, you'll stay with me, won't you, and I showed her what I had for the winter, potatoes and turnips under the floor, fish in the stage, flour and butter and that, and showed where my dad's house used to be, the black ashes still there, and I said I was saving to build it up again, a two-storey house with windows over the bay. And she said she'd stay. And the night before they sailed, her uncle who was captain and head of the crew paid her off and married us right here. We put our hands on the Bible, and it was done.

The fish was still running here then, and every day, I was working bringing them in, and my God, that woman could work too, and we scarcely spoke together for over a week. And then one night, she started to talk to me. Her father had been a mariner out of Trinity Bay. When she was 7 years old, he was lost at sea, and her mother had no means of keeping her youngsters fed, so they went to the aunts and uncles. Some to St. John's, some to Placentia Bay. Her mother died of consumption when she was 10. She remembered it all so clearly still. The way her mother had cried saying good-bye to her. And she said she hated the uncle that took her in.

That winter didn't last any time at all. She used to go with me everywhere, back over the island for ptarmigan and for timber to ship around in the spring. And at night, we'd talk and sing together — and the songs that woman knew! The hundreds of songs she knew! In the spring, though, she didn't want people to know she was here. If anyone came ashore, she'd go and hide. Once, we heard voices right close to the house, and she quick got into the turnip cellar under the floor. I tried to tell her it didn't matter a sheep's fart, but she wouldn't have people looking at her, people I knew from Conche and Englee is what she meant. I don't know what the reason for that was. By ourselves, we were happy as birds.

When the baby was on its way, I was some glad. Made a small bed from young spruce and painted it green. A son or daughter, it didn't matter which. The problem was, she couldn't be having the baby alone. I said I'd get a woman from Englee when the time was near. But she wouldn't agree. Wanted to go to some people of hers in St. John's. And when a boat bound that way came by, they took her along. She told me she'd write, and I was going to go when the season was done and bring her home. And a letter came then, after a couple months, a letter her aunt had wrote saying my wife was dead. My wife and our baby both. I went with the man who'd carried the letter out and got to St. Anthony and finally a boat from there to St. John's. And I found the house of the aunt. But the woman looked at me like I was lord of the plague. Made me stand in the door, and all she would say was my wife and child were buried down to the Belvedere. I went and walked through the rows of crosses and stones, the snow on the ground by then. Her name wasn't anywhere. At the big cathedral, I spoke with the man with the books and lists of names, and he told me he had no record of her being buried there. The bitch of an aunt didn't want to see me again, but I pounded and pounded and made her open the door, and she handed me out a photograph of my wife and said to go back to the graveyard again, that the girl was gone for sure the same as the uncle was. And she shut the door in my face, and that was that.

I took the train across the island then, my only time on a train, all the ponds and barrens covered in snow, and I travelled by snow machine and dog team down from Deer Lake to Englee. But nobody wanted to go to the Grey Islands by then with the coves freezing across. I spent the rest of the winter with people in Englee, cutting wood in the bush and mending nets. I never told anyone why I'd been gone. I was waiting, that's all, waiting and seeing my house that I couldn't get back to. Empty. Frozen and dark.

I'm thinking now about next year, about fixing this place up. Should write to Carm and see if he'd mind. Maybe he'd sell me the place, though Cyril tells me to do what I want, that Carm's beyond all that and won't ever be back. And if everything worked out, I could bring some paint and window glass and tools and fix Carm's old boat too, learn how to do that, and bring Peter and Anna and Karen here. Offer this power to them if I can.

Edna Staebler
from

Cape Breton Harbour

Wednesday, August 15   A family of tourists brought me back to Neil's Harbour before noon. We stopped on the way to watch a doe and her fawn in the woods, to drink at a stream where we saw the swift shadows of trout. We examined a stone replica of the huts used by crofters tending sheep in the Scottish hills — "the lone shieling of the misty island where still the blood is strong, the heart is Highland, and we in dreams behold the Hebrides." We admired the Big Intervale and the grandeur of Sunrise Valley. The tourists spoke about their motor trip; I talked about my fishing village at whose sight I had the feeling of coming home.

There is nothing to do this afternoon: the water is grey as the cloudy sky, gulls fly over the land — a sign of storm — a snapper boat bound for the safety of Dingwall Harbour rises and falls behind the waves. Men sit idly in lee of the stages; women walk with arms and fingers modestly straightened against their thighs as skirts cling and billow; children, like leaves blown across a common, run quickly along with the wind; chickens resent their ruffled feathers erected like fan-shaped sails; cows lie unperturbed by fences, flicking flies with switchbroom tails.

I've slept a little while, I've written letters, I've walked on the stones along the shore. Broken shells, pieces of rope, bits of driftwood, bones of fish, the sole of a little child's shoe have told me that life is full of impressions: things I know someone would love bring a fleeting thought of friends who are far away; often the thought lingers lovingly, poignantly, it does not make me sad, there is no conflict, I am secure in knowing I have friends.

"Always writin', ain't you?" Henry Rider, carrying an empty bucket, sat beside me. "Must be someone you's awful fond of gettin' all them letters."

"Don't you write to your family in Newfoundland?"

"No, I never writes 'em, all that matters is I'm alive; if I ain't, they'd hear soon enough. I'm not much of a hand fer writin', never know what to say and 'tain't easy for me to put it down. I don't know how you doos it so fast. I guess you must a got a lot o' schooling, haven't you?"

"I suppose so."

"That's what I figgered. I says to men, 'That girl's eddicated,' I says, 'her's always writin'; we thinks might be her's igerant 'cause 'er don't know nothin' about what we got round 'ere and is always askin' how we doos things and what's they for, but that's best way for gettin' eddicated,' I says." Henry cut off a wad of tobacco and shoved it inside his cheek.

"Ain't like one feller I knowed had a lot o' schoolin'; nice feller 'e were too, lived in Rose Blanche in summertime, and d'you know what 'e done? He'd get used-up old stamps and stick 'em down into a book. Yes, dear, ye never seen anythin' so foolish like as that man, full growed, sittin' there stickin' them stamps and lookin' at 'em like they was a fortune 'e'd got hold of. One day, I tooked he a packet o' letters I found in old strongbox o' me grandf'er. Well, say, I thought 'e were takin' a fit when 'e seen 'em, and when 'e stopped ravin', 'e took wallet out o' britch pocket and hands me a five-dollar bill. But I give it back. I wouldn't take money for no used-up ol' stamps ain't no good for nobody." Henry stiffly got to his feet and picked up his pail. "I got t' go now and fill this drat bucket for Hattie Buffet. See you around."

Most of the brooks, as the wells of the village are called, have been dried up for some time. The people at the top of the hill were the first to start carrying water about a mile from the spring behind the preacher's house. Now, those living at road level are carrying too. The water in the Malcolms' well is very low: instead of the dipper, there is now a cup beside the pail in the bathroom.

The best place to bathe is in the Pond formed by a stream whose mouth is blocked by a strip of beach, making a pool with water warmer and calmer than the North Atlantic, except when the sea is wild enough to break through the sandbar and mingle its salt water with the fresh. It is glorious for swimming, with firm white sand on its floor — and so well secluded that I can take off my suit in the water and have a bath with Miss Katie's pink soap.

That is what I was doing this afternoon when clumsy big Max crashed down the steep path to the beach. I was still as a fish in the water, and he didn't know I was there; he came up to my things on the stones, gave them a quick going over, picked up a slipper, dropped it, then crossed the sand and looked at the sea. He came back to my coat and stood over it, head inquiringly on one side. I splashed my hand in the water. He saw me then, wagged his great tail and barked.

I've discovered a perfect place from which to watch the sunset; the top of a fence isn't cozy, but after boards and rock and bumpy ground, the surface of a rail is merely a different shape to be impressed on my posterior. Halfway between Alec's house and Mrs. Pride's, I can look at the rosy light on the fishing boats in the bay, I can tell if there is activity on the dock; turning my head, I can watch anyone who comes along the main road and the lane that winds up to the houses on the hill. I am like a decoy; everyone who passes can see me and come to talk to me if they will — and I hope they will.

I hadn't been sitting long tonight when a fisherman came along: "Hain't gone yet, I see. Must loike this place."

"It's so different from what I'm used to; I'm liking it more every day."

"I guess it were some strange for you at first." He leaned against the fence beside me, looking at the bay. A man with a gentle face, blue eyes and sandy hair showing round the back of his swordfishing cap, he is the man who gave me the sword on the night I came to the Harbour. His name — Miss Laurie told me — is Matt Clipper. He turned to me with a grin: "I guess you thinks we talks funny round 'ere, eh? We calls everything 'e, and we says bean 'stead of bin and heyess for eyes. Hit's 'ard on young uns goin' to school, teacher learns 'em one thing and they comes 'ome and we says something helse and they don't know which be roight. I tells mine, teacher knows best and they gotta teach we." Matt Clipper's voice was soft and slow; I longed to put down every word he said, but no writing could reproduce the heartwarming way he said it.

"When you first come, we says, 'That one don't come from Upper Canada, must come from States.' "

"What made you think that?"

"Them from hinland be always findin' things wrong with we, always tellin' us what they got better at home, loike we didn't 'ave nothin'. Americans seems to think Harbour's roight good." He took out a pocketknife and opened it. "We had a couple stay to our house one year, wouldn't moind seein' 'em come back. After they left, they wrote a letter and sent things to the children at Christmas — dolls 'n' that." He took a slice off the fence rail. "We don't git tourists 'ere 'cause there's no room for 'em, season's too short for us to spend money fixin' up places." He cut another shaving. "You never can tell about people neither," he said. "During war, a man and 'is woman come round 'ere in car. I said they was Germans and told Alec, but 'e says, 'Oh, no, they's much too friendly, couldn't be Germans.' Well, say, they had cameras, and they walked round all over this here and snapped and snapped. They got men to take 'em out in boats and asked 'em to go near shore. What's more, they kep' drawin' maps, we ketched 'em at it, maps of whole shore round 'ere they had. I knowed they was Germans, and sure as hell, when they went to Sydney, they was nabbed."

Matt whittled a few slices. "Lots o' people comes round 'ere in summer and wants rides in boats; some even offers to pay fer it. They says, 'Whoi don't you take tourists out instead o' fishin'? You'd make more money.' " Matt raised his head proudly. "We tells 'em we's fishermen, just loike they's lawyers er doctors er whatever they is. Fishin' is our job."

"Where I live, people go fishing for fun."

Matt looked up from his whittling with a twinkle in his blue eyes. "Maybe you thinks we's lazy, layin' round stages loike we doos?"

"I have wondered that," I admitted.

"Fisherman's got to wait fer a cam," he said, "got to have toime fer settin' and mendin' 'is naits. When a man is fishin', 'e works terrible hard; 'e's got to make enough money in six months to last 'im all year. Soon as 'e's got it, 'e can quit if 'e's moinded, no use workin' at fall fishin' if storehouse is filled and ye got money to do ye till spring; woife don't loike fer her man to be out on the water when it's woild and cold." Matt raised his cap and scratched his head with a finger. "You don't need a pile o' money round 'ere," he said, "not loike ye do where you's from. We doos everything for ourself that needs doin': builds our own houses, makes our own boats, fixes our engines; we go huntin', doos our own butcherin', cut and chop our wood." Matt snapped his knife shut. "So long as we got enough to keep us warm and full and droi, we don't need more. I always think if folks be koind and got their health, that's the most himportant."

Two little blond girls with braids came up and pulled at Matt's hands. They wouldn't speak because I was there and they were shy, but somehow, he knew and told me they wanted him to help find the cow that had not come from the hills to be milked. Hand in hand, laughing and talking, they walked down the road toward the Trail — while I stayed on my fence rail with the glowing conviction that I had been given a glimpse of the heart of Neil's Harbour.

A long-faced fisherman came from the direction of the stages, rested his arms on a fencepost beyond me, stared at the water and very soon strolled away. Several people passed by me on the road. Then I saw Andrew Clipper, the lighthouse keeper, coming down the hill carrying his lantern, and I slipped off my rail to follow him.

For me, Neil's Harbour is dominated by the Light. No matter where I wander, it is the focal point of all I see. When I sit on the fence to watch the fishing boats at sunset, the Light beams protectively down on them. When I look from my bedroom window at the cluster of stages, I see the Light above them. From the beach, I see the Light over the jetties across the bay. When I walk along the roads from the Cove or the Trail, I walk toward the Light. Everything in the village has a background of sea, rock or hill, but the Light rises against the sky. Built on the highest part of the Point near the edge toward the open sea, it stands aloof and alone, sturdily guiding and guarding. Its sloping white sides, its red metal cap with the balcony round it have style as they rise into the blue; it is modern, it is classic, it is beautiful; it is the symbol of security for all who live by the sea.

The keeper of the Light, a thick little dark man who looks like a Scottie, took me with him to watch him perform the most responsible job in the Harbour. He unlocked the lighthouse door, filled a can from one of the barrels of kerosene that stood in a small square room, then climbed the narrow stairway to the trapdoor entrance of the metal chamber that houses the Light. There, he removed the duck curtains from the windows and polished the sparkling glass while I looked with wonder at the dim outline of St. Paul's Island beyond faraway Cape North and Smokey Mountain 20 miles to the south.

Turning toward the Light, I examined the heavy, prismatic magnifying glass supported by shining brass, which sends the rays of the two-wicked lamp into the darkness over the sea. "Everything looks so new and clean," I said. "How long has the Light been here?"

"It ain't new, miss," the keeper showed me the thickness of the paint, " 'twere built in 1893, but we keeps it careful and shining like, 'cause lives might be lost if it ain't kep' good. Lots o' fine ships went down off this coast before the lights went up. But only one I knows of got wrecked off the Point since this light come on: the *Velundie,* a large vessel struck on the east side with nobody lost; that were in 1921, and she stayed on rocks till next year.

"The movin' pitcher *The Sea Raiders* was made 'ere because they needed a wreck fer it. They took one o' their women — awful pretty lookin' she was, but painted — and dipped 'er in water and brought 'er in on a stretcher like she was drownded — we watched 'em doin' it — and they asked us to walk across the beach with our hand barrels o' fish, and they took our pitchers in our oilskins just like we was workin', and some people that knowed us seen the pitcher in town and told us we looked right natural."

On my way down from the Lighthouse, I saw Molly leaning in the doorway of her home. "What was you doin' at all day?" she called. "I thought moight be ye'd come round." Warmed by her greeting, I sat on the stoop beside her. "My Gohd," she cried, looking past me, "half me washing's blowed away in the gale." I moved to retrieve it, but she shrugged her shoulders. "Don't bother none, it'll come back." She smiled and nodded her head as diapers and dishtowels clung to the fence. "Lucky it never blowed in with the pig."

A miniature of Molly and a smaller solemn-eyed child with blond curls and an alarmingly red face squeezed between us. "Gwendoline, take that lipstick from Frillie, there ain't nothin' left to it, and last week, it were that tall." She held apart her thumb and fingers, smiling her carefree smile.

"Frillie's an odd name, Molly, where did you get it?" I asked.

"Fred give it to 'er. Oi don't know where it come from, I think he made it oop," she grinned. "Noice though, ain't it?"

We sat for a while in silence as a schooner came into the bay to land a fish at the dock. The children ran down to watch it. "Aren't you afraid the little ones will fall in?" I asked Molly.

"Oh, I goes down and looks now and again, but roight now, with all them men down there, somebody'd fish 'em out quick enough. They couldn't be in more than a little whoile." Molly turned toward the main road. "Fred's drivin' Gladdie's car over to Dingwall tonight, takin' Clipper boys with." We saw the car go up the steep lane that wound around the houses. "Now, if that ain't loike Fred," Molly said, "goin' way up there after the bastards. Whoi couldn't them come down that hill? Can hardly cloimb it with a car, but Fred doos everything for anybody if they asks him to." There was pride and affection in Molly's voice. She sat down beside me. "Oi wonder where to they're goin' at over in Dingwall, must be boats in from Newfoundland with rum."

We didn't talk much after that, but Molly kept smiling with a mysterious half-impish twinkle as if she knew a wonderful secret. And I felt unaccountably as if I knew one too.

When Molly went to tuck her youngest in bed, I walked past the stages where the middle-sized boys were playing a game that might have been cricket if they'd had a ball and bat instead of a rusty tin can and a stick. The men sitting on the grass were encouraging them, and there was a moment of excitement whenever someone hit the can and ran for a goal.

The long evenings at the Harbour are difficult for me. I don't know what to do with myself except to walk along the Road to the Cove where people always stroll; with its grassy banks and concealing spruces, it is the Road for romancing — unlike the open road from the Trail, which can be seen by everyone in the fishermen's houses on the hill.

It was nearly dark when three little girls came strolling. I said hello, and they walked beside me without speaking. They were perhaps 11 years old with wispy blond hair and flimsy cotton dresses. Not knowing what to talk about, I unfortunately reminded them that school would start in a couple of weeks. They groaned. "But maybe it won't," one of them said. "Cove boys broked windows in schoolhouse, and they ain't got glass to fix 'em."

"They ain't got no teachers yet neither," said another. "We needs two, there's over a hunnert to be teached."

"Won't the ones you had last year be back?"

"No, we has different teachers every year, they never comes back, does they, Ellen? They don't loike in winter when we's froze up, can't git out till spring, mail sometimes don't come for three weeks, and they can't hear from their folks. Anyhow, they say it's good to change 'em, then us don't git sassy with 'em loike we doos if we knows 'em too long."

"Last one we had were only 17 year old. She were roight smart too."

"What will you do if you can't go to school?"

They giggled. "Help at home, scrub, wash dishes." Ellen lamented, "We got 12 into our house, Susan and Ada only got eight."

"Where do you belong?" Susan asked me.

I told them.

"Is Ontario far?" Ada, the little one, wondered.

"Roight far," Ellen answered. "D'you do much swordfishing there?"

As we approached the Hall, we heard feet clattering on the outside platform where several young boys were shoving each other around. "Let's go down and tarment en," my little pals suggested. They ran down the slope and stood wistfully on the edge of the dance floor. The boys stood still, and no one spoke. The little girls came back to me. "You might git awful lonesome here by yerself," Susan said.

"I do sometimes."

"You better stay with we," Ellen offered.

"Yes, stay with we," the small one echoed.

We walked back toward the village. Men and boys sitting high on the rocks at the side of the Road flashed a light on us. "Come on," Ellen said excitedly, "let's go oop." They climbed the rocks into the darkness, and I walked on alone. In the wan light, I saw movement at the sides of the Road. Several boys and girls passed me with their arms around each other, a few walking alone said good evening; I heard men come up behind me.

"You look awful lonesome tonight," one said.

"Don't you want company?" asked another.

Farther along, I heard a softly spoken, "Come with me, dear."

I walked faster. There was a restless feeling about the Road; a wondering and waiting and wanting — and a shyness, thank God.

Sunday, August 19 You can tell when Sunday comes in Neil's Harbour: the boats are anchored though the sea is calm, the Point and the wharves are deserted, there are many people on the road. Little boys in clean jerseys look freshly scrubbed, little girls wear hats over proudly shining faces, men have changed their swordfishing caps for wool ones, their heavy clothes for cotton shirts and blue serge trousers, women wearing figured rayon dresses and straw hats carry hymn books. Everyone walks toward the little seaside church where the black-clad Anglican clergyman receives his flock with outstretched arms.

Across the road, the white-steepled church hiding amongst the spruces has no resident preacher. There are only a few Presbyterian families in the two villages; not Newfoundlanders and not fisherfolk, they are old Cape Bretoners and very proud Scots: the Malcolms, the Maclennans, the awesome rich McKays who own half the Cove, the doctor and Gladdie Buchanan who works for the government and reads the *Atlantic Monthly.* The women are clannish and visit one another; though they live in the village, they seem to be not of it.

Our dinner was late today because we had to wait for the deaconess to be brought from Cape North after her service in the church there. She preaches to the Presbyterians of the Harbour and the Cove every other Sunday evening during the summer. Though often smiling with an exaggerated show of pleasure, her face is sadly disfigured by deeply puckered creases. She sighed as she took her place at the table. "There was only a handful at Cape North church today," adding with asperity, "so I gave them a good bawling out to make them feel ashamed of themselves."

Katie, serving our food from the kitchen stove, announced, "We're having chicken."

"Which one?" I asked.

Miss Laurie murmured, "The white rooster."

"Oh, no, not the one that gave you so much pleasure?"

"We haven't had chicken for a long time," Katie said defensively. "We couldn't keep feeding him forever."

"But how will you know when to expect a guest?"

"The little brown rooster will crow on the steps now," Miss Laurie assured me.

I never thought I could enjoy eating anything I had known personally, but I found the white rooster a very pleasant change from codfish.

There is an aimlessness about this afternoon. The men sit together by the stages or walk around as if looking for something to happen, women chatter on front stoops, young men and girls walk along the Road, children play carefully in their Sunday clothes.

Down on the fish wharf, looking at things in the water, five little boys are leaning over the edge. "Look at de baits," one screams as a school of minnows flashes past. "Jeez, can't them swim some pretty?"

"Dey's not swimmin', dey's just goin' along."

"See dat lopster down dere under 'at mess o' fish guts?"

"Wisht I had a pole; Chester, fetch a pole." The smallest boy runs to the shore.

"Dere's mack'rel."

"How can you tell?" I ask. They all stare at me as if I'd asked how they know a cow is a cow.

"No mack'rel where you live?" I'm asked.

"There's no water."

"No wahter atall?" My questioner is Arlie, Molly's son, 7 years old. He is the boy who caught the bird on the windy day, and he is not unlike a tern: his nose, a bit too long for his thin little pointed face, is a beak; his eyes are dark and bright; his hair, cut on the bias over his forehead, is like the black cap of the seabird; he has the same wild look of flight and freedom. "Can you walk anywheres and not go owerboard?" he asks me.

"Yes, there's just pavement and buildings."

"Moi jumpins, must be a funny place." He looks at me curiously, his head on one side.

"I sees a heel!" someone exclaims. We are kneeling, the slim little bodies are taut, the tanned faces eager. "See en down dere in de kalop?" It takes a moment for me to find the snaky body below the swaying kelp.

"Let's git en, Rhindrus."

"Dose heels be hard to keel."

"Here's rock." Freddie throws it. Freddie is Arlie's slightly older brother.

" 'E 'it en, rock were roight on en. Be 'e keeled?" Arlie shrieks with excitement.

"You got to have crowbar to kill dem t'ings."

"My son, you'll never see dat heel again, when you hits 'em, dey goes roight off as far as South Point." For a moment, the children are still; I hear the gentle flip-flop of water against the cribbing of the dock.

"Cheesus, dere's dat cat." Arlie points excitedly to a white form floating near the shore. "She's swelled up beeg as a peeg, ain't she?"

"Be 'er guts hangin' out?" Freddie asks.

"Can't see en," Arlie answers.

"Now what'll 'appen to 'er?" Rhindrus wonders.

"Oh, she'll go on up shore, floies will git onto 'er, and she'll stink awful."

"How'd she get into the water?" I ask.

Arlie tells me. "Her were roight tame, and they ketched 'er and put 'er in bag, put string round 'er and tied rock on. De bobbles come up, and 'er drownded."

"Why did they do it?"

"Her eyes was stuck shut, and her couldn't see none."

"Her were bloind," Freddie explains.

"Were awful thin too," says Rhindrus.

"But 'er's roight beeg and swole now, ain't she?" Arlie exults.

"Let's go to the other side," I suggest, and the children follow me. "There's a big sword," I point to it in the water.

"Freddie, woman wants sword, go git en," Arlie says.

"Oh, moi, ain't 'e a long one? I'll git a pole." Freddie runs off the dock.

"Once I ketched a skulkin and a flatfish," Arlie tells me.

"What's the difference?"

Arlie is dumbfounded by my ignorance. "Don't you know?" He frowns. "Skulkin's got big fins and little horns loike on top," he wriggles two fingers on either side of his head. "Flatfish ain't."

"Dere's dat lopster down dere still eatin'," someone says.

"Lopster's got 'is teeth in 'is claws," Arlie tells me.

"No, 'e ain't," Rhindrus scoffs.

"Well, 'e got little lumps, loike," Arlie argues. He looks at me. "You got lopsters where you's at?" The little boy shakes his head, nonplussed. Freddie has come back with a pole, a spike in one end, a long cord fastened to the other end. "Freddie, where 'er belongs ain't got no wahter, no wharfs nor nutting, only houses," Arlie tells him.

"No fishin'?" Freddie asks. "Where do you git fish to eat?"

"In a store."

"Fish in store? Must be some funny place."

Freddie, looking over the side of the dock, sees the lobster. "Look at dat little booger down dere, I'm goin' to git en." He is gleeful. "Arlie, you hold rope, and when I throws pole, you 'ang on and pull back." Arlie holds the rope in his little fists, Freddie throws the long pole. The pole comes back.

"Freddie's owerboard," Arlie screams.

Freddie can't swim. Twelve feet of water. Should I go in after him?

He comes to the surface. I thrust the pole into his hands. He grasps it. I reach down and pull him up. He sits on the dock shivering convulsively, water streaming from him. Arlie regards him quizzically, then he drawls, "Be wahter cold down dere, Freddie?"

Freddie's teeth are chattering, his hair and face are dripping, he tries feebly to wring water from his Sunday clothes. "You'll ketch it," Arlie warns him; he looks frightened. Arlie turns to me. "Our sister Gwendoline were owerboard in winter; Grandad were on dock, and 'e seed 'er red coat in wahter, and 'e sayed, 'I believe dat's Gwendoline down dere.' 'E went up and called our dad, and when 'e fished 'er out, Gwendoline were roight purple." Arlie looks at Freddie, "But 'er ketched it good when 'er droid out."

There was company in the kitchen when I came home. A radiant young woman sat in the rocker by the front window, a large unbleached cotton tablecloth embroidered in vivid colours spread over her knees. Miss Laurie was holding out a corner of it. "It's beautiful work, Ivey," she said. "When did you find time to do it with a new baby?"

"When Jack's away with boats in Dingwall, there ain't so much to do, the baby sleeps a lot." She smiled at me shyly. "Do you want to take a chance?"

"She's selling chances on it, three for 10 cents," Katie explained as she moved between the pantry and the stove. "I wouldn't want a fancy thing like that myself, it's too hard to iron."

"Some folks likes to use a pretty cloth for a wedding or a christening." The work-reddened hands opened a box of little cardboard squares with numbers on them. We exchanged tokens as the deaconess came into the room.

"What is this?" she asked with her too eager smile.

"It's a raffle," I told her. She flinched at the word, the smile left her face, its creases deepened. "My dear young woman," she said solemnly to the fisherman's wife, "do you realize what you are doing?" The sweet face looked up at her, bewildered. The deaconess asked, "Don't you know that gambling is a sin?"

"But I don't gamble." There was surprise in the young mother's voice. "My man maybe plays a little poker in the stages, but there ain't no harm to it."

The eyes of the deaconess were not compassionate. "My beloved Christian friend," she said sharply, "that embroidery is the work of the devil."

Folding up her cloth, the village woman rose from her chair with composed indignation. "Oh no, it ain't," she said. "I worked it myself, every stitch, to make money for a new linoleum in my kitchen."

After supper, Arlie was waiting for me outside my gate. I walked toward the Point, and he followed at a distance of five paces. We paused to talk about a cow, walked round a dazzling blue sedan that blocked the narrow road. "Some shoiny, ain't 'e?" Arlie observed.

"What koind o' people be them?" the child wondered as a tense little grey man and a bloated young one got out and wandered aimlessly toward the Light. Unlike Harbour men, who keep their shirts tucked in, they wore their loud figured ones hanging over their slacks. A grey-haired, well-groomed woman and a pretty petulant young one emerged from the back of the car and stared at Arlie and me. "What a quaint little boy," the older one gushed and looked toward me for comment. Arlie picked up a stick and ran after a dog. No longer feeling inclined to act as Hostess of the Harbour, I went without a word to sit on the porch steps with Alec and a fisherman who were watching the Presbyterians of the village go to evening service.

"Elsa's gone, aren't you going?" Alec asked me.

"I can't. I haven't a hat."

Alec teased, "Seems odd a woman can't go to church because she hasn't a hat."

"It is so, ain't it?" the fisherman spoke. "Women only wears hats in church, and that's only place men takes theirs off."

Charlotte Clipper, on her way from fetching milk at the Malcolms', invited me to come home with her. Like all the houses I've seen in the Harbour, hers was shining and tidy, with linoleum and hooked mats on the floor and pictures of sailing vessels on the walls. The front room had a large new chesterfield suite that invited admiration.

We were in the dining room having lime juice, layer cake and blueberry pie when Charlotte's husband Big Jim came in from the shore. "Whoi ain't you in front room?" he asked as he sat with us at the table.

"We was," Charlotte told him.

"Did she like the set?" he asked eagerly.

"Yes, she sat on the chesterfield, and she says it's grand."

"It just come on *Aspy* two weeks ago," he explained to me. "It'll be roight comfable to set on when winter comes."

"In winter, you sets by kitchen stove," his wife said firmly.

Jim lit his pipe. "Charlotte, show 'er the bottle that pours out four kinds o' liquor." She fetched an empty divided decanter. "I got that in St. Pierre," Jim said. "You heard o' St. Pierre and Miquelon, ain't you? Islands south of Newfoundland, belongs to France. A grand place with buildings and lots to drink. French people are great for sellin' things: most of their trade is liquor; they'll let you taste what you moight fancy to buy, and afore you know it, you're daid drunk." Jim smiled. "You should see some o' them Frenchmen, they wears flat round caps, loike, and some has wooden shoes. Awful religious they is, great for parades and that. I seen little girls marching with whoite dresses and veils onto 'em, pretty as blossoms. And they got the foolishest grave-yard you could ever see, has cement boxes with portholes into 'em, and if you look in, you can see the coffins where the daid is laid in."

Charlotte shuddered, "Ain't that awful?"

"There used to be a lot o' runnin' back and forth during Prohibition, bringin' in rum. Police watched pretty close all the toime, but still they brought it in handy enough. Wouldn't moind havin' another trip up there one day," Jim rubbed his chin reflectively, and Charlotte breathed a sigh. I said, "I wish I could go too."

"You wants to do a lot o' things, don't you?" Charlotte said.

"We'll git Calvin to take ye codfishin'," Jim laughed. "Ye know, Mother, we's tryin' to make a match between Calvin and this girl," he tittered, and Charlotte shook her head.

"Poor Calvin," I said, "you love to tease him, don't you?"

" 'E knows it's all in fun," Jim sputtered. "You'd never know Calvin were 68 year old, would you?"

"I thought he might be 50."

"That's it, and if ye ever seen 'im cleaned up, you'd git a real surprise," Jim said. "He never shaves, you know, except for a funeral. He lives by himself in his sawmill and gits pretty dirty, but he's a roight foine man and can look good too if 'e wants to. His sister died down in Syd-ney, and Calvin come up here fer me to shave 'im — never done it his-self in his loife — 'e had a tie with him that I gave 'im last toime 'e went to a burying, and 'e wanted me to put it on 'im because 'e didn't know how to tie it. I threw it in foire and got 'im another one. Well, 'e had on his serge suit, and after I got 'im shaved, 'e went up the hill to have a look at old Mr. Bickford that just doid. We forgot all about 'im, and when we seen a man in a blue suit coming down the hill, I says, 'Who's that now?' And Mother says, 'Must be a stranger.' Well, sir, it were Calvin! We just didn't know 'im atall, 'e looked that smart."

Harold Horwood

A Thing So Marvellous to See

Annapolis Basin is a tightly enclosed arm of the sea on the south shore of the Bay of Fundy, which runs northeastward from the Gulf of Maine between the Canadian provinces of New Brunswick and Nova Scotia. The basin is a narrow triangle, eight miles wide at the fishing port of Digby, tapering toward Annapolis Royal, 15 miles away.

Inland from Goat Island, the basin is usually called Annapolis River, though, in fact, it is still part of the sea. It makes more sense to regard the river as starting above Annapolis causeway, though even there, the water is still briny and strongly tidal in a section that is called the French Basin from the fact that the Acadians settled and cultivated its shores and drained and dyked its tidal marshes back in the 17th century.

The Acadian dykes, extending down both shores almost to the region of Port Royal and upriver to Belleisle, are remarkable works containing millions of tons of earth dug by hand and moved into position by hand labour with the help of oxen and horses. These dykes, built to reclaim low-lying land from the sea, are not simple seawalls. From the start, they were fitted with huge valves, allowing the rivers to drain outward into the basin while closing automatically against the incoming tides, an engineering device the French settlers had learned in Europe, farming tidal flats where the sea rose in floods only a little less sweeping than those of Fundy. The peasants who performed this awesome feat, often working knee-deep in water, must have laboured mightily through generations to complete it. Yet they much preferred this kind of work to the labour of clearing forestland with axe and saw and plough as English settlers did everywhere they went, then and later.

The French peasants who arrived here in 1605 were husbandmen who had raised sheep and cattle on the salt marshes of northwestern France. They also grew some grain, but what they wanted above all in Acadia was pasture. Once the salt marsh was dyked and drained and desalted by rainfall and river flow, it required no further work; it would provide excellent pasture for all time to come.

When the dykes were up and the valves in place, the desalting happened automatically; within two years, the salt marsh was a salt-free meadow, growing red clover and purple vetch and timothy in place of the coarse *Spartina* grasses which had been the dominant plants previously. My neighbours who live along the inner shore of the basin are still pasturing herds of animals on the old Acadian meadowland, most of which has never been fertilized in the past three centuries.

It is worth remembering that when those dykes were first built, the plough as we know it had not yet been invented. Except for the ox cart and the stake harrow, neither had any other piece of agricultural machinery. Wooden ploughs, with no mouldboards, sometimes had iron plates to make them more durable, but even the stake harrows still had wooden teeth. A metal spade was a prized possession. Not until the time of Jethro Tull (the turn of the 18th century) did farmers have even simple agricultural machinery. Till then, every farm job except ploughing and hauling was done entirely by hand.

So it seems all the more impressive that the Acadian settlers were able not just to wrest a living from their former salt marshes but to flourish, to become prosperous, to raise large families, to increase from a few hundred immigrants to a population numbering tens of thousands. This is a region where people willing to cooperate with nature can achieve self-sufficiency, even modest affluence.

The salt marshes alone would not have made the Annapolis Basin the best site for a colony in eastern Canada, indeed the only place where an early colony succeeded without support from Europe. The other element in its success was the enfolding hills. North and south along river and basin, the valley is entrenched between steep ridges. Rising to 850 feet, these hills are locally called "mountains," though they are really just wooded hogbacks. With none of the character, much less the height, of mountains, they nevertheless serve to create a very favourable local climate. The sea, flowing in through Digby Gap with tides rising more than 25 feet and flooding upriver for almost 30 miles, softens the winter and extends the summer. At the same time, the enfolding hills protect the region from cold winds, especially from north winds off the Bay of Fundy, whose only access to the valley is by way of the one narrow funnel at Digby.

So the whole region from Digby to Belleisle enjoys a microclimate rather like that of regions some hundreds of miles to the south, less like that of Maine, let us say, than of coastal Connecticut. It is, consequently, a good place not only for raising animals but also for gardening. Such vegetables as tomatoes, peppers and squash flourish mightily on the shores of Annapolis Basin. During the first two weeks of April, the woods are scented by the lilac-coloured flowers of a wild shrub, *Daphne mezereon,* that came from the warm shores of the Mediterranean by way of France or England and soon made itself at home here. The winters are mild enough for broad-leaved evergreens like hollies to flourish and the summers cool enough for crops such as pod peas that cannot stand heat. Gardeners on the shores of the basin regularly grow ornamental shrubs not normally seen north of coastal Massachusetts or New Hampshire. Whoever first planted peach trees on these shores must have been amazed at their success. A few of us even grow melons beside our patches of corn, potatoes and peas.

The combination of sheltering hills, moderating sea water, fertile river-bottom soil and salt marshes created the conditions for Canada's first successful agricultural colony and continues to provide the conditions for home gardening and small farming in this most favoured region. The French pioneers at Port Royal did their experimental gardening somewhere "upriver" near Lequille and built their first gristmill on the Lequille River, which enters the basin at Annapolis Royal. Marc Lescarbot, the Paris lawyer who visited the colony during its second year and later wrote the history of New France, reported success with every kind of crop from Indian corn to marijuana (perhaps grown mainly for fibre).

A region supporting such a lush and varied growth of plants provides equally well for wild animals. White-tailed deer and varying hares are almost pests in this area (some gardeners would omit the "almost"). My own orchard has been visited, without serious harm, by black bears, bobcats, porcupines, raccoons, otters and pine martens, among others. The whole basin—indeed, the whole Fundy shore—is a gathering and feeding ground for flocks of migrating shorebirds that number literally millions.

Unless you've been born here, you can never get used to the tides. Twice a day, they come creeping up to cover rocks that towered far overhead a few hours before, until the basin is filled to the edge of the fields with a great flood. Then it seems to empty itself; the water vanishes over the clam flats; before you know it, what's left truly looks like a river rather than an arm of the sea. Once or twice a month, even the last remaining strips of beach will disappear, and once or twice a year, the water will inundate the salt marshes and come creeping up into the meadows.

Great schools of fish come surging with the tides through Digby Gap and, in pioneer times, were perhaps just as important as the resources of the land. A few fish traps still stand around the basin: towering nets strung on poles, often shaped like corrals, to trap the fish, then net them by the gills. In early times, such traps lined the shores from Annapolis Royal to Digby, but today, most fishing is done from trawlers and long-liners out in the bay.

To one accustomed to the awesome seascapes visible from the hills above Beachy Cove in Newfoundland and to the scarred face of Beachy Cove Mountain, its great slabs of rock dyed red by the setting sun, the Annapolis Basin seems tame and almost pastoral. Yet it is, in its own way, exceptional. The Goat Island "runs," the little coves between Ryerson Brook and Porter's Point, the near and distant hills of the far shore, all combine to create a landscape rather like one painted by Constable at his best.

"A thing so marvellous to see, I wonder how so fair a place did remain uninhabited," Marc Lescarbot said of Annapolis Basin. The French lawyer and historian was thinking of cities and towns; the basin was already inhabited in his time, but to European colonists, Indians didn't count as inhabitants. Even the most sympathetic, like Lescarbot, couldn't help thinking of them as part of the wild fauna, like the deer and the geese. The idea that they might *own* the place and be making full use of it in the best possible way would never have crossed his mind. Now, gazing across the basin from which the Indians have long departed (and from which the French, in turn, were driven at bayonet-point), I wonder if it did not truly belong to them in a sense that Europeans have never been able to understand — in the same sense that it belonged to the lynx and the wood bison and the white-tailed deer.

Especially in the light of evening, before or after sunset, the basin from our vantage point suggests harmony and peace, symmetry and the repetition of pleasant rhythms. On this shore, one is not overawed by the sheer power of nature as one is awed in coastal Newfoundland or Cape Breton during or after a northeast gale. Here, I am impressed less by the power of nature than by its fecundity: aspens that put on seven feet of growth in a single summer, an alder shoot that rises from the ground at the end of April and grows *an inch a day* so that it towers 12 feet high in autumn, a bank of soil left by a bulldozer that clothes itself in a single season in ferns and rushes and the lovely flowers of jewel-weed hanging higher than your head. You feel here that nature will not be put down, that the ugliness, the scars and the devastation are only temporary blemishes that this great tide of life will cover and soften and make beautiful almost in the time it takes the would-be destroyer to turn away and light a cigarette or open a bottle of beer.

The basin is a kind of private world, bounded on the northeast by the villages of Annapolis Royal and Granville Ferry, on the southwest by the town of Digby. North of Annapolis, the valley widens out, becomes flat, almost featureless farmland; south of Digby is the open roadstead of St. Mary's Bay, its arms spread wide to the Atlantic Ocean. The basin, lying between, is a kind of Mediterranean Sea in miniature, separated from the ocean by its own Pillars of Hercules. Inside those walls of stone, the earth is a world apart, where wildflowers bloom in March and grapes ripen in October.

It is easy to fall in love with this small world, as I discovered one day in January after I had lived here for less than two years and had been away for almost four months. A friend picked me up at the ferry dock in Digby and drove me past The Joggins and Bear Island, the reefs of Fool's Run and the channels of the Goat Island Gap to my home at Upper Clements, and I realized, as we drove, how deeply attached I had become to the whole region. I was not merely coming home but coming back to a place that spoke to me at the deepest levels, as Beachy Cove had spoken to me before — a place that had a great deal to say about the phenomenal universe and how it fits together, growing in marvellous harmony out of the unitary universe from which it is derived. Here, if I were willing to be still and listen, I might detect voices speaking out of meadow and marsh, forest and sea, and out of the starlit darkness.

The colony that built Port Royal on the banks of Goat Island Run in 1605 failed because of attacks by privateers from New England. The Habitation was abandoned. But only briefly. Fur traders and other adventurers and peaceful settlers found the area so attractive and the Micmac Indians so foolishly cooperative that they soon established themselves here with little help from the European colonizing companies, which had such a great struggle planting their trading posts in Newfoundland (where they had begun trying it more than 100 years earlier and still weren't succeeding) and in Quebec and in what are now the American states. The struggle to survive here was not a question of combating a hostile environment or fighting off the natives; it was a question of fighting off pirates, privateers and the agents of rival fur companies. The rebuilt Habitation at Port Royal, the restored Fort Anne at Annapolis and the restored gristmill on the Lequille River (now grinding out electricity instead of meal) are all attractive mementos of early colonization, demonstrating its solid and purposeful nature. Europeans came to this place not as mere traders and transients but with the firm intention of making it their permanent home.

In recent years, Annapolis Royal has indulged in a positive orgy of restoration, repairing and redecorating its Victorian and Edwardian buildings in something like their original splendour, even creating new "restorations" such as the Historic Gardens, which have scant basis in history but are masterpieces of landscaping anyway.

The Habitation at Port Royal is a beautiful restoration: hand-hewed beams and planks fastened with wooden pegs, hand-hewed wooden furniture, all as it would have been made in the early 17th century. Except for the lightning rods on the roof, authenticity could hardly have been carried further.

Nobody seems to have thought of restoring the Micmac village of the Chief Membertou, without whom the French colony at Port Royal could not have survived its first winter. The Micmacs, who were the colonists' guides, hunters and canoemen, accepted a kind of patronizing friendship from the French but were later killed and driven off by the English. In Nova Scotia, as in all parts of North America colonized by European settlers, the Indians have had a pretty thin time and have received scant recognition for the great contribution that they made to the nation's development.

As the French power waned, Scots, Irish and especially New Englanders came flooding into southern Nova Scotia; finally, there was an influx of British Empire Loyalists (many of them in no sense British, but all of them hostile to the American Revolution), giving the population its character: settled, conservative, rural, somewhat puritanical, somewhat old-fashioned. Just recently, this deep-rooted population has been spiced by an influx of Canadians and Americans belonging to the artistic subculture: painters, musicians, writers, people practising gardening, handicrafts, alternative life styles and generally belonging to the so-called Aquarian Conspiracy. They have settled among people whose ancestors were born here with less friction than you might expect, perhaps because there is in this region a long tradition of courtesy and tolerance, a tradition that you see at work every day on the streets of Annapolis Royal, where motorists automatically stop for any pedestrian who looks as if he wants to cross the street, even in the middle of a block.

Life around the basin is in many ways as it was generations ago and in many ways different. Rural people today take for granted such things as rapid transit, communications and travel. Halifax is a place you go to shop, perhaps once a month, instead of a place you visit once or twice in a lifetime, if ever. Farmers and innkeepers go to Florida for the winter. Some children ride trail bikes (and some of them get killed doing it). They have "fitness" tests in the schools, and for trail-bike riders, such tests may even make sense. Here and there, a modest-looking house has the interim technology of a parabolic satellite receiver planted in its yard, but to the chagrin of the manufacturers, such "dishes" have not blossomed across the landscape the way TV masts did in the 1950s. People have become justifiably skeptical that the latest technological marvels will remain useful for long or that they add anything to human happiness in the meantime.

The children who live with us here and the children who come to visit do not ride trail bikes. They go running barefoot through the fields and woods. They climb trees. They explore the beaches and splash in the sea. They paddle boats and canoes. They bring into the house such miraculous creatures as rock crabs and red-backed salamanders. All of this was done by Acadian children more than three centuries ago and by Indian children centuries before that and is as filled with magic today as it ever was. Such children need neither trail bikes nor fitness tests; they are living in the world, not in a technological fantasy.

Most people inhabit the shores of this basin not from any sense of necessity but because they wish to live here. That makes a big difference to the character of the people. I met a boy recently in the Fort Anne park. He was maybe 15 or 16 years old, with long hair, immature beard, bare feet, the sort of kid who would have been persecuted as a "freak" a generation ago. He talked to me about Annapolis Royal, how much he liked the village, how he hoped he'd be able to stay, though there was every likelihood he'd have to go away to work. I asked him where he'd come from, and he told me he was born here. He added that he never wanted to live anywhere else. How different from those terrible places one reads about, those rural swamps where every boy and girl dreads above all else the danger of being trapped there, where everyone's youthful ambition is to escape to the bright lights of the nearest city.

There is a sense of contentment here, a sense of being in a place where one wants to be, a sense of mild but pervading satisfaction in the generosity of the earth — and among some of us a wish that we could be left alone here, that we could be assured of another human generation to enjoy the plenitude of the land without the threats of geopolitics and the loom of global disaster.

But perhaps that is the way it has always been in the good places of the Earth. The peasant in the Dordogne Valley, the Hunza in his mountain ravine, has always lived with the threat of destruction from the outside.

In 1979, Corky and I and our two young children, Andrew and Leah, decided to settle here. We had visited every province and state in North America. We had lived in several of them. We built our house on the shore of Fool's Run, overlooking Goat Island and the Habitation, because this, of all the places we had been, was the one we preferred. Fool's Run? Well, you see, there are two passages past Goat Island to Annapolis Royal. Ship's Run, taken by all knowledgeable captains, is on the far side. Fool's Run, strewn with reefs and sandbars, is for seals and loons and people like us, who prefer to travel in canoes.

Acadia is the loveliest place in Canada east of the Rockies. I look across the valley in the rain, seeing the ridges rise, the trees green in the foreground, turning pearly grey the higher and more distant they rise. It looks English. A British landscape painter in watercolours would have fun with it: the perspective from a rooftop, three red-and-white cows for scale and contrast like toys on a child's model of a farm — no human figures in this one; the half-naked peasants, getting ready for their midday frolic in the shadows of the hedge, come out only in the sun; the rain creates pre-Adamic landscapes, echoes of an Earth cleaner than this, less cluttered, when the pace of life was measured by moon-rise and tidefall and the sky was not yet welted with the white stripes of commerce or the blasts of exploding space shuttles.

Here, in mid-July, when the air is scented with wild roses and meadowsweet blooms in the ditches, when the light falls dim and cool through two months' growth of young vines, you could well believe that man and the world grew up together, perfectly suited and matched, until you remember the hellholes of the cities, full of poison and corruption and every known kind of misery. Then you remember that humans are not only "the growing tip of evolution," as Pierre Teilhard de Chardin called them, but also filthy beasts, vicious latecomers to the Earth, perhaps the greatest curse that has ever fallen upon the planet. I will likely die without knowing the resolution of this matter. I will only know it for sure if I die in the nuclear holocaust that so many of our kind are prepared to inflict on the biosphere.

Marion Botsford Fraser

The Lie of the Land

The False 45th Parallel

Big road, this Highway 91 north through Vermont. It looks as if someone got up early and vacuumed it. It is smooth and graded, with clipped edges, and made of pale, spotless materials, and it takes you in an orderly fashion across the line, where it merges with Quebec Highway 55, about 90 miles south of Montreal. It has been landscaped; there are groomed evergreen windbreaks on the median and dramatic stands of birch on outcroppings of dark grey granite ribbed with broad white bands of feldspar. The road undulates according to the internal rhythms of the landform; this is the Vermont Piedmont, east of the Green Mountains and west of the Northeast Kingdom. Below the road on the left, there is a cluster of low red farm buildings. On the right, a sign announces the 45th parallel of latitude, the midpoint between the equator and the North Pole, about three-quarters of a mile south of the boundary.

If you cross the border on this highway, you are halted by flashing lights and channels of traffic, imperious signs and a barrage of tightly belted officials wearing sunglasses and hats, sitting in the narrow boxes Janette Turner Hospital has described as "upturned coffins." Here you find order, regulation and clear-cut national jurisdictions.

But if you leave Highway 91 before the border crossing and head instead for Derby Line, Vermont, you drive into a little valley of curving village roads with sudden dips, past big old houses on well-shaded streets. Canada is just a breath away in the white houses and white churches of Rock Island, Quebec. The boundary line disappears into a cluster of buildings, descends suddenly into the Tomifobia River and only becomes recognizable as a border on the outskirts of Rock Island, running over a small ridge. A few miles along, in Beebe Plain, Quebec, and Beebe Line, Vermont, the border runs beside Canusa Road; the houses on the south side of the street are in Vermont; the houses on the north side are in Quebec. Officially, in order to visit your neighbour in what is simply known as Beebe, you are supposed to go to the border crossing at the end of Canusa Road and come back that way too. (I spent several days in the area, and I only saw one person on Canusa Road.) Up at the end of Canusa Road, the boundary bisects a large granite house before again becoming an occasionally visible line of markers through the bush.

On a map, this is one of three or four straight lines in the entire length of the border. It is an arbitrary 155-mile section, neatly trimming Quebec and touching the states of New Hampshire, Vermont and New York. On the east, the straight line joins the meandering water boundary, Hall's Stream, the northernmost arm of the Connecticut River; on the west, it touches the St. Lawrence River at Cornwall, Ontario. Officially, this is called the 45th parallel section of the line, but the international boundary really never touches the 45th degree of north latitude. Hence it is known as the false 45th; its tidiness is a triumph of cartographical precision but not, as I discovered, a model of surveying accuracy.

This is one of the oldest official borders in North America; it was noted as a boundary line as early as 1606, in the Plymouth Company Charter, and even briefly proposed at one point as the entire boundary from coast to coast. In the 1760s, the 45th parallel was named part of the border between Lower Canada and New York, both British colonies at that time. It was surveyed in the 1770s by John Collins of Lower

Canada and Thomas Valentine of New York. It took shape as a long row of blazed trees, with a large pile of stones every three miles.

In the decade following the survey, there were murmurings on the American side that the boundary was south of the 45th. An American clergyman claimed that the boundary was so far south that the state of Vermont was deprived of more than 17 townships.

In the Treaty of Paris of 1783, after the American War of Independence, the 45th parallel was declared to be part of the international boundary. But in the usual style of treaty-defined boundaries, it was only named, not located on the ground. After the War of 1812, the Treaty of Ghent stipulated that the 45th be resurveyed. It was then discovered that the surveyed line was from ¼ mile to 1¼ miles north of the true 45th parallel. Near Rouses Point, on Lake Champlain, the Americans were building a fort just below the surveyed line to defend themselves from Canadians in what was, in fact, British territory.

Various reasons are given to explain how an official survey, carried out over several years by two skilled and conscientious men, could have been so completely, consistently wrong. Certainly by modern standards, the instruments were primitive, and much of the survey was carried out in harsh winter conditions. The dutifully kept records reveal that the sundries required for one portion of the survey included plenty of rum, wine and six gallons of French brandy. There were confrontations with the Abenaki Indians, who were displeased about the encroachment upon their hunting grounds around the Connecticut River.

In 1831, the king of the Netherlands proposed a compromise whereby the boundary would revert to the true 45th parallel, with a bubblelike arc made around the American fort, later named Montgomery. The Americans would not accept this proposal. In 1842, Daniel Webster and Lord Ashburton settled for the old surveyed line, known as the Valentine-Collins Line, as the permanent boundary.

What on maps looks like a neat, straight line is, in fact, a crooked row of stitches across a patchwork quilt of farmland, woods and small towns. The false 45th parallel intersects cemeteries, houses, beds, even bodies as it stitches itself across the land. Simply walking the line is not possible here. This is a border that belongs in fiction — not Kafka but perhaps D.M. Thomas or John Irving. It is the kind of border you would find in a dream and, upon awakening, be unable to describe. It has its own set of conventions, acknowledged unconsciously in the daily life of villages intertwined like the fingers in a handclasp.

The north-south alignment of the land is powerfully felt even on this gently rolling landscape — the two long lakes, Memphremagog and Champlain, and the Richelieu, Connecticut and Hudson river valleys still defining the movement and settlement of people. On the Quebec side, the area east of the Richelieu Valley is known as the Eastern Townships. In Vermont, the upper right-hand corner of the state is referred to as the Northeast Kingdom.

I made a loop around the Northeast Kingdom on a frosty Sunday morning in late October, listening to Handel and Corelli on Vermont Public Radio, where the Eye in the Sky weatherman talks about Sher-brooke in his picture-story weather forecasts and where Quebec is just another state in the fund-raising drive. CBC stereo, I thought, rarely imagines any audience outside Canada. As I made my way east, criss-crossing the border on quixotic minor roads, I contemplated the idea of a single, undifferentiated culture, all historical distinctions blurred or simplified.

In Stanhope-Norton, I inadvertently slipped into the United States; without warning, it is Vermont. There is no marker; I drove anxiously down a hill and around the backyard of the U.S. Customs building. Next to the car window, the gun hit me at eye level; then the body bent and acquired a face. All American Customs officers must wear guns; for American Immigration officers, a gun is strongly recommended but not mandatory. It will probably become mandatory because "of all the things that have been going on around here recently."

Several years ago, there was a manhunt in the Northeast Kingdom; a man described as a veteran of the Vietnam War, armed with four or five machine guns, was camping along the border, zigzagging along from side to side, eluding capture by moving between countries. This now almost mythical deranged figure suits the Northeast Kingdom, a shabby, rundown corner of poor farms on indifferent land, where hunting shacks and temporary houses with no foundations sit like birds poised for flight on the edges of swamps. In Canaan, where Vermont, New Hampshire and Quebec collide, there is a French church and a large plaque to commemorate those who died in the Korean, Vietnam and Second World wars. Canaan, "the birthplace of Ethan Allan Furniture," had a population of less than 1,100 in 1965; from here, 100 men went to die in Vietnam.

From Canaan, going toward Maine and New Brunswick, the boundary was assigned to Hall's Stream, truly a stream, narrow and flat, rippling across snow-dusted fields. Here again, definition and location of the boundary are out of sync; Hall's Stream has wandered from its course as much as 750 feet since 1845, when the stream was surveyed as the boundary. In 1783, the Treaty of Paris declared that the "northwesternmost head of the Connecticut River" was to join the 45th as part of the border. Several streams laid claim to that distinction through their settlers, and disputes led to the brief, proud tenure of the Republic of Indian Stream, between 1832 and 1836. The republic was subsequently absorbed by New Hampshire, and Hall's Stream became the boundary. It was surveyed in 1845, again in 1914-15 and in 1979, by which time more than half of the 467 turning points in the original boundary line were now on land, the stream itself having moved on. But in the boundary game, as in all sophisticated board games, there are rules of hierarchy; precedent supersedes accuracy, and mathematically defined points outrank mere place names and physical description. Regardless of changes in the physical landscape, "the international boundary remains mathematically fixed."

The once hotly disputed land between Hall's Stream and Indian Stream looks to be a wooded ridge of absolutely no significance whatsoever. The front yards in the little settlements along the stream display a demoralized jumble of poverty. Young girls, their features blotted out with makeup, walk along the highway on a Sunday morning glaring at strange cars and smoking.

I turned west and drove back toward Lake Memphremagog.

This section of the border expands to embrace in its daily compass the entire length of Lake Memphremagog, a long, narrow lake, about 27 miles from stem to stern, in both Vermont and Quebec. People in Georgeville, Quebec, on the northeastern shore of the lake, drive some 30 miles to buy groceries in the mammoth shopping centre at Newport, at the southern end of the lake, and they have an identity as part of the Stanstead-Rock Island border community. To a certain extent, everyone makes use of the proximity to another country. The Americans come over to the doctor and the dentist; the Canadians regularly cross over for gas and to go to the supermarket. Some keep a post office box on each side of the line.

Valerie Cerini and Howard Smith were for several years the editor and the publisher, respectively, of the Stanstead *Journal*, "Quebec's Oldest Weekly." They had an apartment above the *Journal* office in Rock Island and still have an old family cottage at Georgeville. I sat with them one evening at dusk; across Lake Memphremagog, we could see the lights of the red brick stagecoach inn at Knowlton's Landing; it is now called L'Aubergine. Persian cats prowled around us. Howard is mild-mannered, soft-spoken and given to gentle pedantry; Valerie is uncompromising, blunt of manner, warm of heart. They love this area, know its history well and are delighted to talk about it.

"The Anglophones all insist on telling us we're all Loyalists," said Valerie. "Well, we're not, because this part of the border was shut. The Loyalists came into Missisquoi County, and they were in the Maritimes and Ontario, but this section of the border was completely shut."

Howard jumped in. "The whole area that is now the Eastern Townships between 1784 and 1790 was a forest buffer zone, declared by Governor Haldimand to be an Indian neutral state closed to all settlement. And in fact, when a group of Loyalists did come up the Champlain Valley and settled in Missisquoi Bay on the northern end of Lake Champlain, the British government in Montreal tried to burn down their farms and force them out. They fought back. So Missisquoi County is the only Loyalist county; the rest of the townships may have Loyalist families, but they are people who came here *after* the Loyalist migrations."

Valerie seized the initiative. "The only Americans around here are Yankee land grabbers; 1815 is the oldest dated building in Georgeville, and that's the barn up behind the Murray Memorial Centre. The people who came here were opportunists, and they did a little bit of everything. Georgeville was important at least until 1871, big enough to get Lord Dufferin here. And Sir Hugh Allen and the Molsons; they all had cottages."

"They ran a stagecoach from Boston to Montreal, up until the 1860s anyway," said Howard. Valerie took over. "It came through Rock Island, Stanstead, down through Fitch Bay, hopped on a ferry here at Georgeville and went over to . . ."

"Knowlton's Landing," they said in unison, "which is right over there — see, where the light is shining?" Howard pointed across the darkened lake.

The lake is half in, half out of Canada and loosely patrolled compared with the roads. "Well, now the Customs officers are unionized, see, so they no longer do so many lake patrols," said Valerie. "Now, it's the obligation of the person to report. If you have a boat, you take your boat registration and get a boat pass, and then you can flash up and down the lake as much as you want, and they don't care now."

"Which is a far cry from the old days," she added, "when they had the *Anthemis,* the big steamer on the lake. The Customs officers would always come on board and wonder why the ladies had gained 40 pounds on their way home, because they'd been shopping for dresses in Newport!"

To officially enter Canada by road at Rock Island-Derby Line, you cross the small bridge over the Tomifobia River. The border is just beside the 30-mile-per-hour speed limit sign before the bridge; it runs across the brick corner of a dilapidated apartment building and then along the river. I walked down a steep, narrow track just inside Canada, through garbage, debris and brush, to the old Lay Whip Factory on a grassy riverbank. It is a four-storey, pale grey frame building, a wooden shell holding windows as fragile as cobwebs. Dark, stilled machinery is barely visible inside. A pale tan-and-white cat guards the property. The river rushes past, sliding down a staircase of black stone plates; the water curls yellow at the edges of the curves. At one time, a canal steered some of this water through a short detour, into a mill on the opposite bank, but the mill, too, is now an empty, dangerous place.

These factories and the abandoned Butterfield Tap and Die Factory down the road, which is half in Canada, half in the United States, were the small industries around which these border towns flourished in the latter half of the 19th century. Historically, Derby Line, Vermont, Rock Island and its neighbouring village on the hill, Stanstead, Quebec, were key villages in a transportation system and the textile industry. The current Canadian Customs and Immigration office in Rock Island, a dull brick and concrete building, was constructed on the site of one of the old textile factories; there was at one time a pulley system overhead to bring bales of cotton directly and illegally into Canada from a twin factory on the American side.

The Customs officials in Rock Island have plenty of time to talk between cars. "In the 1920s, there were as many as 20 textile factories right here; they were smuggling in custom-made shirts, cloth, shoes, you name it. Then there was a big scandal, and some pretty important people in Ottawa were implicated, and the whole industry shut down overnight."

The attrition visible here is common on both sides of the border; small businesses began as natural extensions of local agricultural activity, expanded as a result of brisk local trading and in response to major events such as the American Civil War and then were left by the wayside in the subsequent rush to mass production to the north and south.

Now, this bend in the Tomifobia River is neither productive nor lovely. It is forgotten. Its history is obscured, built over and built over. The old river buildings, the mill and the factories are frail sentinels; their guts have been worked over by vandals and time. The IGA supermarket and its parking lot sit over the river above the ruins of the mill; under the sidewalks, it is hollow where the canal once ran. The centre of Rock Island is rotted at the heart, and the long, straight ridge on the American side, above Derby Line, is a cemetery.

Residents along the 45th parallel have traditionally exploited, or at least played with, the binational intimacy forced upon them by this line. Buildings, or at least property divisions, usually predated the laying down of the line by surveyors. Nowadays, line houses are refused building permits, existing ones are encouraged to fall down, and transborder intimacy takes the form of neatly squared-off peace parks with controlled access.

But the Haskell Free Library and Opera House in Derby Line, Vermont, and Rock Island, Quebec, built in 1904, was deliberately placed across the boundary line. It was a gesture of international friendship, a good deal less symbolic than most such gestures. Also, it was conceived by a person, not a bureaucratic group, and is therefore idiosyncratic to a degree unimaginable by a committee. The building was offered to the villages by Martha Haskell and her son Horace, as a memorial to husband and father Carlos F. Haskell. It was designed by Rock Island architect James Ball; the opera house, which is the upper half of the building, is a scale model of the old Boston opera house. It is a grand building, in the Romanesque revival style, with an 80-foot hexagonal tower, a glossy slate roof, a lower half built in rough-cut grey granite and an upper half made of a warm, apricot-coloured brick; it is set on a rolling lawn, shaded by copper beech trees.

The library on the ground floor is a series of pleasant rooms finished in shining walnut and mahogany, marble and granite, lit with chandeliers and natural light coloured by stained-glass windows. The reading room is in the United States; the circulation desk and stacks are in Canada. A thin black line is painted on the floor, not, surprisingly, to satisfy the International Boundary Commission but, rather, to comply with the demands made by an insurance company after a fire.

The opera house upstairs is a 450-seat auditorium; about a third of the seats and the stage are in Canada. The black line is carefully marked on the polished wooden floor. The stage is hung with an Italianate pastoral backdrop. In the late 1960s, it was suggested that the Beatles might perform here, at a time when John Lennon was *persona non grata* in the United States.

If you live in Rock Island, to go to the library you must report to the U.S. Customs, then go to the library, then report to Canadian Customs on your way home. The international boundary line, protected by exclusive access to the library from the United States, cannot be exploited. In most of the remaining line houses, the internal configuration of the buildings is of little concern to border officials. There are no longer the ambiguous establishments like Jimmy Hill's Store up at Morses Line, where during World War II, good American housewives would tiptoe across the line on the floor of the store to buy soap and ketchup in Canada; these goods were rationed in the United States.

People walk back and forth across the line here. On either side of the bridge, especially the American side, the Customs and Immigration officials inhabit what look like gas stations. On the American side, too, you are supposed to know that you make a little detour to report to Customs; the station is not stretched across the road, to prevent you from going any farther. This insouciance is counterbalanced by a system of surveillance cameras, sensors and electric eyes, monitoring all the streets in these two little towns where there is not an official crossing. If you were just to walk across the border down there on Sunset Avenue, they say, you'd find the border patrol waiting for you at the bottom of Caswell for sure. For sure.

To the chagrin of local Canadian officials, there is no equivalent Canadian surveillance system; the nearest RCMP constable is posted 25 miles from the border, "and what the hell good is that? People know this area; they know how easy it is to cross." Several Customs officials told me that the Canadians were offered the opportunity of sharing the American surveillance system — "It would have cost us no more than $25,000" — but the Canadian government declined. Canadian officials are sensitive about their impotence: "If you have to intercept someone on one of those back roads at 2:00 in the morning, it would be nice to have a gun. What are you going to do, chase them with a bicycle?"

On the Canadian side ("just went to the library"), I got out of my car and went inside to talk to the officials. The job seems strenuous here, not like those points where three or four people stand in booths in shifts and face a constant stream of rolled-down windows and uncertain, up-lifted faces. To do the job here, you come out from behind the counter, go outside, bend down to the opened window or open the passenger door. It would be pointless to stand outside, waiting for cars. There were some people, though, who were just waved through; no questions, just a glance from the car to the building, a glance returned, an up-lifted hand, and the car would drive on. But it is the kind of town in which people, without even trying to, know exactly where other people will be at any time during the day. After declaring a bottle of wine, I absentmindedly walked away with a pen; later that night, I heard about it over dinner. When I had been in the area for several days, I, too, was waved through sometimes — on both sides of the line.

There used to be two parades, on the first and fourth of July, with two marching bands and two flags. On the first of July, the parade would start up in Canada, in Stanstead, come down the hill, through Rock Island, and stop at the bridge. Here, the Canadian band would change places with the American band, the Canadian flag would go to the back of the parade, and the procession would continue up the main street of Derby Line. On the fourth of July, the same parade would take place in reverse.

There are cracks in the sanguine homogeneity. On the Canadian side, there are English-speaking people who barely contain their bit-terness and contempt for their French-speaking neighbours. They don't like the few brightly painted houses in Rock Island, which strike an elo-quent cultural accent in the predominantly white clapboard picture. The border officials, the small grocery stores, the signs are almost all Francophone. I went to a small shop, where I was the seventh person to be served. Everyone before me spoke and was spoken to in French. Before I said a word, I was spoken to in English.

Yet despite the surface distinctions, courtesies and simmering hostil-ities, the cross-cultural fertilization is deep; beneath the politics, there is a layer of pragmatic unity, like that in a marriage of many years.

Aurore Mosher owns the line house in Beebe, at the end of Canusa Road. She is a plain, forthright woman in her 80s, with solid brown hair and a strong jaw. Her husband, Leon, is 93, formerly a supervi-sor at Butterfield's. Aurore has owned this house for 56 years. She wanted this particular house very badly; it took her three months to buy it from the Stewart estate, and she had to "use the law a little bit to get it." But "I was entitled," she said enigmatically, without elaborating. The original building once contained both American and Canadian post offices. She showed me an old photo, which depicted a simple, well-proportioned granite house. It now has a rambling extension on the American side.

"We are five here," she said, five apartments built into the house and over the double garage. The boundary marker is buried in the grass beside the front door. Leon sleeps in the United States, and Aurore sleeps in Canada.

We were sitting in the gathering gloom of an autumnal afternoon twilight. The sky darkened suddenly; Aurore lit the lamps. Her three sisters were visiting, all wrapped up in caps and scarves and mittens: Albertine and Gloria and the eldest, who dozed inside her warm burgundy wool coat. They all sat with one ankle crossed over the other and hardly spoke a word while I was there, except the eldest, who once said, "We are listening," when Aurore lapsed briefly into French. Her husband speaks not a word of French. He is an American, and she is a Canadian. Sometimes, the American Customs or Immigration officer on duty across the street will come and ask her to translate for them, because they, too, speak no French. And she comes and goes daily as she pleases.

"Oh, if I have a big load, I go to the Customs, and of course, I don't do any smuggling. Of course, if I wanted a fur coat . . ."

Aurore took me outside, walking in her bedroom slippers on the thin layer of snow, to show me the boundary monument planted beside her front steps, part of the garden. She talked about the granite trucks coming all night; all night they come down Canusa Road, she said, with the granite for the Rock of Ages plant up the road. But the house is virtually soundproof, with its walls of thick granite. They never stop, she said, night and day.

In Beebe, granite is used almost casually as a building fabric, not just for churches and big houses. There is a huge granite gateway at the entrance to a small municipal park. Roadside commercial signs look like freestanding gravestones; that of the Emslie Company, for example, is a thick slab of pale grey polished stone with deeply carved letters above the engraving of a truck cab. There are small granite bungalows and, on the outskirts of the village, a row of quarrying companies, where the granite is left lying around the yards in loose piles, like lumber. Through one such yard, I saw a small herd of cattle wandering at dusk.

As I drove toward Graniteville, I could smell a tension in the autumnal landscape. Hunters in fluorescent orange vests hung with guns and knives pulled up in gangs beside small cemeteries on the back roads. They wore red-and-black wool trousers and red caps and stood motionless behind trees, smoking cigarettes, sudden figures in a landscape. I watched comrades spilling out of pickup trucks to admire the white-bellied carcass of a young female deer, splayed and stiffening beside the road. When I stopped beside the Stanstead Granite Company quarry, I heard several shots, the sound bouncing off a slate-grey sky.

The Stanstead Granite Company quarry looks like a set design for a production of *Das Rheingold*. An enormous rough bowl is being hewed out of the crust. I stood at the edge, beside an aluminum shed that contains the controls for the hydraulic system whereby the rock is cut and moved. In the centre of the bowl stands a very tall metal ridgepole, with wires radiating out and anchored around the edge of the bowl. A long metal arm is attached to the pole, so it resembles an inverted compass. Deep in the curves and ledges and ridges of the faceted rock, there are tiny wooden ladders leaning on the sides of the bowl — I can imagine the Nibelung dwarfs placing their tackle around slabs of cut granite. There are many small dark pools of water laced with ice, and the only sound on a Sunday evening is that of a pump, constantly draining the water out of the bowl.

This is the northern rim of a granite industry that since the early 19th century has been carved out of the hills south of here, down the central ridge of Vermont. This was one of the first industries to draw French-Canadian labour south into Vermont. The border counties still have a population that in some areas is 30 percent French Canadian by birth; this population forms most of the Vermont farming community.

Derby Line, Rock Island, Stanstead and Beebe all get their water from Vermont; there is a watershed about 10 miles south of the line, and the rivers flow north. This area drains into the St. Lawrence, through Lake Champlain and Lake Memphremagog. In 1985, the area was one of a number of sites being considered by the American Department of Energy (DOE) for a nuclear dump. Twenty-five of the 125 possible sites were within 50 miles of the Canada-U.S. border, five of them in New Hampshire and Vermont, within the watershed.

A group of local residents from both sides of the border formed a vigilante group called Citizens Against Nuclear Dump Usage — CANDU, for short. (The name itself antagonized Canadian politicians because they disliked the intended implication of a connection, in some mocking sense, between this citizens' group and the Canadian nuclear reactor.) The group's sole objective was to prevent the sites within the watershed from making the short list for further and more detailed consideration. Chick Schwartz and Jean Choquette were prime movers in this group, and I spent a morning with them at Chick's farmhouse, between Rock Island and Beebe. Chick is an engineer, originally from Atlanta, Georgia, who has become a ceramics artist and sculptor; he lives here with Marsha, his beautiful, warm wife, who is a potter, and their four big sons. Jean is a Canadian Customs officer, a fiery and outspoken Québecois. It seemed an unusual alliance.

The proposed site that most concerned them was centred about five miles south of the border, in the middle of a lake from which the border communities draw their water. It consisted of a 20-acre burial site contained within a 20,000-acre no-man's-land. There was to be a shaft, about a thousand feet deep, leading to 400 acres of underground chambers — in effect, a mine. Only instead of being used to remove precious metals, it would hold nuclear waste. Twenty trucks (semis) would pass through the area every day, hauling nuclear waste to the dump. At the time of the first phase of the search for a nuclear dump, no geological analysis had been done. But the American Department of Energy imagined a shaft blasted down through granite, an apparently impervious substance within which nuclear waste would be held in containers designed to last for 300 years.

"Plutonium's half-life is 26,000 years," said Chick. "So in effect, they were saying, we'll protect everybody for 300 years. After that, the river in Montreal will be polluted, and Montreal probably will therefore be off the map. Because all the water flowed into the Canadian watershed."

"If they had gone maybe 10 miles south," said Jean, "they would have gone into the Connecticut basin, where all the water flows south, into the States."

"The DOE had 20-some maps, showing population and mines and forests and water. And on every one of them, the land above the Canada-U.S. border was white. There was not a river; all rivers stopped miraculously as soon as they came to the border. You could almost imagine a waterfall there, going over the edge, the border!"

"And Lake Memphremagog — all you could see was the little back bay of Newport. The map didn't show the 25 miles or so of the lake that goes into Canada."

The issue of the nuclear dump site became a transborder concern; in fact, initially the Canadians were not even invited to local hearings, but finally it was they who mobilized the Vermont citizens and apparently informed the Canadian government of the plan. CANDU drew broadly based, nonpartisan public support. And its most powerful arguments came from the people who knew the local geology best.

"A lot of the people who came to the meetings had worked in the granite quarries their whole lives," Chick said. "Men who had retired 10 years ago were giving impassioned speeches to these guys from the DOE. About how when you sink a shaft into granite, water comes pouring up like a geyser."

"When you look at a tombstone," said Jean, "okay, it's beautiful. It's been polished. But when you look in a mine or a quarry, everywhere there is water."

"And the DOE map," said Chick, getting heated, "supposedly showing all the lakes on the potential sites, did not even show Island Pond, Vermont, which is not only where Rock Island, Quebec, gets its water but where Derby Line, Vermont, gets *its* water. And that wasn't even on their map."

At dawn on the following day, I left Rock Island-Derby Line. To go east toward Lake Champlain along the 45th parallel, you must choose a route around Lake Memphremagog; I took the Newport route and came back into Canada at North Troy. The old Mansonville crossing is closed; it now sits at the end of a dirt road that runs through rills and gullies and over the bright, cold tributary streams of the Missisquoi River. Just before the old Customs house, which has been converted into a private cottage, the road runs beside an old covered bridge. It is a substantial bridge, painted that familiar soft red iron-oxide colour; its interior was warm and dry on a cold, wet November morning. Some of the old bridges bear a sign mounted in 1983, written only in French, which describes the history of these bridges, their construction according to various patent designs, the Town, the Howe, the Kingpost. The signs invoke the mythology of these *ponts baladeurs, ponts hantés,* host to first cigarettes, first kisses and the legends of hidden treasure and phantom cavaliers.

Around the corner from the bridge, on a hill, is a little forgotten cemetery, like hundreds I have seen in this part of Quebec, all the stones facing west in crooked lines. Metcalf, 1864, 1874, many Elkinses, Whitcombs, Henrys, Skinners — old Loyalist families, I imagine. One broken stone, its pieces stacked like broken pottery against a sister stone, is pure white and granular on the inside, like a piece of sugar icing. There are no bouquets, just lovely old stones, in the summer brushed by daisies, red currants, wild phlox and Queen Anne's lace. No church; the cemetery is loosely hemmed in by wire and a wild hedge.

There are numerous small roads here marked "cul-de-sac" that end in a fence and a sign: *Chemin et pont fermé.* People in Quebec and Vermont remember the 1976 Montreal Olympics as the time during which many of these small crossings were eliminated for security reasons.

Near Franklin, Vermont, I found Almon Richard, whose family land sits right on the border. His pale green mobile home, not at all mobile, has settled in a field that in summer is covered with a rash of brilliant yellow wild mustard. Today, the field is leeched of colour. A red sleigh sits on the roof, perhaps abandoned by Santa Claus. Almon has that tough, drained look of an ex-drinker, slightly shaky hands, a sharp laugh and fingers yellowed from many cigarettes. He is alert, responsive, yet unutilized. His wife has recently died of cancer; Almon has had at least one stroke and several biopsies. Today, his colour is good, his eyes bright. He sits at the kitchen table in the trailer, surrounded by hunting trophies, the tanned skins of otter and raccoon and memorabilia from the Fenian raids. He is the first Democrat in his family, and he is known for his skill in training dogs for hunting and for his knowledge of local history.

Almon is like an old turtle, with a tough shell, like an armour around a thin bright light. The past, his own and that of his family, is of far greater interest to him than the present, which seems empty, silent, the day inching along with the inexorable slowness of the minute hands on the bronze-faced kitchen clock. His best days were when he and his father were working the farm together; he talks a lot about his father.

"We got into trouble a couple of times, my father and I, through red tape, you might as well say; the Americans are great for red tape. They get hold of a little thing and they won't let go of it, take it to the Supreme Court. Well, we took 'em, my father and I, in the '60s, I think.

"There was an outbreak of hoof-and-mouth disease in Saskatchewan. 'Course, they quarantined the area. That's a very bad disease to get in livestock, nobody wants it. So the United States decided they'd put an embargo on all livestock crossings. They had crews that went along the border, the Department of Agriculture did. Walked the border to see if there was any cattle going back and forth. You couldn't get any through. So they came here, saw my father and me. I was running the farm at the time.

" 'Have you got any Canadian land?' they said.

" 'Well,' I said, 'I've got some Canadian land I use. I don't own it, but I've got a right-of-way through there, and my cows go through there night and morning.'

" 'Oh,' he said, 'fence that off.'

"I said okay. 'Then there's a little bit of Canadian land, part of that meadow.'

" 'Oh,' he says, 'never mind that little bit.'

"Well, the first time I turned my cows out in that field, the border patrol happened to come through; the cows were just over the border about 15 feet. On our own land, that little bit they told me not to fence! The border patrol went and got the Department of Agriculture, and they more or less drove some over. They got 13 cows into that one-tenth of an acre, seized them, and they were supposed to be shot right there. But the American officials called the Mounted Police to come and hold them cows because they were on Canadian soil and they hadn't gone through Customs.

"Then they called all the big shots. There were 10, 15 cars in the yard, officers everywhere, and the Mounties were holding the cows. Then they says to me, 'What are you gonna do? If you leave your cows there, the Mounted Police are going to seize them, and if you bring them across here, we are going to seize them!'

"Well, I said to myself, maybe it would be easier for me if the United States government seized them, not the Canadian government.

"Well, the red tape started there. They tried to shoot them a couple of times, but I'm a little smarter than they, got ourselves a good lawyer and served an injunction against them, so they couldn't shoot them. Went to court, for a year or more, and we were winning! The federal judge in Vermont was for us against the lawyers from Washington. Our governor was for us; our senator was for us. And we had to isolate these 13 cows, put them in a different barn, because they were the government's cows, for a whole year.

"Finally, I guess they saw they were losing. They approached their lawyer and said that if we would drop all charges against them, they would drop all charges against us.

"My father was in his 60s, and he was sickly. He had served in the legislature over here in Vermont, and he was always a law-abiding citizen and believed in his government. It broke his heart to have his government calling him a liar and this and that and having to go to court. Finally, he said we quit. So they wouldn't pay us anything; the court cost us thousands. My father said, well, to hell with it.

"I know that's what killed him; he died within a year. And after that, when they caught any cows, they didn't shoot any. They didn't dare!"

He laughed, a sharp laugh. "Made history there. There's always something going on!"

In the late 1860s, it was the Fenian raids. The Fenian movement was first formed in Ireland as a rebellion against English rule; after the American Civil War, it became a movement in the United States, its militia members mostly ex-northern soldiers. Because Britain had tacitly and perhaps otherwise supported the South in that war, there was considerable tension between British and American governments, which the Fenians were able to exploit. This was also a particularly volatile period for Canada, poised nervously on the brink of Confederation.

"The U.S. government knew about the Fenian Brotherhood, knew they planned to capture Canada and force England to free Ireland. The U.S. was mad at England, so they just closed their eyes and let it go. The Fenians formed an army and even went to the legislature in Washington, D.C. There were several thousand people involved; they were rumoured to have several million dollars, and they had a formal government set up.

"Everyone that came over here, chore girl or what the hell they were, joined the movement. They took part of their wages, see."

The Fenian raids took place in 1866 and again in 1870, at selected points along the border, into Quebec, at Niagara Falls and up the Red River Valley in the west. The valley east of Lake Champlain was seen as strategic, halfway between St. Alban's, Vermont, a major railway centre, and Montreal, which the Fenians hoped to capture. In 1866, the Fenians met little resistance in Quebec; they camped on the Eccles farm, just across the line from the Richard land, captured four or five towns, burned barns and stole brandy and livestock, until troops were sent down from Montreal.

"General Joseph O'Neill was head of the whole thing. He wasn't here the first time, but the second time, this was the only place they hit. Well, anyone with common sense could see it; hell, it was useless." Almon Richard laughed and drew slowly on his cigarette.

"But O'Neill was going to make one last stab. They had this McLaren, who they thought was a Fenian, but he was really an English spy, keepin' tabs on them. So when the Fenians came the second time, in 1870, the Canadians were waitin' for them. The Fenians walked right into the ambush. They just stepped across the border, and it was over in one day."

"Now, was your family living here at that time?"

Almon savoured his cigarette.

"Oh, yes. You see, it was one of the stories I'd always been told (you know how stories are handed down in a family), and I had always wondered if it was true or just kept being blowed up to make it sound better. My great-grandfather lived in the brick house down here, that's the homestead, built in 1853, about 200 feet from the border. When the Fenians came through the second time, in 1870, he got the women-folk and everybody out of the house. His sympathies were with the Canadians, because they were neighbours, his friends. And he did more business over there; he was in the smugglin' business or the trading business, besides the farming.

"The Fenians wanted to come in the house and get up in the attic with the windows facing north. Going to get up there with binoculars and look the area over, but he wouldn't let them in the house. They were here a day or so before the raid. Well, somehow Joe O'Neill himself got in the house and up in the attic. Then the Fenians started firing on the house. Well, something was attracting the fire. So, my great-grandfather, he went up in the attic, and there was O'Neill with the glasses. That's what got the attention of the Fenians; they were firing at their own man!

"Well, what I was told was that my great-grandfather threw O'Neill down the stairs and kicked his ass out the door and told him not to come back.

"And later that same day, he was standin' out on the porch, my great-grandfather was, when the Fenians shot at him. The bullet went right between his legs and through the front door.

"Well, that was the story that was always handed down to me, and it sounds good. But when we were diggin' in the Montreal library a few years ago, we found this history book, and it was right in there, the same story! Verified it. Well, somehow, I felt better about it then."

Tagged by a young, barking leopard mountain cur, we drove up to the old house, where Almon's great-grandfather had fended off the

Fenians. It is a handsome red brick house with black shutters and a fanlight over the front porch. Almon's ancestors were Dutch Loyalists from the Hudson Valley, who headed for Canada after the American Revolution and only got as far as Vermont. The family name was Reikhardt. They would have come straight up the Hudson River into Lake Champlain, then along the Missisquoi River to this land. The family still owns about 400 acres, in woods and pasture.

I looked briefly into the house: stripped pine floors, stereo and television, toys, the trappings of a young family — Almon's son and his wife.

I didn't think to ask Almon how much time he has spent away from here. He was born in a wooden house on this property, almost on the border; it has burned down. (The family is like the Traffords of New Brunswick in its tenacity, but the Trafford elders, older, have held onto the reins, for whatever different circumstances and reasons.) Almon's sons no longer farm the 400 acres; they are contractors. For them, living here, said Almon, is like living on the edge of the world.

We walked up the steps onto the front porch, past the dozing cats, up to the varnished wooden door. "Here's the bullet hole; see, he was standing right there, and the bullet went right through his legs. It's more splintered on the inside, see, where the bullet come out. The Fenians had two cannon; one of them blew up, and there was a piece of the barrel right here. I left it on the front porch for a doorstop, but I guess somebody stole it on me."

In the shed beside the house, there is a trapdoor, hidden under machinery and traps; there is a tunnel to the basement of the house. Almon thinks maybe this was a stop on the underground railway.

Then, with the leopard mountain cur, we walked across the border.

"We can't walk freely like we used to. I still walk across when I feel like it. I don't care; they can take me if they want. My brother-in-law is in the Customs, and he says I could be fined $1,000."

"Do they have a surveillance system along here?"

"They have had; they had a hidden camera or an electric eye or maybe a camera too. 'Course, kids and people activated it, so they finally took it out. I know my grandson and a Canadian neighbour boy about his age were playing together back and forth. The officer finally caught them one day going through. 'Boys,' he says, 'I know I can't stop you going back and forth, but would you go around in the field, instead of going down the old road? It would be a lot better for us.'"

"What about during Prohibition?" We were standing beside the 1842 boundary marker that stands in waist-deep grass on Almon's land.

"Oh, it was always active here. Let's see, I was born in 1920, and Prohibition ended around 1933. What I remember is these big cars, Cadillacs and Packards, going through, loaded with booze, and the Customs chasing them. We lived in the big brick house then. My father wouldn't cooperate with them. You can't; when you live on the border, you gotta be neutral somewhat. You can't squeal on anybody, either, so you don't say anything half the time. For your own good, or your house will burn, or your barn will burn, or some damn thing.

"Anyway, one morning, we got up, and there was a big roadster sitting back of the house out of sight. Pretty near a new one. All loaded down; you could tell from the springs. We opened up the rumble seat, and it was all full of sandbags. That was the decoy car; they'd send that one through first, and the Customs would go after it, and then a couple more would come through with the real stuff.

"Then, of course . . ." He hesitated briefly. "Well, during the war in the '40s, I couldn't get in the service because I was a farmer. There was smuggling going on then, and I helped in that, and I'm not ashamed to say so. I figured I was helping my country. It was meat mostly. You might as well say black market. I helped my country, made a few dollars. I didn't figure that as a crime, really, but if you get down to brass tacks, it was, really. I wasn't paying any duty. I was just running a cheaper customs house, that's all."

We crossed a slanted wooden bridge over Chickabiddy Creek and into Canada. Through the rusty tangle of what Almon calls wild bamboo, past the final burst of goldenrod stuffing, cloud-white on blackened stems, at rest before flight. There was snow in the air and an icy west wind pouring up the valley. When the west wind was blowing, Almon's father would bring visitors to the break that is the border, and he could say, you see, it really is a lot colder up there in Canada.

We walked past the noisy farm of Hector Messier just beyond the trees; he has a system for sucking the moisture out of corn that is going all the time. "He's a separatist," said Almon, "not like his father." Hector came past the bright turquoise house in a bright turquoise truck and stopped to talk to Almon about the hunting, a 200-pound 10-point buck shot close to here the other day, and the Lebanese men with the bomb, caught crossing the border from Canada over to Richford.

Here and down at Morses Line, there were once tiny villages, rather like Pigeon Hill now, I think, but there are few visible remains. There are five houses now in this valley; Hector Messier is the name on the yellow plastic mailbox in front of the bright blue house. E. Piette and H. Sylvestre are the names on the house beside the bridge with a rack of horns on the door. Beside the garage with the bright blue doors sits an abandoned rail passenger car, red, rusted, with a broken back. Across the road from a barn with snowshoes laced over the door is the Fenian raid monument. Almon opened the gate, and the leopard mountain cur bounded up the small hill.

Contemporary engravings — *Action at Eccles Hill* by John Henry Walker and *Volunteer Camp at Eccles Hill* by A. Vogt (the latter published in the *Canadian Illustrated News,* June 11, 1870) — show a considerable community in the valley, this little hill covered with small canvas tents, and the tall trees are not there at all.

The monument is massive and simple, in the style of prehistoric megalithic statues. On a base of loosely piled boulders and platters of shale sit two roughly dressed blocks of granite, one on the shoulders of the other. The clean white text cut into the granite reads:

THE CANADIAN VOLUNTEERS
AND HOME GUARDS
HERE REPULSED
THE FENIAN INVADERS ON THE
25TH MAY 1870

A miniature cannon is mounted on a block of concrete. The monument was erected in 1902 by the Dominion government, under the supervision of the Missisquoi Historical Society. A nice twist of proprieties. The knoll is grassed, with boulders lying around; Almon sees these as hiding places for the red-sashed Canadians waiting for the Fenians. Except for a jay, a pewter squirrel rippling along the grey maple branches and the snuffling dog, it was silent. The rocks were furred with moss, the dead leaves ankle-deep. A distant shotgun sounded, and leaves fluttered like snowflakes to the ground.

The sky seemed to be moving overhead, thick grey-and-white backlit clouds billowing rapidly eastward. Patches of sunlight passed quickly across the fields as if caught up by the wind. A stream glittered, a tamarack hummed with sudden golden light. The fields roll into the valley and are folded into the stream, as furled ribs of amber, green and gold.

The cedars, invisible for half the year, in autumn give a rich, warm green texture to the far hillside, because the maples are stripped bare. Beyond the grey curtain of branches, I could just see the Richard house and the old wooden silo, built of stacked two-by-fours, stark and open like a mediaeval tower and rigid in a mass of crumbled rock and blackened timber, the remains of an old stable.

I drove around the Canadian end of the valley later, having crossed the border formally at Morses Line. There is a tiny crooked sign pointing to Eccles Hill, but the monument itself is unheralded. In a maple woods, thousands of skinny striplings were competing to become big trees, and old sugaring huts were visible through the grey latticework. Again, windblown light swept over the ridge and set bright coins rattling on the tips of the poplar trees. The fields glowed briefly, a bright green pile. In an apple orchard of short fat trunks, the thick, braided boughs were pruned into arches that almost touched the ground. The new stems sticking straight up were tender and thin, with no colour at all. The leaves formed a taffeta underskirt of burnt orange against the shuttered maple grove.

Alistair MacLeod

The Closing Down of Summer

It is August now, toward the end, and the weather can no longer be trusted. All summer, it has been very hot. So hot that the gardens have died and the hay has not grown and the surface wells have dried to dampened mud. The brooks that flow to the sea have dried to trickles, and the trout that inhabit them and the inland lakes are soft and sluggish and gasping for life. Sometimes, they are seen floating dead in the overwarm water, their bodies covered with fat grey parasites. They are very unlike the leaping, spirited trout of spring, battling and alive in the rushing, clear, cold water, so electrically filled with movement that it seems no parasite could ever lodge within their flesh.

The heat has been bad for fish and wells and the growth of green, but for those who choose to lie on the beaches of the summer sun, the weather has been ideal. This is a record year for tourists in Nova Scotia, we are constantly being told. More motorists have crossed the border at Amherst than ever before. More cars have landed at the ferry docks in Yarmouth. Motels and campsites have been filled to capacity. The highways are heavy with touring buses and camper trailers and cars with the inevitable lobster traps fastened to their roofs. Tourism is booming as never before.

Here on this beach, on Cape Breton's west coast, there are no tourists. Only ourselves. We have been here for most of the summer. Surprised at the endurance and consistency of the heat. Waiting for it to break and perhaps to change the spell. At the end of July, we said to ourselves and to each other, "The August gale will come and shatter all of this." The August gale is the traditional storm that comes each August, the forerunner of the hurricanes that will sweep up from the Caribbean and beat and lash this coast in the months of autumn. The August gale with its shrieking winds and crashing, muddied waves has generally signalled the unofficial end of summer, and it may come in August's very early days. But this year, as yet, it has not come, and there are only a few days left. Still, we know that the weather cannot last much longer, and in another week, the tourists will be gone and the schools will reopen and the pace of life will change. We will have to gather ourselves together, then, in some way and make the decisions that we have been postponing in the back of our minds. We are perhaps the best crew of shaft and development miners in the world, and we were due in South Africa on the seventh of July.

But as yet, we have not gone, and the telegrams from Renco Development in Toronto have lain unanswered, and the telephone calls have been unreturned. We are waiting for the change in the weather that will make it impossible for us to lie longer on the beach, and then we will walk, for the final time, the steep and winding zigzagged trail that climbs the rocky face of Cameron's Point. When we reach the top of the cliff, we will all be breathing heavily, and then we will follow the little path that winds northward along the cliff's edge to the small field where our cars are parked, their hoods facing out to sea and their front tires scant feet from the cliffside's edge. The climb will take us some 20 minutes, but we are all still in good shape after a summer of idleness.

The golden little beach upon which we lie curves in a crescent for approximately three-quarters of a mile and then terminates at either end in looming cliffs. The north cliff is called Cameron's Point after the family that once owned the land, but the south cliff has no name. Both cliffs protect the beach, slowing the winds from north and south and preserving its tranquillity.

At the south cliff, a little brook ends its journey and plummets almost vertically some 50 feet into the sea. Sometimes after our swims or after lying too long in the sand, we stand underneath its fall as we would a shower, feeling the fresh water upon our heads and necks and shoulders and running down our bodies' lengths to our feet, which stand within the sea.

All of us have stood and turned our naked bodies unknown, unaccountable times beneath the spraying shower nozzles of the world's mining developments. Bodies that when free of mud and grime and the singed-hair smell of blasting powder are white almost to the colour of milk or ivory. Perhaps of leprosy. Too white to be quite healthy; for when we work, we are often 12 hours in the shaft's bottom or in the development drifts, and we do not often feel the sun. All summer, we have watched our bodies change their colour and seen our hair grow bleached and ever lighter. Only the scars that all of us bear fail to respond to the healing power of the sun's heat. They seem to stand out even more vividly now, long running pink welts that course down our inner forearms or jagged sawtooth ridges on the taut calves of our legs.

Many of us carry one shoulder permanently lower than the other where we have been hit by rockfalls or the lop of the giant clam that swings down upon us in the narrow closeness of the shaft's bottom. And we have arms that we cannot raise above our heads and touches of arthritis in our backs and in our shoulders, magnified by the water that chills and falls upon us in our work. Few of us have all our fingers, and some have lost either eyes or ears from falling tools or discharged blasting caps or flying stone or splintering timbers. Yet it is damage to our feet that we fear most of all. For loss of toes or damage to the intricate bones of heel or ankle means that we cannot support our bodies for the gruelling 12-hour stand-up shifts. And injury to one foot means that the other must bear double its weight, which it can do for only a short time before poor circulation sets in to numb the leg and make it too inoperative. All of us are big men, over six feet tall and near 200 pounds, and our feet have, at the best of times, a great deal of pressure bearing down upon them.

We are always intensely aware of our bodies and the pains that course and twinge through them. Even late at night when we would sleep, they jolt us unexpectedly as if from an electric current, bringing tears to our eyes and causing our fists to clench in the whiteness of knuckles and the biting of nails into palms. At such times, we desperately shift our positions or numb ourselves from the tumblers of alcohol we keep close by our sides.

Lying now upon the beach, we see the external scars on ourselves and on each other and are stirred to the memories of how they occurred. When we are clothed, the price we pay for what we do is not so visible as it is now.

Beside us on the beach lie the white Javex containers filled with alcohol. It is the purest of moonshine made by our relatives back in the hills and is impossible to buy. It comes to us only as a gift or in exchange for long past favours: bringing home of bodies, small loans of forgotten dollars, kindnesses to now dead grandmothers. It is as clear as water, and a teaspoonful of it when touched by a match will burn with the low blue flame of a votive candle until it is completely consumed, leaving the teaspoon hot and totally dry. When we are finished here, we will pour what remains into 40-ounce vodka bottles and take it with us on the long drive to Toronto. For when we decide to go, we will be driving hard and fast, and all of our cars are big: Cadillacs with banged-in fenders and Lincolns and Oldsmobiles. We are often stopped for speeding on the stretch outside Mt. Thom or going through the Wentworth Valley or on the narrow road to Fredericton or on the fast straight road that leads from Rivière du Loup to Lévis, sometimes even on the 401. When we say that we must leave for Africa within hours, we are seldom fined or, in odd instances, are allowed to pay our fines upon the spot. We do not wish to get into the entanglement of moonshine brought across provincial lines and the tedium that accompanies it. The fine for open commercial liquor is under $15 in most places, and the transparent vodka bottles both show and keep their simple secret.

But we are not yet ready to leave, and in the sun, we pour the clear white fluid into Styrofoam cups and drink it in long burning swallows, sometimes following such swallows with mouthfuls of Teem or Sprite or 7-Up. No one bothers us here, because we are so inaccessible. We can see any figure that would approach us from more than a mile away, silhouetted on the lonely cliff and the rocky and treacherous little footpath that is the only route to where we are. None of the RCMP who police this region are in any way local, and it is unlikely that they even know this beach exists. And in the legal sense, there is no public road that leads to the cliff where our cars now stand. Only vague paths and sheep trails through the burnt-out grass and around the clumps of alders and blueberry bushes and protruding stones and rotted stumps. The resilient young spruce trees scrape against the mufflers and oilpans of our cars and scratch against the doors. Hundreds of miles hence, when we stop by the roadsides in Quebec and Ontario, we will find small sprigs of this same spruce still wedged within the grillwork of our cars or stuck beneath the headlight bulbs. We will remove them and take them with us to Africa as mementos or talismans or symbols of identity. Much as our Highland ancestors, for centuries, fashioned crude badges of heather or of whortleberries to accompany them on the battlefields of the world. Perhaps so that in the closeness of their work with death, they might find nearness to their homes and an intensified realization of themselves. We are lying now in the ember of summer's heat and in the stillness of its time.

Out on the flatness of the sea, we can see the fishermen going about their work. They do not make much money anymore, and few of them take it seriously. They say that the grounds have been overfished by the huge factory fleets from Russia, Spain and Portugal. And it is true that on the still, warm nights, we can see the lights of such floating factories shining brightly off the coast. They appear as strange, movable, brilliant cities, and when they are far out, their blazing lights seem to mingle with those of the stars. The fishermen before us are older men or young boys. Grandfathers with their grandsons acting out their ancient rituals. At noon or at 1:00 or 2:00, before they start for home, they will run their little boats into our quiet cove until their bows are almost touching the sand. They will toss us the gleaming blue-black mackerel and the silver herring and the brown-and-white-striped cod and talk to us for a while, telling us anything that they think we should know. In return, we toss them the whitened Javex bottles so that they may drink the pure clear contents. Sometimes, the older men miss the toss, and the white cylindrical bottles fall into the sea, where they bob and toss like marker buoys or a child's duck in the bathtub until they are gaffed by someone in the boat or washed back in to shore. Later, we cook the fish over small, crackling driftwood fires. This, we know too, cannot go on much longer.

In the quiet graveyards that lie inland, the dead are buried. Behind the small white wooden churches and beneath the monuments of polished black granite, they take their silent rest. Before we leave, we will visit them to pray and take our last farewell. We will perhaps be afraid then, reading the dates of our brothers and uncles and cousins, recalling their youth and laughter and the place and manner of each death.

Death in the shafts and in the drifts is always violent, and very often the body is so crushed or so blown apart that it cannot be reassembled properly for exposure in the coffin. Most of us have accompanied the grisly remains of such bodies trussed up in plastic bags on trains and planes and automobiles and delivered them up to the local undertaker. During the two or three days of the final wake and through the lonely all-night vigils kept in living rooms and old-fashioned parlours, only memories and youthful photographs recall the physical reality that lies so dismembered and disturbed within each grey, sealed coffin.

The most flattering photograph is placed upon the coffin's lid in an attempt to remind us of what was. I am thinking of this now, of the many youthful deaths I have been part of and of the long homeward journeys in other seasons of other years. The digging of graves in the bitterness of February's cold, the shovelling of drifts of snow from the barren earth and then the banging of the pick into the frozen ground, the striking of sparks from steel on stone and the scraping of shovels on earth and rock.

Some 20 years ago, when first I went to the uranium shafts of Ontario's Elliot Lake and short-lived Bancroft, we would have trouble getting our dead the final few miles to their high white houses. Often, in winter, we would have to use horses and sleighs to get them up the final hills, standing in chest-high snow, taking out window casings so that we might pass the coffin in and then out again for the last time. Or sometimes, in the early spring, we would again have to resort to horses when the leaving of the frost and the melting of the winter snow turned the brooks into red and roiling rivers and caused the dirt roads that led into the hills to become greasy and impassable. Sometimes in such seasons, the underground springs beneath such roads erupt into tiny geysers, shooting their water upward and changing the roadbeds around them into quivering bogs that bury vehicles up to their hubs and axles.

And in November, the rain is chill and cold at the graveside's edge. It falls upon our necks and splatters the red mud upon our gleaming shoes and on the pant legs of our expensive suits. The bagpiper plays *Flowers of the Forest,* as the violinist earlier played his haunting laments from the high choir loft. The music causes the hair to bristle on the backs of our necks and brings out the wildness of our grief and dredges the depths of our dense dark sorrow. At the graveside, people sometimes shout farewells in Gaelic or throw themselves into the mud or upon the coffin as it is being lowered on its straps into the gaping earth.

Fifteen years ago, when the timbers gave way in Springdale, Newfoundland, my younger brother died, crushed and broken amidst the constant tinkle of the dripping water and lying upon a bed of tumbled stone. We could not get him up from the bottom in time, and his eyes bulged from his head and the fluids of his body seeped quietly onto the glistening rock. Yet even as we tried, we realized that our task was hopeless and that he would not last, even on the surface. Would not last long enough for any kind of medical salvation. And even as the strength of his once powerful grip began to loosen on my hand and his breath to rattle in his throat, we could see the earthly road that stretched before us as the witnesses and survivors of his death: the report to the local authorities, the statements to the company, to the police, to the coroner, and then the difficult phone calls made on badly connected party lines or, failing those, the more efficient and more impersonal yellow telegrams. The darkness of the midnight phone call seems somehow to fade with the passing of time or to change and be re-created like the ballads and folk tales of the distant, lonely past. Changing with each new telling as the tellers of the tales change, as they become different, older, more bitter or more serene. It is possible to hear descriptions of phone calls that you yourself have made some 10 or 15 years ago and to recognize very little about them except the undeniable kernel of truth that was at the centre of the messages they contained. But the yellow telegram is more blunt and more permanent in the starkness of its message, and it is never, ever thrown away. It is kept in vases and in Bibles and in dresser drawers beneath white shirts, and it is stumbled upon sometimes unexpectedly, years later, sometimes by other hands, in little sandalwood boxes containing locks of the baby's hair or tucked inside the small shoes in which he learned to walk. A simple obituary of a formal kind.

When my brother died in Springdale, Newfoundland, it was the 21st of October, and when we brought his body home, we were already deep into fall. On the high hardwood hills, the mountain ash and the aspen and the scarlet maple were ablaze with colour beneath the weakened rays of the autumn sun. On alternate days, the rain fell, sometimes becoming sleet or small hard hailstones. Sometimes, the sun would shine in the morning, giving way to the vagaries of precipitation in the afternoon. And sometimes, the cloud cover would float over the land even as the sun shone, blocking the sun out temporarily and casting shadows as if a giant bird were passing overhead. Standing beneath such a gliding cloud and feeling its occasional rain, we could see the sun shining clearly at a distance of only a mile away. Seeing warmth so reachably near while feeling only the cold of the icy rain. But at the digging of his grave, there was no sun at all. Only the rain falling relentlessly down upon us. It turned the crumbling clay to the slickest of mud, as slippery and glistening as that of the potter's wheel but many times more difficult to control. When we had dug some four feet down, the earthen walls began to slide and crumble and to give way around us and to fall upon our rubber boots and to press against the soaking pant legs that clung so clammily to our blue-veined legs. The deeper we dug, the more intensely the rain fell, the drops dripping from our eyebrows and from our noses and the icy trickles running down the backs of our necks and down our spines and legs and into our squishing and sucking boots. When we had almost reached the required depth, one of the walls that had been continuously crumbling and falling suddenly collapsed and, with a great whoosh, rolled down upon us. We were digging in our traditional family plot, and when the wall gave way, it sent the box that contained my father's coffin rolling down upon us. He had been dead for five years then, blown apart in Kirkland Lake, and at the time of his burial, his coffin had been sealed. We were wildly and irrationally frightened by the slide and braced our backs against the splintered and disintegrating box, fearful lest it should tip and fall upon us and spill and throw whatever rotting relics remained of that past portion of our lives. Of little flesh but maybe green decaying bones or strands of silver matted hair.

We had held it there, braced by our backs in the pouring rain, until timbers were brought to shore up the new grave's side and to keep the past dead resting quietly. I had been very frightened then, holding the old dead in the quaking mud so that we might make room for the new in that same narrow cell of sliding earth and cracking wood. The next day at his funeral, the rain continued to fall, and in the grave that received him, the unsteady timbers and the ground they held so temporarily back seemed but an extension of those that had caused his life to cease.

Lying now in the precarious heat of this still and burning summer, I would wish that such thoughts and scenes of death might rise like the mists from the new day's ocean and leave me dry and somehow emptied on this scorching fine-grained sand.

In Africa, it will be hot too, in spite of the coming rainy season, and on the veldt, the heat will shimmer and the strange, fine-limbed animals will move across it in patterns older than memory. The nomads will follow their flocks of bleating goats in their search for grass and moisture, and the women will carry earthen jars of water on their heads or baskets of clothes to slap against the rocks where the water is found.

In my own white house, my wife does her declining wash among an increasingly bewildering battery of appliances. Her kitchen and her laundry room and her entire house gleam with porcelain and enamel and an ordered cleanliness that I can no longer comprehend. Little about me or about my work is clean or orderly, and I am always mildly amazed to find the earnings of the violence and dirt in which I make my living converted into such meticulous brightness. The lightness of white-and-yellow curtains rustling crisply in the breeze. For us, most of our working lives are spent in rough, crude bunkhouses thrown up at the shafthead's site. Our bunks are made of two-by-fours sometimes roughly hammered together by ourselves, and we sleep two men to a room or sometimes four or sometimes, in the development's early stages, in the vast "ram pastures" of 20 or 30 or perhaps even 40 men crowded together in one huge, rectangular, unpartitioned room. Such rooms are like hospital wards without the privacy of the dividing curtains, and they are filled, constantly, day and night, with the sounds of men snoring and coughing or spitting into cans by their bedsides, the incoherent moans and mumbles of uneasy sleepers and the thuds of half-conscious men making groaning love to their passive pillows. In Africa, we will sleep, mostly naked, under incongruous structures of mosquito netting, hearing the sometimes rain on the roofs of corrugated iron. In the near 24-hour winter darkness of the Yukon, we have slept in sleeping bags, weighted down with blankets and surrounded by various heaters, still to wake to our breath as vapour in the coldness of the flashlight's gleam.

It is difficult to explain to my wife such things, and we have grown more and more apart with the passage of the years. Meeting infrequently now, almost as shy strangers, communicating mostly over vast distances through ineffectual say-nothing letters or cheques that substitute money for what once was conceived as love. Sometimes, the cheques do not even come from me, for in the developing African nations, the political situation is often uncertain, and North American money is sometimes suddenly and almost whimsically "frozen" or "nationalized," making it impossible to withdraw or remove. In times and places of such uneasiness, shaft crews such as ours often receive little or no actual money, only slips of paper to show our earnings, which are deposited in the metropolitan banks of New York or Toronto or London and from which our families are issued monthly cheques.

I would regain what was once real or imagined with my wife. The long nights of passionate lovemaking that seemed so short, the creating and birth of our seven children. Yet I was never home for the birth of any of my children, only for their fathering. I was not home when two of them died so shortly after birth, and I have not been home to participate or to share in many of the youthful accomplishments of the other five. I have attended few parents' nights or eighth-grade graduations or father-and-son hockey banquets, and broken tricycle wheels and dolls with crippled limbs have been mended by other hands than mine.

Now, my wife seems to have gone permanently into a world of avocado appliances and household cleanliness and the vicarious experiences provided by the interminable soap operas that fill her television afternoons. She has perhaps gone as deeply into that life as I have into the life of the shafts, seeming to tunnel ever downward and outward through unknown depths and distances and to become lost and separated and unavailable for communication. Yet we are not surprised or critical of each other, for she, too, is from a mining family and grew up largely on funds sent home by an absentee father. Perhaps we are but becoming our previous generation.

And yet there are times, even now, when I can almost physically feel the summer of our marriage and of our honeymoon and of her singing the words of the current popular songs into my then attentive ears. I had been working as part of a crew in Uranium City all winter and had been so long without proper radio reception that I knew nothing of the music of that time's hit parade. There was always a feeling of mild panic then, on hearing whole dance floors of people singing aloud songs which had come and flourished since my departure and which I had never heard. As if I had been on a journey to the land of the dead.

It would be of little use, now, to whisper popular lyrics into my ears, for I have become partially deaf from the years of the jackleg drill's relentless pounding into walls of constant stone. I cannot hear much

Alistair MacLeod

of what my wife and children say to me and communicate with the men about me through nods and gestures and the reading of familiar lips. Musically, most of us have long abandoned the modern hit parades and have gone, instead, back to the Gaelic songs remembered from our early youth. It is these songs that we hum now on the hotness of this beach and that we will take with us on our journey when we go.

We have perhaps gone back to the Gaelic songs because they are so constant and unchanging and speak to us as the privately familiar. As a youth and as a young man, I did not even realize that I could understand or speak Gaelic and entertained a rather casual disdain for those who did. It was not until the isolation of the shafts began that it started to bubble up somehow within me, causing a feeling of unexpected surprise at finding it there at all. As if it had sunk in unconsciously through some strange osmotic process while I had been unwittingly growing up. Growing up without fully realizing the language of the conversations that swirled around me. Now, in the shafts and on the beach, we speak it almost constantly, though it is no longer spoken in our homes. There is a "Celtic Revival" in the area now, fostered largely by government grants, and the younger children are taught individual Gaelic words in the classrooms for a few brief periods during each month. It is a revival that is very different from our own, and it seems, like so much else, to have little relevance for us and to have largely passed us by. Once, it is true, we went up to sing our Gaelic songs at the various Celtic concerts that have become so much a part of the summer culture, and we were billed by the bright young schoolteachers who run such things as MacKinnon's Miners' Chorus; but that, too, seemed as lonely and irrelevant as it was meaningless. It was as if we were parodies of ourselves, standing in rows, wearing our miners' gear, or being asked to shave and wear suits, being plied with rum while waiting for our turn on the programme, only then to mouth our songs to batteries of tape recorders and to people who did not understand them. It was as if it were everything that song should not be, contrived and artificial and nonspontaneous and lacking in communication.

I have heard and seen the Zulus dance until they shook the earth. I have seen large splendid men leap and twist and bend their bodies to the hard-baked flatness of the reddened soil. And I have followed their gestures and listened to their shouts and looked into their eyes in the hope that I might understand the meaning of their art. Hoping to find there a message that is recognizable only to primitive men. Yet

82

though I think I have caught glimpses of their joy, despair or disdain, it seems that in the end, they must dance mainly for themselves. Their dancing speaks a language whose true meaning will elude me forever; I will never grasp the full impact of the subtleties and nuances that are spoken by the small head gesture or the flashing fleck of muscle.

I would like to understand more deeply what they have to say, in the vague hope that it might be in some way akin to what is expressed in our own singing. That there might be some message that we share. But I can never enter deeply enough into their experience, can never penetrate behind the private mysteries of their eyes. Perhaps, I think sometimes, I am expecting too much. Yet on those occasions when we did sing at the concerts, I would have liked to reach beyond the tape recorders and the faces of the uninvolved to something that might prove to be more substantial and enduring. Yet in the end, it seemed we, too, were only singing to ourselves. Singing songs in an archaic language as we, too, became more archaic and recognizing the nods of acknowledgement and shouted responses as coming only from our own friends and relatives. In many cases, the same individuals from whom we had first learned our songs. Songs that are for the most part local and private and capable of losing almost all of their substance in translation. Yet in the introduction to the literature text that my eldest daughter brings home from university, it states that "the private experience, if articulated with skill, may communicate an appeal that is universal beyond the limitations of time or landscape." I have read that over several times and thought about its meaning in relation to myself.

When I was a boy, my father told me that I would never understand the nature of sex until I had participated in it in some worthwhile way and that there was little point in trying to grasp its meaning through erotic reading or looking at graphic pictures or listening to the real or imagined experiences of older men. As if the written or the spoken word or the mildly pornographic picture were capable of reaching only a small portion of the distance it might hope to journey on the road to understanding. In the early days of such wistful and exploratory reading, the sexual act has to be described as "like flying." A boggling comparison at the time to virginal young men who had never been airborne. In the future numbness of our flight to Africa, we will find little that is sexual if it is to be like our other flights to such distant destinations.

We will not have much to say about our flight to those we leave behind and little about our destinations when we land. Sending only the almost obligatory postcards that talk about the weather continents and oceans away. Saying that "things are going as expected," "going well." Postcards that have as their most exciting feature the exotic postage stamps sought after by the younger children for games of show and tell.

I have long since abandoned any hope of describing the sexual act or having it described to me. Perhaps it is enough to know that it is not at all like flying, though I do not know what it is really like. I have never been told, nor can I, in my turn, tell. But I would like somehow to show and tell the nature of my work and perhaps some of my entombed feelings to those that I would love, if they would care to listen.

I would like to tell my wife and children something of the way my years pass by on the route to my inevitable death. I would like to explain somehow what it is like to be a gladiator who fights always the impassiveness of water as it drips on darkened stone. And what it is like to work one's life in the tightness of confined space. I would like somehow to say how I felt when I lost my father in Kirkland Lake or my younger brother in Springdale, Newfoundland. I would like to say how frightened I am sometimes of what I do. And of how I lie awake at night aware of my own decline and of the diminishing of the men around me. For all of us know that we will not last much longer and that it is unlikely we will be replaced in the shaft's bottom by members of our own flesh and bone. For such replacement, like our Gaelic, seems to be of the past and now largely over.

Our sons will go to the universities to study dentistry or law and to become fatly affluent before they are 30. Men who will stand over six feet tall and who will move their fat, pudgy fingers over the limited possibilities to be found in other people's mouths. Or men who sit behind desks shuffling papers relating to divorce or theft or assault or the taking of life. To grow prosperous from pain and sorrow and the desolation of human failure. They will be far removed from the physical life and will seek it out only through jogging or golf or games of handball with friendly colleagues. They will join expensive private clubs for the pleasures of perspiration, and they will not die in falling stone or chilling water or thousands of miles from those they love. They will not die in any such manner, partially, at least, because we have told them not to and have encouraged them to seek out other ways of life which lead, we hope, to gentler deaths. And yet because it seems they will follow our advice instead of our lives, we will experience, in any future that is ours, only an increased sense of anguished isolation and an ironic feeling of confused bereavement. Perhaps it is always so for parents who give the young advice and find that it is followed. And who find that those who follow such advice must inevitably journey far from those who give it to distant, lonely worlds which are forever unknowable to those who wait behind. Yet perhaps those who go find in the regions to which they travel but another kind of inarticulate loneliness. Perhaps the dentist feels mute anguish as he circles his chair, and the lawyer who lives in a world of words finds little relationship between professional talk and what he would hope to be true expression. Perhaps he, too, in his quiet heart sings something akin to Gaelic songs, sings in an old archaic language private words that reach to no one. And perhaps both lawyer and dentist journey down into an Africa as deep and dark and distant as ours. I can but vaguely imagine what I will never know.

I have always wished that my children could see me at my work. That they might journey down with me in the dripping cage to the shaft's bottom or walk the eerie tunnels of the drifts that end in walls of staring stone. And that they might see how articulate we are in the accomplishment of what we do. That they might appreciate the perfection of our drilling and the calculation of our angles and the measuring of our powder and that they might understand that what we know through eye and ear and touch is of a finer quality than any information garnered by the most sophisticated of mining engineers with all their elaborate equipment.

I would like to show them how professional we are and how, in spite of the chill and the water and the dark and the danger, there is perhaps a certain eloquent beauty to be found in what we do. Not the beauty of stillness to be found in gleaming crystal or in the polished hardwood floors to which my wife devotes such care but, rather, the beauty of motion on the edge of violence, which by its very nature can never long endure. It is perhaps akin to the violent motion of the huge professional athletes on the given days or nights of their many games. Men as huge and physical as are we; polished and eloquent in the propelling of their bodies toward their desired goals and in their relationships and dependencies on one another but often numb and silent before the microphones of sedentary interviewers. Few of us get to show our children what we do on national television; we offer only the numbness and silence by itself. Unable to either show or tell.

I have always wished to be better than the merely mediocre, and I have always wanted to use the power of my body in the fulfilling of such a wish. Perhaps that is why I left the university after only one year. A year that was spent mainly as an athlete and as a casual reader of English literature. I could not release myself enough physically and seemed always to be constricted and confined. In sleeping rooms that were too low, by toilet stalls that were too narrow, in lecture halls that were too hot, even by the desks in those lecture halls, which I found always so difficult to get in and out of. Confined, too, by bells and buzzers and curfews and deadlines, which for me had little meaning. I wanted to burst out, to use my strength in some demanding task that would allow me somehow to feel that I was breaking free. And I could not find enough release in the muddy wars on the football field or in the thudding contact of the enclosed and boarded rink. I suppose I was drawn, too, by the apparent glamour of the men who followed the shafts. Impressed by their returning here in summer with their fast cars and expensive clothes; also by the fact that I was from a mining family that has given itself for generations to the darkened earth.

I was aware even then of the ultimate irony of my choice. Aware of how contradictory it seemed that someone who was bothered by confinement should choose to spend his working days in the most confined of spaces. Yet the difference seems to be that when we work, we are never still. Never merely entombed like the prisoner in the passive darkness of his solitary confinement. For we are always expanding the perimeters of our seeming incarceration. We are always moving downward or inward or forward or, in the driving of our raises, even upward. We are big men engaged in perhaps the most violent of occupations, and we have chosen as our adversary walls and faces of massive stone. It is as if the stone of the spherical Earth has challenged us to move its weight and find its treasure, and we have accepted the challenge and responded with drill and steel and powder and strength and all our ingenuity. In the chill and damp, we have given ourselves to the breaking down of walls and barriers. We have sentenced ourselves to enclosures so that we might taste the giddy joy of breaking through. Always hopeful of breaking through, though we know we never will break free.

Drilling and hammering our way to the world's resources, we have left them when found and moved on. Left them for others to expand or to exploit and to make room for the often stable communities that come in our wake: the sewer lines and the fire hydrants and the neat rows of company houses; the overorganized athletic leagues and the ever hopeful schools; the Junior Chambers of Commerce. We have moved about the world, liberating resources, largely untouched by political uncertainties and upheavals, seldom harmed by the midnight plots, the surprising coups and the fast assassinations. We were in Haiti with Duvalier in 1960 and in Chile before Allende and in the Congo before it became associated with Zaire. In Bolivia and in Guatemala and in Mexico and in a Jamaica that the tourists never see. Each segment of the world aspires to the treasure, real or imagined, that lies encased in its vaults of stone, and those who would find such booty are readily admitted and handsomely paid, be they employed by dictator or budding democracy or capitalists expanding their holdings and their wealth. Renco Development on Bay Street will wait for us. They will endure our summer on the beach and our lack of response to their seemingly urgent messages. They will endure our Toronto drunkenness and pay our bail and advance us personal loans. And when we go, they will pay us thousands of dollars for our work, optimistically hoping that they may make millions in their turn. They will wait for us because they know from years of many contracts that we are the best bet to deliver for them in the end.

There are two other crews in Canada as strong as, perhaps even stronger than, we are. They are in Rouyn-Noranda; and as our crew is known as MacKinnon, theirs are known by the names of Lafrenière and Picard. We have worked beside them at various times, competed with them and brawled with them in the hall-like beer parlours of Malarctic and Temiskaming, and occasionally, we have saved one another's lives. They will not go to Africa for Renco Development because they are imprisoned in the depths of their language. And because they speak no English, they will not move out of Quebec or out of northern or northeastern Ontario. Once, there was also the O'Leary crew, who were Irish Newfoundlanders. But many of them were lost in a cave-in in India, and of those who remained, most have gone to work with their relatives on high-steel construction in New York. We see them sometimes, now, in the bars of Brooklyn or sometimes in the summers at the ferry terminal in North Sydney before they cross to Port aux Basques. Iron work, they say, also pays highly for the risk to life; and the long fall from the towering, swaying skyscrapers can occur for any man but once. It seems, for them, that they have exchanged the possibility of being fallen upon for that of falling itself. And that after years of dodging and fearing falling objects from above, they have become such potential objects themselves. Their loss diminishes us too, because we know how good they were at what they did and know, too, that the mangled remnants of their dead were flown from India in sealed containers to lie on such summer days as these beneath the nodding wildflowers that grow on outport graves.

I must not think too much of death and loss, I tell myself repeatedly. For if I am to survive, I must be as careful and calculating with my thoughts as I am with my tools when working so far beneath the Earth's surface. I must always be careful of sloppiness and self-indulgence lest they cost me dearly in the end.

Out on the ocean now, it is beginning to roughen, and the southwest wind is blowing the smallish waves into larger versions of themselves. They are beginning to break upon the beach with curling whitecaps at their crests, and the water that they consist of seems no longer blue but, rather, a dull and sombre grey. There are no longer boats visible on the once flat sea, neither near at hand nor on the horizon's distant line. The sun no longer shines with the fierceness of the earlier day, and the sky has begun to cloud over. Evening is approaching. The sand is whipped by the wind and blows into our faces and stings our bodies as might a thousand pinpricks or the tiny tips of many scorching needles. We flinch and shake ourselves and reach for our protective shirts. We leave our prone positions and come restlessly to our feet, coughing and spitting and moving uneasily like nervous animals anticipating a storm. In the sand, we trace erratic designs and patterns with impatient toes. We look at one another, arching our eyebrows like bushy question marks. Perhaps this is what we have been waiting for? Perhaps this is the end and the beginning?

And now I can feel the eyes of the men upon me. They are waiting for me to give interpretations of the signals, waiting for my sign. I hesitate for a moment, running my eyes along the beach, watching water touching sand. And then I nod my head. There is almost a collective sigh that is more sensed than really heard. Almost like distant wind in far-off trees. Then suddenly, they begin to move. Rapidly, they gather their clothes and other belongings, shaking out the sand, folding and packing. Moving swiftly and with certainty, they are closing down their summer even as it is closing down on them. MacKinnon's miners are finished now and moving out. We are leaving the beach of the summer sun, and perhaps some of us will not see it anymore. For some of us may not return alive from the Africa for which we leave.

We begin to walk. First along the beach toward the north cliff of Cameron's Point and then up the steep and winding zigzagged trail that climbs its face. When I am halfway up, I stop and look back at the men strung out in single file behind me. We are mountain climbers in our way, though bound together by no physical ropes of any kind. They stop and look back too, back and down to the beach we have so recently vacated. The waves are higher now and are breaking and cresting and rolling farther in. They have obliterated the outlines of our bodies in the sand, and our footprints of brief moments before already have been washed away. There remains no evidence that we have ever been. It is as if we have never lain nor ever walked nor ever thought what thoughts we had. We leave no art or mark behind. The sea has washed its sand slate-clean.

And then the rain begins to fall. Not heavily but almost hesitantly. It is as if it has been hot and dry for so long that the act of raining has almost been forgotten and has now to be slowly and almost painfully relearned.

We reach the summit of the cliff and walk along the little path that leads us to our cars. The cars are dusty, and their metal is still hot from the earlier sun. We lean across their hoods to lift the windshield wipers from the glass. The rubber of the wiper blades has almost melted into the windshields because of heat and long disuse, and when we lift them, slender slivers of rubber remain behind. These blades will have to be replaced.

The isolated raindrops fall alike on windshield and on roof, on hood and on trunk. They trace individual rivulets through the layers of grime and then trickle down to the parched and waiting earth.

And now it is two days later. The rain has continued to fall, and in it, we have gone about preparing and completing our rituals of farewell. We have visited the banks and checked out all the dates on our insurance policies. And we have gathered our working clothes, which when worn continents hence will make us loom even larger than we are in actual life. As if we are Greek actors or mastodons of an earlier time. Soon to be replaced or else perhaps to be extinct.

We have stood bareheaded by the graves and knelt in the mud by the black granite stones. And we have visited privately and in tiny self-conscious groups the small white churches that we may not see again.

As we have become older, it seems we have become strangely more religious in ways that border close on superstition. We will take with us worn family rosaries and faded charms and loop ancestral medals and crosses of delicate worn fragility around our scar-lashed necks and about the thickness of our wrists, seemingly unaware of whatever irony they might project. This, too, seems but a further longing for the past, far removed from the "rational" approaches to religion that we sometimes encounter in our children.

We have said farewells to our children too and to our wives, and I have offered kisses and looked into their eyes and wept outwardly and inwardly for all I have not said or done and for my own clumsy failure at communication. I have not been able, as the young say, "to tell it like it is," and perhaps now I never shall.

By 4 o'clock, we are ready to go. Our cars are gathered with their motors running, and we will drive them hard and fast and be in Toronto tomorrow afternoon. We will not stop all night except for a few brief moments at the gleaming service stations, and we will keep one sober and alert driver at the wheel of each of our speeding cars. Many of the rest of us will numb ourselves with moonshine for our own complex and diverse reasons: perhaps to loosen our thoughts and tongues or perhaps to deaden and hold them down; perhaps to be as the patient who takes an anaesthetic to avoid operational pain. We will hurtle in a dark night convoy across the landscapes and the borders of four waiting provinces.

As we move out, I feel myself a figure in some mediaeval ballad who has completed his formal farewells and goes now to meet his fatalistic future. I do not particularly wish to feel this way and again would shake myself free from thoughts of death and self-indulgence.

As we gather speed, the land of the seacoast flashes by. I am in the front seat of the lead car, on the passenger side next to the window. In the side mirror, I can see the other cars stretched out behind us. We go by the scarred and abandoned coal workings of our previous generations and drive swiftly westward into the declining day. The men in the backseat begin to pass around their moonshine and attempt to adjust their long legs within the constricted space. After a while, they begin to sing in Gaelic, singing almost unconsciously the old words that are so worn and so familiar. They seem to handle them almost as they would familiar tools. I know that in the other cars, they are doing the same, even as I begin silently to mouth the words myself. There is no word in Gaelic for good-bye, only for farewell.

More than a quarter of a century ago, in my single year at university, I stumbled across an anonymous lyric from the 15th century. Last night, while packing my clothes, I encountered it again, this time in the literature text of my eldest daughter. The book was very different from the one that I had so casually used, as different perhaps as is my daughter from me. Yet the lyric was exactly the same. It had not changed at all. It comes to me now in this speeding car as the Gaelic choruses rise around me. I do not particularly welcome it or want it, and indeed, I had almost forgotten it. Yet it enters now regardless of my wants or wishes, much as one might see out of the corner of the eye an old acquaintance one has no wish to see at all. It comes again, unbidden and unexpected and imperfectly remembered. It seems borne up by the mounting, surging Gaelic voices like the flecked white foam on the surge of the towering, breaking wave. Different yet similar, and similar yet different, and in its time unable to deny:

I wend to death, knight stith in stour;
Through fight in field I won the flower;
No fights me taught the death to quell—
I wend to death, sooth I you tell.

I wend to death, a king iwis;
What helpes honour or worlde's bliss?
Death is to man the final way—
I wende to be clad in clay.

George Johnston

Bee Seasons

Packages A warm day in February. Out to the hives to see who are flying and who not. Fred seems to have lost four hives out of 60, perhaps five: a good winter. Bruce thinks he has lost six. Bees are flying from all three of mine.

The time has come to order replacements and augmentations. Fred wants three 2-pound packages, I want one, and Bruce wants six 3-pound packages.

Fred thinks two pounds is enough, and he is my authority. Two pounds of bees with a good queen will make comb honey, he says. Bruce does not agree. He wishes they would put starline queens in packages, then there would be enough.

Fred has the merest contempt for starline queens. I got one once, he says. She made a hive of cross bees, you could hardly work with them. Bruce does not agree. He had starlines, and they made quiet bees, and the bees made lots of honey too. If Fred would only order him two more from that place in the States again. Fred is Bruce's authority too, with reservations.

Fred has been working with bees since he was 10.

He is not Walter's authority. Damn fool wants to make money, says Fred. He has been takin' courses and thinks he can start right in with a lot of bees. He don't know nothin'.

Has he got equipment?

Made his own supers out of junk. Then an old fellow in Ontario sells out, and Walter buys his extractor and uncappin' gear cheap. You ought to see what he fixed up for a honey house.

Well, good luck to him.

We got to pick up his bees, says Fred. He asks if he can come, but I tell him we are full up. You want to listen to him?

I agree that I do not. The nuggets in Walter's talk are sparse, for a 3½-hour drive, counting lunch.

Instead of listening to Walter, we listen to Bruce. He has painted or taped or sanded in every other house on the way.

That Mrs. Thurston, he says. I could not do nothin' to please her. She tries to get out of payin' me. They say her husband was a terror. One day, she could not stand it no more, she tells him to shoot himself, and he does, out in the field behind the house. Was that not an awful thing? Then she took up with a Fraser on the Second Concession Road, an old bachelor, you know the one. Kept pigs.

We pull into the yard at 11 o'clock. It is a cool, sunny April morning. An odour of hot beeswax and sawn wood comes from the plant on the south side. The offices and warehouse are on the north side. An odour of bees comes from the packages, which have been driven overnight by truck from Georgia and are now standing in angular heaps on the ground, labelled and humming. Thousands of hangers-on who have come, too, are buzzing through the air among the beekeepers and their pickup trucks and cars. Talk is loud and jocular. Beekeepers are here from many parts of Quebec and from New York and Vermont. It is a yearly event. Fred would not miss it. He knows many of the beekeepers, and everyone seems to know him. The staff enjoy bantering with him.

Who is this Walter, Fred? Friend of yours?

Damn fool. Thinks he knows about bees.

Beginner?

Fred nods.

We do not want to sell him all these packages. But he will not take no.
Let him find out, says Fred.

Lunch is a yearly event too. Bruce wants to pay, but that is not allowed.
Everyone pays.

He buys us a beer on the way home.

Walter is standing in his yard waiting, veiled and gloved. His brother
is standing farther off, veiled and gloved too, a distrustful eye looking
out through his veil. We are late. We have stopped at two sawmills.
The air has turned cool. Walter's hives are made of weathered wood,
and they have a grey look in the greying light.

Can you help me? he asks.

Fred steps to the back of the truck, lowers the gate of the animal box
and hands the packages out one by one to Bruce and me. Walter
watches as we set them on the ground. Then Fred pries the can of sugar
syrup out of one package and takes the queen cage.

Hold this, he commands Walter. See the hole where I took the can out?
Shake the syrup through it onto the bees. Do not put it on the screen.
Then shake the bees into your frames.

He demonstrates, as he speaks, with the package, prying the lid loose
to get the last of the bees out. We have neither veil nor gloves, but the
bees are sticky and sated with syrup; they swarm over the frames and
down between them. The few that fly about pay no attention to us. Fred
sets the syrup can upside down on the top bars. Then he pokes a fine
nail from the lid through the sugar plug in the queen cage and hangs
the cage between two frames.

Now put your cover on, he says.

Can you stay and help me? Look at all these packages!

Fred is late for chores.

Can you? Or you?

I am late too, and so is Bruce.

If they are not all in tonight, the rest will keep till tomorrow.

I feel sorry for Walter as we climb back into the truck. His brother is
waving a wandering bee away. I told you not to wave at them, says
Walter in a melancholy tone of voice.

Swarm   Phone! Quinns have a swarm, and they have company, and
we have company. Review the procedure for them please.

Take the spare super with the drawn comb and the bottom board, put them under the swarm, and shake the bees into it.

Back to lunch. I am telling the story about the chihuahua and the bicycle, and the phone rings again. The swarm is on a big branch high up, and there is no shaking it loose.

Swarms are like birth and death, they take no account of plans and are not to be put off, though their challenge weakens as the summer wears on; after mid-July, it may be ignored, as a phone may be let ring until it stops.

Is it a big swarm?

Pretty big.

Light the smoker. I shall be there in 20 minutes.

Jamie is in white coveralls and veil, and he is tying a rusty pail to the end of a long and heavy pole. Bees may be gathered in a rusty pail but not in a shiny one. Seamus is blowing smoke into the air, and the company are standing by in the field. The swarm is noisy on the branch, a fuzzy brown growth, as awkwardly placed as can be, 25 feet up over a stone pile on which the super, with its drawn comb, teeters.

Up the extension ladder goes Jamie, confident in my assurance that a new swarm is peaceful. Hughie, clad in shorts and cotton jersey, wields the rusty pail on the heavy pole, and Jamie brushes the bees into it. We empty two pailfuls into the super, and they seem to be settling there. Hughie gets stung and retreats. The bees have been mostly brushed from the branch, and the air is full of them, flying in excited zigzags. Their hum is loud. Next thing, Jamie may be heard hooting as he runs for the house. Bees have got under his veil and given him a thorough stinging. He breaks out in welts and begins to show alarming symptoms. Jeannie, who is a doctor, keeps watch on his pulse and his breathing; she gives him antihistamine. She concludes that his symptoms are no longer alarming, but he is a casualty now and not a participant. He bathes himself with soda to calm the itch that he feels all over. The swarm is still noisy. Hughie puts on Jamie's armour, and we return to it. It is a brown growth hanging from the branch as before, and the super is empty except for a few indecisive bees. We are unwilling to leave it unhived after Jamie's sufferings, but we can see that a new strategy is needed. Get the swede saw, clear away the lower branches and undergrowth, and move the super to a less teetery position off the stone pile and as near where the bees will land as we can guess.

Hughie's turn to climb the ladder, and this time, it is saw, saw, saw at the branch, close to the trunk. At last it comes, crack, crack and crash, and the air is full of eccentric beelines and noise, and there are heaps of bees on the stones, near enough that many may be shaken and scooped onto the frames. By and by, the super is thick with them. Put a lid on it.

Hurrah!

Perhaps.

It is never better than perhaps with a swarm.

Jamie, what about this climbing of ladders? It was my idea and I am sorry, and next time, we must ponder. Is a July swarm worth a face full of stings? For two days, you look like a beaten prizefighter.

Skunk   A whiff of skunk in the evening air.

Little as one is inclined to action, the whiff demands it.

Out to the hives. The honey flow has begun, and the twilights are bright and long. Grass in front of the bottom boards has been pushed down and pulled aside.

He claws at it, Fred says. Out come the bees to investigate, and he eats them. He can thin out a hive like nothin'.

Reluctantly, I fetch the cage trap and bait it with an egg.

Skunks have their part to play, and I regret collisions with ours, for if the skunk takes the bait, both our parts become fateful. Skunks have a fearsome weapon with which Fred has had encounters and I not. Supposing I catch a skunk, what then? Having placed the egg and set the trip engine for the gate, I am committed. Skunk cannot be left caged to starve, nor released, nor shot except from a range at which my aim is not sure. I should like to ask Fred for advice, but pride restrains me. Early morning. Who would not hope through the binoculars to see the trap empty? Fred, for one. He knows already that it is not and is on hand to see what I do and assist. Cage traps are new to him; he has bought one but not used it.

The skunk is shifting about inside, half hidden by a nest of grass he has clawed up into it through the wire-mesh floor. A gentleman skunk, as we establish later. Female skunks are ladies. Lady and gentleman skunks are elegant in their black and white. This gentleman eyes us. The trap is a rectangular box, wire mesh on sides and bottom, metal gates at either end. One gate is left closed, the other closes on the skunk when he or she crosses the trip engine. The top is a metal rectangle with the handle in the centre. I have tied 20-foot lengths of baling twine to the handle and laid them out straight from both gates. I plan to have Fred and me each take an end of twine, pull it tight, raise the trap in the air by this means, transport it to a deep pool in the brook and there drown the skunk.

An inadequately thought-out plan. The twine will not lift the trap however hard we pull. I am at a nonplus. A hundred yards of pasture must be crossed before we come to the pool. Fred offers to throw a raincoat over the trap and manhandle it down.

No, I say, I cannot be responsible for such a risk.

I retire to my workbench and construct a sledge of plywood with a long piece of baler twine tied to one end. Somehow, we get the trap pushed and pulled onto it.

One of Fred's best stories is of my struggle across the hundred yards of pasture pulling the sledge well behind me. He is ready to help, but his bulk is shaking with laughter. There is not much he can do anyhow. The same laugh comes back at this point in the story when he tells it and remembers how I walk into the pool to my middle and far out on the far side, pulling sledge and trap into the water at last.

One learns. Learning is life, and hard lessons are best, one might say only. The next skunk was a lady. I threw a tarpaulin over her, trap and all, and lifted her by hand into my wheelbarrow. There were others, ladies and gentlemen. They take their tumbril ride well; I tell myself that they may be enjoying it.

Then I learn something more: skunks do not climb, not even a low fence. I put this knowledge to work and fence the fronts of my hives. Now, when the hay is cut and skunks take off at dusk over the shorn fields, hoping for a feed of bees — or whatever else comes their way, an egg, a chick or two or a setting hen — I think of them with benevolence and leave the trap in the woodshed.

The ground shakes. Fred. Something has reminded him of my first skunk.

Queens   The queen picks her drone, says Walter. She knows which one.

He has watched a nice drone around the corner of the hive, a fat one, waiting. The queen comes out and then goes in again. She knows about him.

The books tell us that the virgin takes off on her mating flight and a crowd of drones, from different hives, with her. Perhaps she does another mating flight, and another. What goes on up there? They say that she mates more than once with different drones, perhaps four or five, and then she has thousands of eggs, enough for two or three years, her life.

How can they know all that? asks Walter. Do they get up there and watch? In a balloon or something? I watch at the hive. Bees know when a virgin is going to mate. They run up and down the combs, up and down, up and down. The hive gits stirred up. You can't tell me she don't know. I seen this fat drone.

Fred says Walter is a liar. Walter's lies make him mad. They make him mad because they are boring. Walter begs to go up to Bedford with us for supplies, three of us in the cab of Fred's pickup, an hour and a quarter there, hour and a quarter back and lunch in the town. All right, we say. Once. Walter talks. Everything he says is hard to believe, boring. The way he talks is boring too, fishing for words and winking and blinking and swallowing and nodding his head.

A queen's life is not to be envied; it is as fate-bound and regulated as a human life. It begins as a worker egg. Something moves the workers to nourish its womanliness and so make the it that it would normally become into a queen. No royal blood and no inheritance. Not a woman, unless it has been selected, seemingly at random, and specially fed. An egg, and an it egg at that.

A drone egg is decisively male.

A brief encounter or four or five, aloft on a flight whose moment she decides, and the virgin is deflowered. Henceforth, her life is eggs, except for a spell at the end of summer. Workers attend her, groom her and watch her, they stroke and lick her, and they bring up her children. She moves her long body across the combs at a queenly pace and with a flickering motion, while her attendants fuss around her. She has a battery of scents that give direction to the hive.

One says, It is time to think of swarming, make queen cells.

Another says, Winter is coming, turn the drones out of doors.

Another says, I am past my prime.

These scents have become known to the men who study bees and by them given the name pheromones. Fred and Walter and Steve and I refer to them, though our pronunciation is uncertain. When we meet in town or at an auction or a wedding anniversary party, we ask one another, How are your bees? We may ask, What is the pheromone these days? if we feel like pronouncing it.

Virgins may now be artificially inseminated. I think it is too bad. My attitude is unacceptable, but I persist in thinking it is too bad. My notion that there may be a fleeting bliss in the mating flight is no more than that, no better than my faith in human goodness, groundless and unproductive, but I give it up unwillingly. And Walter's drone waiting around the corner of the hive. The virgin knows about him. I should like it to be true.

Extraction   Mid-August, time to take off the last of the honey. Jamie and I arm ourselves and light the smoker.

Jamie's wrists are nimble. He pries out a frame and, with a flick, throws the bees, a buzzing throng, on the ground in front of the hive, all but a few, which I brush off. I pry a frame out and give it my kind of flick. Soon, the air is full of bees, and the ground is crawling with them. We have pulled up our socks over the cuffs of our trousers.

It is a calm, sunny midday. Many bees are foraging, though the nectar supply has dwindled. A sting here and there each, but for the most part, the bees are unresentful. The frames are full of honey and well capped, their surfaces are pebbly with white wax. They are heavy; a deep super of eight frames is as much as I want to lift, but Jamie handles it easily.

Other demands call us when we have taken off, though this warm weather is right for extraction. When we get back to the honey house a few days later, the air has turned cool, the honey is sluggish, and hungry bees are gathering at the windows. I have neglected to repair the screens.

Uncapping goes badly. My knife is dull, and the fork I bought a few years ago, and prefer when the weather is warm, lets me down today: it gets gummed up. Turning the extractor is no easier. Jamie cranks hard and works up a sweat in the cool air.

Quite a few bees, says Fred, looking in.

There must be a thousand. They come in around the door. We stuff the openings with newspaper; then the vibration of the extractor shakes the newspaper back out again. In come the bees through the woodshed and the north passage. The air is full of them. Some are in the extractor. Many are drowning in the collector bucket. Honey is slow to move through the straining cloth, and bees drown in it. Hundreds are in the windows, wanting out. If we open a window to let them out, more hundreds fly in.

Fred observes my struggle with the cappings and offers his electric knife. I have resisted electric knives after reading somewhere of melted wax getting into the honey.

That don't hurt none, says Fred, and I succumb.

He comes back with the knife and offers the use of his electric extractor. Why not?

Well, we have everything set up. Inertia—or otherwise, dogged-ness—decides. Many thanks just the same.

A small operation, 160 pounds. Clover, sweet clover, vetch, creeping charlie, wild thyme and goldenrod. We keep some apart that seems to be mostly buckwheat, not dark but a distinct flavour of buckwheat, very good.

Fred has no time for buckwheat or goldenrod, but we like it. His favourite is basswood. Mine too, when we can get it.

Bees. In the evening, they hung in two swarms under the windows. I swept them into a bucket and put them out. For days, they flew about in the honey house and got into the honey as I canned it up. I had to keep picking them out.

Wintering   Cold today, though it is still October: dark skies, freezing air and gusting winds. Showers of rain and snow. Three days ago, we sat on the edge of the verandah and drank our afternoon tea in warm sunshine. Small sow thistles dotted the lawn with yellow. Foragers from our hives work at our feet, making the heads bob a little as they light on them and part their petals. Their wings make a pleasant monotone. Wintering seems far in the future.

Now, it is upon us. We heft our hives and note that some of them are light. It has been a poor summer: nectar enough but too little foraging weather. We shall have to do some feeding, two to one of sugar and water. Fred says honey is best. To be sure. Yet the experts tell us that sugar syrup is better than nectar from the fall flowers—goldenrod, Michaelmas daisies and wild asters. It has too much protein, which gives the bees diarrhea.

Fred has designed a simple, ingenious and sufficient winter cover, a plywood box lined with tentest that fits down over the hive and shields it against freezing winds without stopping a circulation of air. A small entrance at the top allows the bees to fly out on a warm day and, as the term for it is, cleanse themselves. A layer of fibreglass insulation on top of the inner cover collects moisture, and hardware cloth stapled across the lower entrance keeps out mice. Mice are glad to find a hive of full combs to nest in. There, they may be warm and well fed while they chew the comb to pieces and starve the bees.

Comes a cool November afternoon, and we lug the covers out and put them on. They are not heavy but awkward; their bottom edges bang against our shins. We are glad of them just the same and find them easier than wrapping with tar paper on a windy November day. Now we sit back. The bees either make it through or they do not. The queens have stopped laying now, and the drones have been driven out to die. Workers and queens are clustering near the fronts of the lower brood chambers, eating honey and generating warmth. As the winter wears on, they move slowly back and upward, and by spring, they are at the top and somewhat to the back of the upper brood chamber. We give them little thought as we stoke our fires and venture out for winter chores or pleasure. On an open day, we may pass the hives and stop by for a look. We put our ears to the top entrance and listen for wing movements as the bees shift place in the cluster. If there is snow, it is likely to be spotted with yellow and brown around the hives where the occasional flying bee has dropped its feces. Dead bees will be spotted about too, who have ventured out when the air is too cold.

Comes a blizzard with drifting snow. A few of the hives are quite covered and stay covered for many days, sometimes for two or three weeks. One year, we dig in to see. There is the hive, in a snow room that its warmth has made. Bees have been flying in this room. It was late winter, near the end of February. The queen, we knew, was beginning to lay again in her cluster, in her brood chamber, in the middle of her snow room.

Norman Levine

Into the Bush

The man in the Algoma office was right: there were improvements. Though the machinery had changed — instead of the old steam engine, there was a new diesel, freshly painted with a large black grizzly bear on its sides — the two coaches carrying the passengers had not. Their insides were still like old worn-out billiard tables with large patches eaten out of the green. The seats were hard and uncomfortable. Gas brackets hung from the ceiling. In the centre of the ceiling, a couple of naked light bulbs. Two men got on, dressed in heavy lumberjack shirts and tall boots laced high up. They spoke in French. They went through the first coach that was going to Wawa and into the second one.

In the first coach, there were five of us, all sitting in separate seats. Opposite me was the girl in her fur coat. Her top lip protruded and was pinched just underneath the nose as if she had had an operation there. She was plump, her eyes inquisitive, but when you looked at her, they became defensive. Behind the girl was an elderly couple, both short and stout. The man had coarse straight white hair cut short on top of his head. His head looked much too big for his body. He wore a cheap secondhand black suit. He took off his jacket and showed fireman's braces holding up his trousers and a loud tie of painted palm trees. His wife was taller, a shapeless body, a sad, tired face; she had a print dress on, with a clasp, *Mother*, pinned to the dress by the neck. Behind me, in the last seat of the coach, was a well-built middle-aged man, a handsome Slavic face, high cheekbones, a long thin nose, wearing a cheap blue suit.

We started to move at 7:15 with the familiar two deep notes. I could see the muddy river, the logs piled high on the banks, snow melting everywhere, leaving stains as it turned to water and the earth to mud. The place looked like a junkyard. Old buckets, tires, cardboard, twisted wire, old rusty tins, mounds of rubbish. On the other tracks were freight cars and tankers: an Algoma Central attached to one marked Chesapeake and Ohio, another to Missouri Pacific. Past old brick buildings with narrow windows and mud around them. And men in old coats, overalls and Windbreakers and ski caps, walking to work with black lunchpails, driving to work in new, brightly painted cars, parking them outside the grimy buildings and going inside. The coach smelled of disinfectant.

In less than five miles from the siding, we were in thick forest. And the rest of the morning and early afternoon was one vast repetition.

We crossed trestle bridges, curved by small, partly frozen lakes and moved slowly through miles of pine, hemlock, spruce and birch. Sometimes, the trees were so thick, they did not let the light through. Every 15 minutes, there was a stop. Eton. Frater. Canyon. Magpie. Cases of milk bottles were taken off from the baggage car for the logging camps deeper in the bush away from the line. Often, the train did not stop, it just slowed down while the conductor held out to the waiting man on the ground a small bundle of newspapers, a mail-order catalogue, a circular, a few letters. And by these whistle stops hemmed in by the trees were a few shacks painted a dull brown, smoke coming from the chimneys, an outhouse not far away. But then the trees swallowed the clearing and the perimeter of stumps. And then more trees and more trees and the melting snow between the trees like an animal skin that was shrinking as it dried up.

We moved from a crest of a ridge with a river below, the ice breaking up, thick massive blocks jammed one on top of the other, while the muddy water flowed swiftly around and under the ice. Then down through a valley with large rocks above us. And icicles hanging from the rocks thick and long and tapering to a fine point that was turning into water. On one side of the slope where the sun was shining, the snow and the ice was melting and the water came down as a torrent and over the track, washing away the top layer of soil in its path, uprooting trees and rocks.

The sun had not yet touched the other side of the slope, and the water, which had flowed yesterday, then froze during the night, remained frozen: a streak of thick grey ice with small trees and rocks locked in the ice on the lower slopes while the top hung down with massive grey icicles. It would run again later in the day, then freeze again during the night.

Then more trees, close together, very thick and straight, especially the pine and the spruce, hiding the light. Then we stopped again by a few log cabins, the snow piled high on the roofs, and a tall Finnish-looking woman in a heavy coat and flying boots came through the snow and met the two men in lumberjack shirts who got off the train. Then back through tunnels of evergreen, by rocks, water, ice and snow.

The scenery, for all its magnificence, did not excite me. It had the beauty of something primitive, hostile and indifferent. There was no warmth to be had out of this landscape, it hadn't been lived in. To try to understand it, one would have to reduce it to human terms: it represented wealth—that meant possession, and man reduces this hostility and indifference by hacking into it, cutting straight lines and curves, imposing the only sense of order that he knows.

"*T'rawnah-Star, T'rawnah-Star.* Funnies. Western. Get your last read. Get your last read." A small boy, Italian—the shrewd face looked 16 or 17, but his short, spare body made him look younger—came through the compartment wearing a white apron and carrying magazines and newspapers and shouting. The Slav in the back was sprawled out in his seat snoring. The girl had long ago taken off her fur coat. It was warm in the coach. No ventilation. We shared a bar of chocolate. She said she was a Scottish nurse going to work in the hospital at Wawa. She had worked in the bush in Labrador and in Newfoundland, and she was coming here because the pay was better and it was a little closer to civilization. I told her it was isolated.

"It couldn't be as cut off as the logging camps in Labrador or the one in Newfie," she said. "Sometimes, we didn't get mail for weeks."

We watched the trees go by.

She said you could tell a spruce by the bit on the top that always faced the same direction. She had picked that up from the loggers in Newfoundland. We sang a few songs: *A Wee Dock and Doris, The Nut Brown Maiden, My Bonny Lad.* She had a soft, resonant voice. Her face was very pale. She asked me if I was married. I said I was. She said she had had a boyfriend, he was an engineer in the RAF. He was killed in the war. The old couple who sat behind her came over and listened while she sang. They were going to visit their daughter in the bush. He used to work for the railroad, and they gave him a free pass when he retired, so now, they came up twice a year to see their daughter. They were Irish, and they both had badly fitting store teeth. His clicked when he talked, while hers appeared to float in her mouth.

Outside, young birches moved in the wind. White praying branches and peeling bark. Their fragility stood out in all this massiveness. They were white and stark, snow about them.

By noon, the journey had gone on much too long. It was too much the same. The coach was stuffy. The retired couple had slumped in their seats, mouths open, asleep.

The nurse fell asleep leaning against the window looking outside. The total distance was 183 miles, and we had travelled half of it in nearly six hours when the young boy in white apron came walking through again. "Anybody want to eat? Anybody here for lunch?" I went to the head of the coach. There were four tables with chairs and a small kitchen partitioned off by a dirty black curtain. Stacks of funnies were on the floor, Western stories, dime detectives, love stories — and a large cardboard box overflowing with opened tin cans. The boy came out from behind the curtain. "You want tomato or vegetable soup?" I said I'd have a hot dog and coffee. He overboiled the hot dog in a large pot and brought me a cracked cup of stale coffee. Then he went back to his funny.

At Hawk Junction, we had a 10-minute stop. Young boys were waiting for the train, and as soon as it stopped, they climbed in, ran through the coach, went into the toilet, drank the water out of the glass container at the head of the coach until it was dry. Then they threw the paper cups and fought each other for the choice seats by the windows.

I went out to exercise my legs. Everything was still. The air cool and fresh and the smell of trees. The light clear. The forest spilled over its silence into this clearing. It was the largest clearing that we had come to. The trees were all around it. And huddled inside were wooden houses; a few had signs saying that they were hotels and general stores. Some men in overalls and Windbreakers were standing by the back of trucks at the siding watching the train, the kids and the passengers. A couple of black mongrel dogs were playing in the snow. It was like most of the other stops along the line, a railway workers' settlement.

When I returned inside, the kids had squeezed into all the empty seats. They were playing a game of "going somewhere." One said that this time, he was going to Toronto. Another said that this time, he was going to New York. Another one said he was going to Montreal to see the Canadiens play for the Stanley Cup. Several others agreed to go with him. Then the brakeman came on board, and without being told, they climbed off, stood by the siding, threw snowballs at each other and watched as the train pulled away.

The landscape had remained so much the same for so long that one hardly took notice of it now, but after Hawk Junction, the train began to climb a sharp gradient and to go even slower. And as we approached the crest, the landscape suddenly changed.

It looked like a battlefield. One of those melodramatic pictures of World War I. Trees, with branches and leaves and bark and pine needles, disappeared. And all that remained standing were scattered black charred trunks. Sometimes, there was only half a trunk, split, broken, burnt, and stumps around it. And they stood up from the rock; black, gaunt vertical lines; a grey and yellowish grey rock broken by patches of white snow. And where the snow melted, the water was the colour of rust. All vegetation was killed by the sulphur that the wind carried from the Sinter Plant. You could see the direction of the wind. It was like a scar in the landscape. In the distance, on either side, I could see more hills with the blue-black outline of growing trees on them. But here, everything was dead. The rocks the colour of ashes and the burned-out remnants of trees sticking up like a field of gibbets. And it seemed as if we were deliberately crawling through this cemetery, until we came around a bend and I saw the Mine rising like a large back tooth that was decayed and split in its centre.

The Mine   I first came to the Mine on a hot June afternoon in 1948. With two others from university, we decided to go and work the summer in the bush where we knew the pay was good and where I would be able to save some money, as I wanted to come over to England.

We did not get to the Mine until sundown. The train was slow and made this journey only three times a week. A cream-coloured bus with a blue sign, "Algoma Ore Properties," painted on its side waited by the siding. Some men were inside. The driver sat like a sparrow over the wheel, a jockey cap on his head. He wore an orange sweater with "Helen Mine" in blue across the front. "Students?" he said. We told him we were. "Hop in."

We came to a lake with wooden houses on one side and a dirt road. The bus stopped by a general store. Several men with black lunchpails climbed in. They called the driver Jack in various accents. He punched small cards that they held up as they entered the bus.

We drove around the lake and up a hill. Above us, a steel cable carried large buckets of iron ore from the Mine to the Sinter Plant. We stopped at the top of the hill beside wooden buildings. I asked the driver where the office was. He said to follow him. He carried a mail sack over his shoulder.

"Where you from?"

Bob and I said Ottawa; Ian said Montreal.

"Play ball?"

We said we did.

He remained silent as we went through a wooden gate and into a frame building partitioned off for several offices. The bus driver dropped the mail sack on the floor, and a girl came out of one of the partitions. "Hi, Glorie. Students." And he went out. She came to the counter, unsmiling, and took some paper. A skirt and a sweater, and on her sweater at the neck, she wore a black cross. She took our names and home addresses. Then she told us to go to the cookhouse, the next building away, and ask the cook for our lunchpails.

We crossed the rough ground and saw a man with glasses, grey hair, stripped to the waist, holding a white apron. He stood by the cookhouse near several large barrels filled with garbage and looked toward the horizon. It was a stiff sky, and all the hills were black.

He brought us into his office and gave us black lunchpails. "It's all right," he said. "It will come off your first cheque." He spoke with a Scottish accent. Then he told us to scratch our names on the lunchpails with a nail, that supper was at 7:30, so that we still had half an hour to get a place to sleep. We walked out through the dining hall. Twenty large, unpainted tables, benches on both sides. The first table near the door had chairs and flowers and a sign, "STAFF ONLY." He showed us a wooden building about 30 yards away, at the edge of a cliff. "Go to Room 9 and ask for Jim Wordle."

The cable stretched over the cookhouse, and I could hear it creak as the buckets kept passing overhead. Where the cable crossed between cookhouse and office, a steel net was suspended above the ground.

We found number 9 in a plain building smelling of paint. Outside the door, a bundle of dirty laundry was tied together by a shirt. Some time passed between our knock and the door being opened. At first, I thought he was a boy, then he switched the room light on, and I could see that he was old, unshaven and sleepy. He could not be much more than five feet, a thin frame covered by a dirty white shirt buttoned tight at the neck, collar crumpled, and grey trousers that were too small. He wore no shoes but heavy woollen socks. His fly buttons were undone.

We told him what we wanted. He went to a cupboard and pulled out a large piece of cardboard. He sat down on his bed and began to examine the large writing on one side of the board. I looked around the room. It stank of old age. Shelves covered an entire wall. In these shelves, toothpaste, soap, razor blades, shoelaces and chocolate bars were propped up in the open boxes. Above his bed, pasted to the wall, was a map similar to the one hanging in the company's office in Sault Ste. Marie. Covering most of the map's face were pictures of boxers, hockey players, movie stars, old Christmas cards, pin-up girls and an old calendar advertising life insurance.

"Yours will be 42," he said to Bob and myself, and to Ian he gave number 43. "You'll be with a Finn. He's away in the Soo having a blow." He said this with difficulty, for he had no teeth. They were sunk in a glass of water by his bed. He licked the end of the pencil and printed our names large on the cardboard. "You can get most things from me." He showed us the cupboard built into the wall where he returned the piece of cardboard. Inside sprawled hundreds of paperbacks and magazines. "Mystery, cowboy, sex stories, funnies, no need to pay. It'll come off your cheque."

Number 42 was a square room freshly painted white with one window directly opposite the door. Two iron beds, two dressers, all new. A light hung from the ceiling. I tried to raise the window but was able to move it only a few inches. I could see a side of a hill right below us and what looked like a small lake that was dry. The outside air tasted cold and fresh. Bob and I unpacked and had changed into old clothes when we heard a bell tolling. There was nothing urgent about the sound. A slow sound, silence, then the sound again. We went out of the room and looked out of the window in the passage. Men were pressed tight to the door of the cookhouse. Others were running toward it. Suddenly, the door opened, and those that were there disappeared inside. By the time we reached the cookhouse, the tables were crowded with men eating. Latecomers, like ourselves, were running from one table to another until they found a place on a bench.

At my table, they were speaking German. The only one not speaking was deformed. He sat opposite me. Stubbles for fingers on a wrist that was raw. A large red handkerchief, tied around his head, went underneath his chin. He used this handkerchief to hold his jaw together. To eat, he would loosen the knot above his head, and with one stubbled hand, he would slide the food from the table to his mouth while the other worked the jaw up and down.

"You a Canadian?"

A few nicotine-stained teeth, wide gaps between.

"Yes."

"Look at these monkeys eat."

As a platter of food was placed on the table, often before it reached the table, hands snatched whatever they could get. In less than 10 minutes, it was all over. The men, still chewing, stood up from the benches and went with their dishes to a large sink in the kitchen, where a thin Slavic woman took the plates and plunged them into greasy water. An arrow painted on the wall behind her showed the direction to the kitchen door. By the door, black lunchpails were lying open on a table. I saw the men who were going on the next shift look for their pails, then examine the lunch inside.

Outside, the men stood in silent groups by the side of the cookhouse. On the side of the cookhouse facing our bunkhouse, a wooden booth was built on to the main wall. It stuck out like an ear. Steps without handrails led to a door. Someone shouted, "Here he comes." I saw Jim Wordle coming from the office to the cookhouse, his hands full of letters and newspapers. He gave the letters to the first man, then went up the ladder to the booth and flung the papers inside. "Shout them out." Another man took the envelopes and began to call out names. Letters passed from hand to hand. After all the names had been read out several times, the DPs went through them again.

The three of us were put on shovelling muck for the first few weeks, then promoted to operate a machine. There were about a dozen students here for the summer, from different universities, mostly undergraduate engineers. We were the smallest group. The largest were the DPs and the various kinds of Canadians.

The DPs had been hired at the camps in Europe. They had to pass a medical and sign a contract that they would work at the Mine for three years. Then they would be free to go wherever they wanted. Very few could speak English, and the only common language was German. They marked off each day on their homemade calendars with an X. A few had their wives with them. They worked as waitresses in the cookhouse. But they lived separate lives. They slept in different bunkhouses. They met if, by chance, their one day off a week coincided.

There was a Polish film director, Konrad, who had had his front teeth knocked out by the Nazis. He taught me the words of the *Horst Wessel* song. There was the fair-haired architect from Lithuania with his prize edition of *Faust* that he kept carefully wrapped in several pieces of paper, in despair because he could not see himself coming out of here alive. There was the plump Polish philosophy student working in the blacksmith's shop, reading Nietzsche and Goethe. There were teachers, ex-army officers, tradesmen. The intellectuals among them suffered the most; at least, they were more lucid about their despair. They did not go drinking or bootlegging or play crap on payday or go fishing. They remained in their rooms lying on their beds, writing letters to Europe. And waiting, like the others, for the next shift, the next meal, the next paycheque.

Most of the Canadians who were here were born in Europe. They could not understand why university students came to a place like the Mine. We told them, to make money. But they thought: If you have education, you can make money without having to do labouring work. That was why they were saving up money so that their children could go to university and not have to come to places like this. Our presence confused them. Those who had their families with them lived in the company town by the lake; the bachelors, at the camps at the Mine. There were seven camps at the Mine. Each camp consisted of one bunkhouse. And the bunkhouses were divided into small rooms, two men to a room.

The management lived in wooden bungalows on top of the hill. They were mainly Anglo-Saxon and Scottish, various engineers from the small towns of Ontario. Quiet, dull, provincial. A few came from South

Africa and Australia. There was one Englishman who had been in Canada about 10 years. He said proudly that when his children were born, he had some water flown over from his church in Sussex for them to be baptized. During the summer when their daughters came here on holiday from the private schools, the students were then invited to picnics along the lake, to dances in the wooden bungalows that went on late into the night, when you walked outside and saw the sky shot through with northern lights.

But the highly skilled miner, the one who worked at the rockface, was a transient. The bush telegraph worked amazingly well. They would arrive with their kitbags as soon as there was an expensive level to be cut, a slope or a drift. They stayed as long as the bonus made it worthwhile. Then they would be off to another mine. They were professionals. They took pride in their equipment and in their work. Their only other interest was making more money. When the paycheque came every two weeks, they would come back to the bunkhouse drunk on bad whisky they called rotgut, screech, poof. Then disappear. They were not very talkative or articulate. Of all these men, the only one I got to know was Max.

Biography   He was born in Poland. He came over to Canada in his early 20s. He still spoke English with a heavy accent. He was big, with a barrel chest, a bullet head accentuated by having the grey hair cut short. He had a strong face with black, thick eyebrows and dark eyes. He always looked worried. His room was across the corridor from mine in the bunkhouse, and we often sat on the same bench at the dining table. On one of my days off, I went up to the Mine.

The day was hot. The earth between the rock was dry and cracked open. Patches of grass were scorched brown. Small blackflies came in clusters and bit the skin. The only sound was the creaking noise the tramline made. Past the office building, a dirt road led to the top of the hill, where the open mine stood ugly and massive. The peak of the hill was peeled back, stripped, hacked out, the colour of rust. All around me, as far as I could see, were a series of similar hills with blue lakes set in them. But they were untouched. The rock was grey-blue and intact. And scattered trees sprouted from their sides and tops.

Max was sitting with a few others outside the dryer, fully dressed to go underground, looking toward the horizon. "You know," Max said, "God must have made this boosh, all right. Look at the hills and the lakes. It's good boosh. The best boosh I have seen."

Once, we went out blueberry picking in the dips of the rock where the grass was burnt. He led the way, scrambling over the hot surfaces of the rock until we came to a ridge, and there was a fine patch of ripe blueberries. We picked and ate the blueberries, then we took off our shirts and lay in the sun. I asked him why he had come here. He did not answer right away.

"I come to the boosh because I got a wife. When I meet her, I only want a poke. Then she tell me a baby made. So what the hell. In the end, we marry. But it's a big swindle, fixed from the start. I only wanted a poke. But what do I get in the bargain? I get a wife, a child. She tells me now I got responsibilities. I say, to hell. I don't want to be with her. When we are together, we say nothing except quarrel. I like her in bed. But not for a friend. So I come here. Make good money. Send her more than half. Then I miss her. Three or maybe four months, and I begin to forget what a bitch she is. So I go back. But I know right away it's no good. We quarrel. I come back to this boosh. This time, I stay."

For the rest of the summer, we ate, worked, slept and watched the dollars mount up every two weeks. On days off, we cut each other's hair, went blueberry picking, fought the blackflies and the mosquitoes, escorted the daughters of the management for canoe trips on the lake or picnics or else just lay on the bed and looked up at the ceiling until it was time for the next shift or the next meal.

We had to take a day off a week (union rules allowed only 48 hours a week; the union was affiliated to the one in the United States), but nobody wanted to. If we could only work that extra day, we would get time and a half. The union leader was called Bogie, a nearsighted, slow-moving, timid man. A French Canadian who went around with an oilcan, oiling the moving machinery at the charge bins, the conveyor belts, the crusher and the coke plant. He also had a sideline. He was the representative of a mail-order-catalogue firm in Winnipeg. If you wanted anything, you went to Bogie, and he would measure you up for a suit or get you a pair of shoes, a tie, socks, underwear.

At the end of the summer, we each had over $400 with us. We bought a bottle of rotgut and drank it. We smoked cigars. We took the seaplane back to the Soo.

Matt Cohen

Country Music

There was an old lady who lived near a dump. The old lady got tired of looking out her window at the dump, so she spent two whole summers cleaning it up and planting flowers on top. I was driving down the road one day, and where there used to be a dump, I saw a garden. I got out and went over to look at it. There were plastic flowers, and from close up, you could see the edges of rusted tin cans growing out of the soil.

The old lady waved at me from her window, so I went in and had a cup of tea with her. Yes, the old lady said, I guess those Frank brothers are pretty crazy. They take after their father, Old John MacRae. He was even crazier, but he only showed it once or twice. Once was right after the war, he had come back to live with us on the family farm, even though he wasn't wanted. One day, he got so mad, he ate a half a sack of potatoes. Wasn't sick either. Best appetite and biggest belly in the history of the township. He said he would finish the sack, but he wanted to leave himself something for dinner. Then he walked out of the house and wasn't seen for a week. He was my own brother too. I don't even know if I wanted him to come back. He did, though. Came back and finished off the potatoes.

Patrick Frank used to drive his old Ford truck into town every Wednesday afternoon to buy groceries and hang around the hardware store. He liked to shoot a game of pool there, but they closed the hall after Joe Canning tried to set fire to the owner. He walked in with a can of kerosene, poured it over Mr. Liston and lit it. Now, Mr. Liston builds cottages for tourists and owns the drugstore. Joe Canning is in jail for setting fire to a barn. Patrick Frank is parked in a field forever. He wanted to buy one of the tables after the pool hall closed, but they were sold, all at once, to someone from Toronto.

Patrick Frank's twin brother Mark is known to be the crazier of the two. Once, he got so drunk lying in the hot summer sun that he passed out on the side of the road. Pat Frank and Billy Clenning saw him there, so they went and got a can of black rustproofing paint, some deluxe off-white wall enamel that was in the barn and an old roll of wallpaper and took off all his clothes and decorated him. Mark Frank was so drunk that when he woke up, he didn't even realize what had happened, until he tried to pull down his wallpaper to have a crap. But that wasn't the incident that made everyone think he was crazy.

Driving out from town, along the road that goes to town, you come to a place where there are a whole bunch of little roads going out from the main road. The little roads lead to cottages and farms. At the place where the big road starts turning into little roads is a general store. Since the turn of the century, the store has been burned five times and gone through a dozen owners, but right now, it is a lucrative business in the summer. People around here are terrible liars, one woman told me. When Mark Frank found he had been decorated, he was so happy that he went to the store to show it off to everyone. A retired engineer and his wife from Florida were buying baked beans and maple syrup, when in walked Mark Frank wearing nothing but paint and a strip of wallpaper down his backside.

Howdy, folks, said Mark. One false move, and I'll shoot you dead.

You meet some crazy people where you least expect them, and sometimes it makes you wonder how they got that way. And of all the crazy people in the county, it was agreed that Pat and Mark Frank were the craziest. Welfare drunks, that's what they were, welfare drunks. Pat Frank was tall and fleshless as a desert runner. He played fiddle at all the parties for 30 years. Held it against his chest and made up songs to go with it.

I was leaning against an old half-ton truck, watching Mark Frank cut through another half-ton truck with a welding torch. There wasn't just one half-ton truck or two, there were more than I could count. Saved them for tires, he said, for tires and trailers like the one he was making me by cutting off the box of a truck that hadn't moved for 20 years. He was sober all that summer, so he said, at least, while his brother was in the hospital. Used to play the fiddle like no one you ever heard, always had a smart answer for anything you might say. When he picked him up off the floor to take him to the car, you couldn't believe how light he was. The man had disappeared from drinking.

People out here are terrible liars. That's what one woman told me. We were sitting on her front porch, and she was telling me lies. Now, she's married to a prosperous farmer, but once, she was known to be going out with Mark Frank. After he turned into his true self, which anyone could have predicted, she used to get teased about how she almost married him. I can see you now, her husband would say, you'd be drinking and singing away just like the rest of them. I bet you wish you married him instead of me.

And every time he says that, she blushes and says, well, who was that floozy you used to take to the movies? I guess you only needed one, when she gave you what you wanted.

And every time she says that, he just grins and slaps the table. Now, you know that isn't true, he says. I never bothered taking her to the movies.

People out here are terrible liars, the woman said to me. You can't trust a thing they say. Now, that old lady, the one up the road, she's an aunt to the Frank twins, and she told them that their father would have married the widow Frank if he hadn't been crazy. Why, he only went and saw her because he was in a state of shock. It was his unconscious mind that made him do it. When he realized what he had done, he got out of there so fast, you couldn't have believed it.

What's this unconscious mind stuff?

It's what a person has in his head that he doesn't know. Like the way a cow always goes for a garden.

When Pat Frank got out of the hospital, he would have killed himself if he hadn't passed out first. A man can't drink too much when he's been in bed for two months. You have to get used to it. Mark Frank and I were passing a wine bottle back and forth in his junkyard. Now, people like you, he said, you come out to the country, but you see things through city eyes.

I don't know, I said. Right now, I can hardly see a thing.

That's right, he said. Only good thing to be said for you is that you know it.

I bought the wine, I said.

But the bottle was empty. He threw it through the windshield of an old Chevrolet that had been waiting for it these past 15 years. Never mind, he said. He reached into his shirt and pulled out a mickey. Now, you look over at that house there, and what do you see?

What house? All I could see was a bump in the field.

That's my mother's house, he said. Stood there for 50 years without moving. Burned down two winters ago. Only problem is, he said, hogging the bottle, you can't live in it now.

Tell me about your aunt, I said.

The old lady?

Yeah.

I don't know, he said, there isn't anything to tell. Only see her once a year at Christmas. If the snow's not too bad.

What does she do all day?

I don't know, he said. Listens to the telephone. Can't make a phone call without her breathing down your neck. I tell her to get off the line, but it doesn't do any good.

The old lady who lived by the dump had been married to a man named Tom Gorman. No one remembered anything at all about him except two things. The first gets told about three times a month: one time when a shed was burning, he picked up a 200-pound pig under each arm and carried them to the house. The remarkable thing about this was that the man was lame. The second thing, which people have forgotten about, is that he hated John MacRae, his wife's own brother, one-time lover of the widow Frank and father of the craziest twins in the county. And because the old lady is the widow of the man who hated their father, the twins only visit her once a year and not even that if the snow's deep.

This and more Billy Clenning, comrade-in-arms of the Frank brothers, told me as we sat by the lake sampling his homemade wine.

Right from where we sat, we could see the old sugarhouse that John MacRae had built, the only thing he ever did in his life except spend a night with the widow Frank.

Billy Clenning's father and lame Tom Gorman had been pretty good friends. Especially good friends in a place where people never get too close. To celebrate their friendship and the spring every year, they boiled down some maple syrup. They would sit and drink and keep the fire going for a couple of weeks. It made them enough syrup and sugar to carry them through the year and sell a bit besides.

There are places you can walk, pockets and valleys, where you can't see any signs of the last 50 years: no hydro poles or metal fences, not even roads, except for old ruts that might have been gouged by a wagon. So that's what it was like when John MacRae decided, after 10 years in the war and in the city — from here, the two are almost the same — to make his return to the old homestead. In that 10 years, he had never sent any communication at all. He showed up, in his fashion, one Sunday at church — dressed up in city clothes and sporting a moustache. There is a picture of him in his fancy clothes and moustache in the old lady's kitchen. She pointed it out to me one day when we were playing cards. He is sitting on top of an old pine hutch in a gilded frame, posed in a rocking chair with one leg crossed perfectly over the other, his leather shoes gleaming. They must have dragged the chair out onto the lawn so there would be enough light. Bits and pieces of the house are in the background. And I also noticed, to tell the truth, that the old lady cheated, even though we were only playing for a cent a point.

Everyone was glad to see John MacRae when he arrived at the church. Afterward, he and his suitcase got driven over to his sister's farm. Maybe they even took the picture that day. In the picture, he is trying to look like a country squire on a mission of mercy.

At first, things went pretty well. He and Tom Gorman never got to be friends, but John MacRae was healthy enough to work, and though he didn't do much, he came in handy. He was still young, only 32, and he let it be known that he had a little money in the bank and was just waiting around deciding where to buy.

John MacRae was what you could call a slow man. He had waited 10 years to come back to the farm, and after a while, it looked like he might wait another 10 before he got married and bought a place of his own. In the meantime, he enjoyed himself. He did a few chores, and he ate his sister's cooking. He constructed a huge sugarhouse to replace the old one that Tom Gorman and Billy Clenning's father had been using. Maple sugar, he said, was like money in the bank. There was nothing you could sell like maple sugar.

Down the road lived the widow Frank. She was just a bit older than John MacRae, and it was thought that eventually, he and she would see what was necessary and get together. The only person standing in the way was the young daughter of the widow Frank. About 17 years old and pretty, she started to come visiting the Gorman farm. Not exactly officially, but you could tell it was John MacRae she was after. He wasn't too old for her: he had city clothes, and he had seen the world. Maybe she thought he would elope with her. Two years passed. John MacRae put on some weight and lost some teeth. His city clothes wore out, and he didn't change his overalls from one week to the next. The pretty young Frank girl from down the road visited less often. She got married and moved away. He visited her mother, the widow Frank, a couple of times, but his heart wasn't in it.

To console himself, he ate. With everything he ate, he had maple syrup or maple sugar. Pretty soon, he was all stomach and hardly any teeth at all. His moustache grew wild and caught in his mouth when he was chewing. He spent so long over dinner that he hardly had time for an afternoon nap. The widow Frank told one of her neighbours that he was getting disgusting before his time and that as far as she was concerned, she didn't care if she never saw him again.

When the widow Frank announced that she was through with John MacRae, she destroyed Tom Gorman's last hope for peace in his own house. He was so mad that if he hadn't been lame, he would have kicked John MacRae from the house to the road. Not only was John MacRae eating twice as much as any normal man, but he was teaching the children bad habits and driving his wife crazy.

This and more Billy Clenning told me as we moved on to the second bottle of the historic recipe. Of course, people around here are terrible liars, the woman said. They've lied so much, they've forgotten the truth. One time, Pat Frank was at a wedding eating everything in sight. Someone asked him to play the fiddle. Well, he'd forgotten it. It's invisible, he said. Then, for the rest of the day, he walked around making noises like a bullfrog and trying to sing through his nose. Even to this day, he won't admit he forgot it.

And that time, she was telling me the truth, because I asked Pat Frank about it one day after he came home from the hospital. Oh, no, he said, I didn't forget it. It had shrunk up, and I had it in my pocket. He coughed. He was so thin, his cheeks had collapsed completely. He wasn't the same man at all, Mark said. No point trying to stop him drinking now.

Winters are always long in the country, but John MacRae's last winter there was long indeed. When the weather's bad, you are cooped up in the house, and when it's good, there's so much to do, you can hardly enjoy it. In the morning, again at noon, then from dark until bedtime, the family was in the kitchen. Probably John MacRae's picture was up on the wall even then. What must he have thought, looking at it? Perhaps he never bothered.

If the snow hadn't melted early, they might not have been able to get into the bush to make syrup. But by March, it was almost gone. Early that month, John MacRae, glad to be out of the house and away from Tom Gorman, went out and tapped the trees: bored the holes in the bark and set in the narrow metal spiles. The weather stayed good, and Tom Gorman and Billy Clenning's father went and got everything ready for boiling down the sap. The very most important step was to bring enough homemade wine to last the two men at least three weeks. During their annual drunk, they cemented their friendship, prepared for the long summer ahead and fed the fire inside the huge arch John MacRae had bought for the sugarhouse.

In those five unwanted years, John MacRae had learned at least one thing. He had learned to stay out of the way when the serious drinking began. His job was to organize the kids, Billy Clenning included, into carrying the sap to the storage tank and splitting the wood. And while John MacRae stayed out of sight, the two men, after spending a couple of days plotting to throw him out in the spring, forgot him and passed on to more pleasant topics. They even, and Billy Clenning heard them, said they might let him hang around another summer if he could be got to do a little work. After all, he had built the big new sugarhouse, and even if he was lying about the nest egg, they were doing okay selling maple syrup every season. In fact, they admitted, they made more than twice as much as they ever had before the new house was built. And so it went. The women did what they had to and let the men be, and the kids sneaked in whenever they could to watch their fathers drink and swear.

One day, near the end, when the men had run out of wine and were roaming about, the old lady and John MacRae were in the sugarhouse alone. They were finishing off a batch of syrup, and the sap was boiling away thick and hot. Suddenly, there was the loudest scream you ever heard, and the old lady, young then and John MacRae's sister, came running out of the shack shouting that Uncle John had fallen into the evaporator pan.

Well, Billy says, by the time he got there, Uncle John was rolling around in the snow trying to get cooled off. When he stood up, all the syrup had turned to taffy, and Billy says he was the most amazing thing he ever saw. A big fat man standing up with a thousand strands of taffy coming out of everywhere and stretching, like a huge tent, right to the ground.

As it turned out, he survived. Tom Gorman and Billy Clenning's father cut the taffy off him with their pocketknives, and what the kids and dogs couldn't eat, they broke into small pieces and sold that summer at the church bazaar. He couldn't walk, they had to hitch up the horses and drag him home. Though he was badly burned, he only complained once: that was when they cut off his moustache. A few weeks later, he was better, and except that he had turned a bit crazy, you wouldn't have known that it had taken two strong men four hours to cut him loose from his cocoon. But the experience had unstrung him. Fat and ugly as he was, he walked down the road one April day and proposed to the widow Frank right on her front steps. She invited him in, one thing led to another, and when he came out, they were married by God and engaged by intent. But like I said, John MacRae had turned a bit crazy. After a couple of days of being engaged, he must have forgotten it had happened, because the last anyone saw of him, he was heading down the road at 6 o'clock in the morning, carrying his old suitcase and wearing his city suit. Whatever he'd come for, he'd got.

In due course, the twins were born. The widow Frank gave them her first husband's name and admitted that she was just as glad John MacRae had disappeared, and as far as she was concerned, she didn't care if she never saw him again.

People around here are awful liars, the woman said. Now, someone sooner or later is going to tell you that when John MacRae came out of the sugarhouse, he said his own sister had pushed him in. He probably fell in drunk. Still, she said wistfully, you should have seen him when he came out. Just a big mountain of taffy, I guess he looked good enough to eat.

How do you know?

I was there, she said. I used to sneak around after Billy Clenning.

In the fall, Pat Frank died. After the funeral, Mark Frank and I sat down in the cemetery to do whatever you do after a funeral. I wonder if you see anything when you're dead, he said.

I don't know. Right now, I can hardly see a thing.

All you city people are the same.

Your nose is too long.

It is?

It's too long for the rest of your face. If it was a little longer, it would be noble; if it was a little shorter, it would fit in with the rest. But as it is, it's hopeless.

I never noticed it.

That's because you're cross-eyed.

You know what? he said. You're right. I'm cross-eyed from looking at my nose that's too long. I never knew it. How long do you think this has been going on?

It was the first thing I noticed.

And you never said anything?

No.

Soon we'll all be dead.

Soon enough.

Me, the old lady and Pat. There won't be anybody left at all.

No.

If old MacRae hadn't of been so crazy, we'd have been dead long ago.

You wouldn't have been born.

He arced the bottle into the gravestone that had been waiting for that very moment, waiting for almost a century. It had been waiting so long, it was half toppled over and eaten away by doubt. The bottle crumpled against it and made a neat pile of glass. You know the old lady? he said. If I wasn't so dumb, I would have killed her years ago.

Maurice Henrie
from

La chambre à mourir

The Milkwagon   The wooden wheels with their steel bands crush the stones in the gravelled yard, and the noise — monochord, magical — never fails to wake me up. As I rush to get dressed, I hear the deep thundering of the metal milk pails at the bottom of the well as they bang against the stone-and-metal casing. The men are hauling the pails, full of last night's milk, out of the icy water, where they had been left overnight to cool. They lift them out of the well by hand and heave them on the back of the wagon, to which the big blond mare has already been hitched. Then Jean-Paul comes into the house for his tobacco and matches. He'd never say so, but he is also coming in to get me, his indispensable morning passenger.

"Are you coming to deliver the milk today?" he asks, needlessly.

And together, we head off for the cheese factory.

Fog, thick as porridge but at the same time translucent, luminous, lies over the earth, fending off the feeble attacks from the sun. The road opens up ahead of us and closes immediately again as we pass. Suddenly, the noise of our milkwagon seems to increase, and out of the phosphorescent fog appears a team of phantom horses that, at first glance, look identical to our own. We were passing one of our neighbours who is already returning from the cheese factory, his pails emptied of milk and then refilled with whey, which the factory gives away free and the farmers take home to feed to the pigs.

Through the thunder of eight iron-shod hooves and eight ironbound wheels clattering over a road of huge crushed stones packed in clay, the drivers salute each other by touching the brims of their straw hats with their index fingers and exchange totally incomprehensible greetings, relying more on the movement of each other's lips than on the words that issue from them. Sometimes, the driver of the other wagon stands up, turns our way, cups his hands around his mouth and shouts a question at us. When this happens, Jean-Paul invariably assumes an air of deep concentration, seems to reflect for a moment, then shouts back: "I think so," or "As far as I know," managing to sound both affirmative and exclamatory at the same time. When the fog has swallowed the other wagon, I turn to Jean-Paul with the inevitable question:

"What did he ask you?"

"I haven't the faintest idea," he says, smiling.

The Death Room   When she reached the door, Grandmother seemed to hesitate a moment before entering the room. Jacqueline, who was following close behind her, noticed and asked, "Are you feeling bad again?"

Without answering, Grandmother continued into the room and sat down on the big bed, whose white eiderdown barely moved under her weight. She took a deep breath, placing her hand over the pit of her stomach. The pain was getting worse.

"I seem to be feeling better already," she said.

Jacqueline looked at her skeptically but remained polite.

"Well, even so," she said, "it'll be a lot easier to look after you down here. It's too much trouble running up and down those stairs to your room every time you want something."

Grandmother inclined her head in a weak sign of acquiescence, then, with a low groan, stretched out full-length on the cold bed. She lay still, her eyes fixed on the ceiling. For the past two weeks, a growth had been forming in her chest, becoming bigger and bigger each day, until now, it seemed about to smother her.

Jacqueline half opened the room's single window, which gave out onto the barnyard, then left the room, closing the door noiselessly as she went.

Alone, Grandmother seemed to regain her self-control. Through the window, she could see the grey shingles of the barn roof and the three lightning rods, their clear glass balls glinting in the afternoon sun. And she could hear the sounds of the farm coming up from the yard: The rooster's boastful crowing, the flapping of his wings — when she went down to gather the eggs, he would strut along her path, barely deigning to get out of her way, taking tiny, stately steps, turning back on himself constantly, as if deliberately trying to make her angry. The quick, dull clank of the stainless-steel milk cans being washed in the cement tank by the hired hands before being filled and lowered for the night into the cold water of the wells. The quick, welcoming mews of the barn cats to whom, under Jean-Paul's disapproving eye, Jacqueline gave warm milk every summer night straight from the pail. And then, when a sudden breeze moved the thin curtains, Grandmother could smell the million-and-one farm odours rising up from the fields, the buildings and the animals. The same smells that so offended the people from the city who showed up uninvited on Sundays to stroll around in the fields, poke around in the yards and even stick their noses into the empty buildings.

But when Grandmother turned her head away from the window through which drifted so many tender memories, her eyes fell on the severe whiteness of the room's walls, hung with the stiff portraits of her ancestors. They regarded her from their oval frames, the glass bulging out like eyes, silent and impervious. Especially old Moise and his wife Mathilde, whom she had known when she first got married and had moved into this house. She had looked after them assiduously in their old age and couldn't think why they looked down on her now with such cold, distant and severe expressions.

Moise and Mathilde had been dead for more than 30 years. Each of them in turn had died in this white room. Grandmother remembered she had brought them in here with more or less the same words Jacqueline had just used with her: it was close to the kitchen, it made the job easier for those who had to look after them. It had also been in this room that Grandmother had watched two of her own infant children die, one from jaundice and the other from pneumonia. And more recently, she had also seen and touched the still body of Germaine, her husband's youngest sister, whom God had seen fit to call to Paradise on the day of her 18th birthday. They had laid her out on this very bed.

Grandmother's isolation from the rest of the house suddenly felt insupportable to her. She sat up on the bed. After a moment's reflection, she got to her feet and went over to the door, through which she could see a corner of the kitchen.

"I'm not going to let myself be shunted off like this at my age," she thought.

With a weak but still authoritative voice, she called Jacqueline.

"Apart from the fact that it's the prettiest room in the house," Grandpa said, "it means the youngsters don't have to spend half the day traipsing up and down those damned stairs. Even the doctor said it was easier on him to have you down here."

"If the others can climb stairs, so can the doctor," said Grandmother firmly. "Climbing a few stairs never killed anyone. I've climbed them myself more often than all the rest of you put together, and I'm not dead yet."

Still, after climbing the 12 steps slowly, one at a time, she had to rest at the top for a moment to get her wind, leaning heavily on Jacqueline's arm. When she could breathe again, she walked quickly to her own room, her slippers flapping against the linoleum, marched over to the window and flung open the two shutters. Through the branches of the apple tree — so close she could almost reach out and pluck a sour, green apple from its heavily laden boughs — she heard the impatient snorting of the young pigs as they waited for Jean-Paul to finish pouring out the table scraps from dinner. She smiled, suddenly feeling much better. She pulled back the bedclothes and climbed into bed.

"Is it tonight the doctor's supposed to come again?" she asked.

But Jacqueline had already gone back downstairs to the kitchen.

The Dandelions Grandfather watched the hillside in Mathias' field with a jaundiced eye. For three days now, it had exploded into brilliant colour — a rich, buttery yellow — that covered the ground and sparkled in the morning sunlight. But come evening, it had folded back in on itself, returning again to what it had always been, an ordinary green pasture.

"I've never seen anything like it," said Grandfather. "Mathias' fields've never had any trouble growing weeds, but all those dandelions — I can't remember seeing so many before."

On the fourth day, the yellow paled a bit and was sprinkled here and there with white, especially where the hill was south-facing and the sun beat down on it from dawn to dusk.

On the fifth day, it rained.

On the morning of the sixth day, the hill was transformed into a mass of white cotton. The only yellow left was in a few thin patches of late dandelions that grew in the more shaded areas. Around noon, when the dew had dried, a playful wind came along to tickle the sides of the hill, and the great dispersement began.

It was the dog who noticed it first. He took to barking, though somewhat hesitantly, as if he couldn't quite figure out what to make of this aerial invasion. In the barnyard, the chickens lifted their heads, bent their long necks into question marks and, with fixed, glassy, attentive stares, tried desperately to come to their own opinion about the phenomenon. The rooster instinctively assumed his responsibilities as a deputy minister; he took two steps to the left, three steps to the right, then, contrary to form, declared at the top of his voice that he didn't have the slightest idea what was going on. And as for the half-dozen heifers in the rocky paddock, they observed all these disturbances placidly enough through the bars of the fence, then raised their tails and scampered off to the far end of the field, throwing out their feet in all directions at once and kicking up globs of wet earth as they went.

Alerted by the goings-on, Grandfather gulped down his tea, jumped up from the table and ran out onto the side verandah to get a better view of the spectacle. And what a spectacle it was. The air full of fine, silky dandelion heads, released from the field below and sliding horizontally through the sunlight. The slight breeze blew them steadily toward a secret destination, millions of minuscule parachutes floating west to east so that they seemed to be hurrying for shelter between the house and the darkened drive shed, against which their whiteness stood out sharply.

"You'd think it was snowing in the middle of summer," Jacqueline said, running her fingers through her hair and over her neck to rid herself of the light, fluffy balls that stuck to her skin and tickled.

The organic snowstorm persisted. The seeds rose so high in the air that we could see huge clouds of them flying over the roof of the barn, swirling around the lightning rods. They even seemed to change the colour of the sky to a slightly paler shade of blue. Closer to the ground, the fleecy balls zigzagged between the buildings. Caught in a series of cross-draughts, they accelerated swiftly or, with equal suddenness, slowed down almost to the point of hanging motionless in the air. Then, in suspended animation punctuated by a few fruitless attempts to regain flight, they seemed to give up altogether and sank slowly to the ground, brushing the rough boards of the drive shed and the barn as they fell. Others gave themselves up to the downward spirals of tiny tornadoes, only to be ambushed by the barn cats, who pinned them to the ground with their quick claws and then lost them in the plantain and galinsoga.

"It's a bad sign," grumbled Grandfather, scratching his neck and rubbing the stump of his right arm with his left hand, as if trying to wipe off thousands of itching, invisible seeds. "Means we're going to be overrun with dandelions next year. Doesn't matter much in the fields, but they're a goddamned pain in the neck when they get into the garden. A lot of extra work pulling them up, spraying them with herbicide, and still you never get rid of the buggers. It'll drive Toinette crazy, so it will; she never could abide weeds in her vegetable patch."

The silken storm diminished visibly after half an hour but was still fairly strong at milking time, the little white pompoms continuing to bounce around the buildings, making us snuffle and sneeze and piling up in drifts in the sheltered corners, out of the wind. The magical migration was over, though. After a while, no one took much notice of the odd seed that still settled down from the sky.

No one, that is, except Grandmother.

She had been standing beside her basket of freshly washed laundry, waiting for the storm to pass so she could hang the clothes on the line to dry. She'd been afraid the dandelion seeds would cling to the wet cloth. When she judged the time was right, she stuck a few clothespins in her mouth, draped one corner of a sheet over the line and, holding the rest of it out at arm's length, put the first pin in place. When the whole sheet was firmly secured by four pins, she pulled on the clothesline mounted on pulleys so that the sheet swung out freely over the newly planted vegetable garden. Then she cast another anxious glance at Mathias' field, which by now had returned to its usual shade of green. Something new caught her eye: just where the dandelions had been thickest, she saw two or three black-and-white cows grazing, their heads lowered between their forelegs and their tails whipping from side to side as they moved slowly across the verdant meadow.

"If that Mathias had only put his cows out to pasture a few days early this spring," Grandmother said that evening at supper, "he wouldn't have sown half the county with his blessed dandelion seeds."

Wayne Grady

Tobacco Road

The farms are small, averaging only 40 acres of tobacco, and they display an almost Dutch fanaticism for neatness, perhaps because many of the farmers came here from Europe after World War II. Not a cow, not a pigpen, no tumbledown chicken coops, no muddy dogs herding muddy sheep; just row after row of green tobacco plants separated by light brown soil, what agronomists call fox sand: more than 90 percent sand, the rest silt. The traditional cattle-below-and-hay-above barns of Ontario's mixed dairy districts are replaced by sprawling glass greenhouses and rows of green tobacco kilns with red shutters. The effect is of windowless houses on a giant Monopoly board. Ninety-five percent of the tobacco grown in Canada is grown in Ontario, and 72 percent of that is grown by the 1,800 farmers who live within a 20-mile radius of Delhi.

Paul Van Londersele owns two farms. One is about three miles east of Delhi on Highway 3 and is run by his son-in-law John Scott. The second is a mile farther out of town and is run by his son Dan. Paul Van Londersele's father came to Canada from Belgium in 1926 and headed for Saskatchewan. Four months later, he decided, his son says, "that there was no future out West," so he came East and eventually settled in Delhi.

There was a future in Delhi. A few years earlier, a soil specialist from the Dominion Experimental Station in Ottawa had taken soil samples in Norfolk County and determined that the area was fit for nothing but tobacco. In 1922, he planted a small crop of flue-cured tobacco in Lynedoch, a few miles south of Delhi; that first crop grew well but was destroyed by hail. The next year, he purchased the old Chrysler farm nearer Delhi for $20 an acre. When he planted 20 acres of tobacco, his neighbours thought he was crazy. When he sold his crop for 60 cents a pound — about $27,000 — they stopped laughing and started ploughing. The "green gold rush" was on. In 1929, the Imperial Leaf Tobacco plant was built, and in 1930, it bought 10 million pounds of tobacco from local farmers. Paul Van Londersele's father was one of them.

The farm hasn't changed much since the 1930s. To the left of the lane is a relatively modest white frame farmhouse; across the lane is a low shed and a huge greenhouse. The lane spills into a yard in front of the pack-barn, then veers left between two rows of green-and-red tobacco kilns.

Arn Sayeau, the mayor of Delhi, pulls into the yard and parks his four-year-old Ford between the greenhouse and the pack-barn, where the cured tobacco will be stored until it is sold in October. He gets out and walks up to the first kiln. One of its windows is open, and an elephant wagon has been drawn up to it. Through the window, Dan Van Londersele's work boots can be seen on the lowest rafter, at about eye level. The inside of the kiln is a dark golden cave, and the smell of freshly cured tobacco rolls out into the air in sweet, rich waves.

"Hello, Dan," the mayor calls up into the kiln. "Your dad about?"

"Hi, Arn," Dan replies without stepping down from the rafter. He gets an average of two tourists a day stopping by the farm, mostly American farmers on vacation. "Dad's over at John's place checking on the kilns." He pronounces the word "kills." He passes a stick of cured tobacco through the window to his wife Mary Ann who stacks it on the elephant wagon. "Should be back any minute."

"How's it look?" asks Sayeau.

"Coming along not too bad," Dan says, which is Ontario farmer talk for the best damn tobacco crop in years. "Had a bit of trouble getting that old steam truck started, but she's all right now, I guess." He points to a 20-year-old truck that is solid rust, not a speck of paint left on it. A 1,000-gallon water tank, also solid rust, sits on the back of it. Before a kiln can be emptied, a certain amount of moisture has to be put back into the leaf so it won't crumble. Dan's priming crew is finished for the day — they usually start around six in the morning and have the day's kiln filled by two in the afternoon — and Dan and Mary Ann are getting this kiln emptied and ready to be refilled in the morning.

Mayor Sayeau sticks his head through the window and looks up. "You got any Frogs working for you this year?" he asks.

"Yep," says Dan. "I've got two fellows from Quebec. The rest are local lads." He jumps down and looks up toward the house. "Here's Dad now."

Paul Van Londersele drives his car up the lane and parks beside the kiln. He's not as tall or lean as his son, and he has a paunch that makes him look like a boa constrictor that has just swallowed a mule, but there is a strong family resemblance. His crew cut, dark glasses and open sports shirt suggest a Southern plantation owner. There is no mistaking the air of authority with which he pulls a cured leaf from the elephant wagon and examines it. The leaf is golden, soft and pliable as chamois.

Van Londersele has installed bulk kilns on his other farm. These are modern kilns about the size and shape of truck trailers. Instead of being tied onto sticks, the tobacco is laid out in metal frames that have steel rods running through them. Each frame is squeezed shut, with the rods puncturing the tobacco, then swung up on a chain and slid along metal runners into the kiln with the tobacco hanging down vertically. The idea makes Van Londersele shake his head in amazement. "When I was a kid, my old man would take a stick to me if I even bent a tobacco leaf," he says. "Now, we're running steel rods through them."

He has also bought a one-row automatic harvester that strips away the leaves from a tobacco plant with small rubber discs and conveys them up on a belt into a hopper at the top. This is called the "tangled leaf" method. The machine requires only two workers — one to steer it and one to spread the leaves out evenly in the hopper. With bulk kilns and the harvester — a total investment of about $150,000 — Van Londersele has cut his work crew on the Scott farm from 10 last year to 3 this year, all of them local students from Delhi. Norm Sheidow, an extension agronomist at the Delhi Research Station west of town, had said earlier that automation is risky. "The more equipment you have," he argued, "the more equipment breakdowns you get. Some of this new equipment is difficult to repair and hard to get parts for. Even if one of those $38,000 machines is down for half a day, you've got three workers waiting around doing nothing. It's costing you $150 a day." So why is Paul Van Londersele going automatic?

"It's the union talk," he says, throwing the leaf back on the wagon. "If the union comes in, every farmer in the district will go automatic. We won't stand for it."

Although it is only midafternoon, the taproom in the Diplomat, Delhi's only hotel, is half full. The room is almost pitch-black. The predominant language is the all but impenetrable patois of Quebec's South Shore, the Rimouski and Rivière-du-Loup regions that lie between Quebec City and the Gaspésie. It is a defiant, hard-edged, nasal *joual* that had earlier leaked into Acadia and on down to Louisiana and Alabama: a language designed for home consumption but used to being exported, almost a private code, a barrier against intrusion.

For 10 months of the year, Delhi has a population of 3,800, mostly retired tobacco farmers and the 200 employees of the local Benson & Hedges storage plant. From mid-July to mid-September, that figure increases by about 8,000 — the number of seasonal workers who flock to Delhi for the harvest. Three-quarters of them come from Quebec. The rest are offshore workers brought in from the Caribbean by Employment and Immigration Canada or students from Europe shipped over by arrangement with the governments of Canada and six European countries.

The average age of the migrants in the Diplomat is about 19, but by their dress and manner, they might have stepped directly out of the late 1960s — long, straight hair held back in ponytails, sparse moustaches, thin arms sticking out of T-shirts that have "Harley-Davidson" or "Kiss" or stylized marijuana plants scrawled across their chests. Even in the false midnight of the Diplomat, they look tanned and healthy, farm kids. They sit around the red Arborite tables in groups of five or six, sprinkling salt into their draft beer, bumming cigarettes, passing joints, checking out the taproom for any stray farmers who may be looking for pickers, arranging for a place to sleep.

A few of them will spend the night upstairs on the floor of a friend's room: a double-occupancy at the Diplomat costs $40 a week, but there's no charge if you sleep on the floor. Army-surplus backpacks with tan work boots and plastic groundsheets tied to them are sprinkled about on the floor, and the jukebox, an ultramodern, computerlike affair with tiny blue lights chasing each other madly through the darkness, is playing something by Split Enz.

Daniel (no one bothers much with surnames) raises his empty bottle and waves it above his head. "Raymond," he calls to the waiter, "*une p'tite molle.*" Raymond plunks down a small Molson's Export, and Daniel pours it lovingly into his glass.

"*Que Dieu bénisse la vache,*" he intones, "*qui donne du si bon lait.*"

"*Si la mère chez nous donne la pareille,*" Pierre joins in, "*je serais toujours à bresse.*"

The recitation is like a grace, or thanksgiving — "May God bless this cow, who gives us such good milk. If Mamma at home gave half as good, I'd still be at her breast" — and is followed by laughter and the clinking of glasses. Daniel wipes his moustache and says he has found a job with a labour contractor named Joe Guitar, who hires out toppers and suckerers to a dozen different farmers around Delhi in exchange for a percentage of their wages — the farmers pay him, and he pays the workers.

In most cases, a tobacco crew is made up of 10 people: five pickers, or "primers"; a table gang — three women who tie the tobacco leaves together to be put into the kiln; one kiln hanger, who hangs the tied tobacco on the kiln rafters; and one foreman, usually the farmer himself ("Papa Boss") or his son, who also drives the wagon that brings the tobacco in from the field.

Before the plants can be harvested, the fields must be hoed and the plants must be topped and "suckered" (have their second-growth leaves, or suckers, removed before they can weaken the plant). The primers, table gang and kiln hanger are paid by the kiln — this year, it's about $50 for each kiln filled — whereas the toppers are paid by the hour, and suckerers are paid by the row or sometimes by the acre. A fast suckerer can earn as much as $70 a day.

Daniel is fast. He's 22, and this is his third summer working tobacco. He comes from a little town a few miles southeast of Quebec City. Every June, he hitchhikes to Delhi, works the harvest, then heads out West to look for work on a mushroom farm in British Columbia. After that, he swings back through the United States, picking grapes or other soft fruits, then spends the winter in Florida. This year, he wants to save $2,000 and go to Montreal to buy a motorcycle. Or he may go back to Europe, where he spent two years roaming around.

"One time, I was in a bar in Sydney," Daniel says, "on Cape Breton Island, and I heard two men talking at the next table. One man said he was looking for someone to work on his ship, which was leaving that night for Liverpool. I leaned over and tapped him on the shoulder, and when he turned around, I said, 'You found him.' "

Pierre is from Hull. He's a little older than the others, less boisterous, clearly a leader. He lives upstairs in Room 2. He's wearing Adidas shorts and a sort of basketball singlet that shows off his muscular shoulders and upper body. Most of his skin is covered with scar tissue. "In Hull, I tried construction for a while, when they were moving all those civil servants out of Ottawa. I used to work 12, 15 hours a day. I'd get home so tired, I couldn't eat. One night, I came home and fell asleep smoking a cigarette. I was in the hospital for two months. After that, I said to hell with this and came back to Delhi. At least this way, I get to see my family for eight months of the year."

Pierre has a photograph of his wife and her sister and his two children, sitting stiffly in the living room of a high-rise apartment, looking at the camera as if it were a bomb. Daniel also produces a photograph. "This is Sylvie," he says, "my daughter." The photo is of a blond 2-year-old in a red jumpsuit, staring solemnly into a Polaroid camera. She has red pupils because of the camera's flash. Daniel is not married, but he has two friends in Montreal who are. The husband found out he was sterile, so the couple invited Daniel to come and live with them for a few weeks. After a while, the wife became pregnant, and Daniel moved back in with his brother. He doesn't see Sylvie that often. The last time he was in Montreal, he stopped in and took the snapshot.

Alain Guitar, the younger brother of Joe, the labour contractor, is a kiln hanger. Big and burly, with dark blond hair and moustache and a missing front tooth, he works at a farm a mile from town. "A good kiln hanger is worth his weight in gold," he says, "because they're hard to keep. They're always taking off somewhere, going to another farm that pays more. You can work with only four primers if you have to, but if your kiln hanger doesn't show up in the morning, you're out of luck. I've known some kiln hangers throw themselves off a top tier and fall 32 feet to the ground, break their legs, then go back to Quebec and wait for their Workmen's Comp. cheques to come in."

For every acre of tobacco planted, a farmer should have 100 square feet of greenhouse. Dan Van Londersele's two greenhouses measure 19 feet by 100 and 19 by 70. Their shape is that of an aluminum A resting on a concrete U. Every March, the U is spread with two inches of fresh muck, a black, highly organic soil that's trucked in from nearby marshlands. Because the muck is full of insects and weed seeds, it must be sterilized. The old method is to steam the muck, using huge boilers that pump steam at 180 degrees F through hoses into metal pans inverted over the seedbeds. The new method is to use chemical disinfectants. Even the walls and ceiling are sterilized.

The tobacco is planted in the greenhouses in early April, at a rate of one ounce of seed to every 2,000 square feet of seedbed. The seeds are almost unimaginably small: a single ounce contains 350,000 seeds, enough to seed 20 acres of tobacco. Farmers come home from the seed store carrying enough seeds for a 50-acre crop in a box about the size of a pack of cigarettes. In the greenhouse, the seeds are mixed with water and sprayed in a fine mist over the seedbed.

While the seedlings are growing, the fields are prepared for transplanting. The winter crop, usually rye planted the previous fall, is ploughed under to a depth of eight inches, and the fields are lightly cultivated with a springtooth harrow. When the seedlings are six inches tall and the threat of a late frost is past (about the end of May), the seedlings are pulled from the greenhouse and transplanted to the fields.

At one time, the transplanting was done manually, with two people, usually the farmer and his wife, sitting on a low planter pulled along by a tractor. Two-row automatic planters now require four workers, who feed the seedlings onto a wheel. The machine marks the rows, applies fertilizer (up to 1,500 pounds per acre of nitrogen, phosphorus and potash), deposits the seedlings, adds water to the roots and cultivates between the rows. It's easier on the back and quicker: a two-row automatic planter, spacing the plants at 24-inch intervals in rows that are 42 inches apart (to give a population of 6,223 plants per acre), will do about five acres on a good day.

The amount of tobacco that may be planted is determined by an august group of elected representatives called the Ontario Flue-Cured Tobacco Growers' Marketing Board. This group allots a certain poundage (or quota) to each farmer. A farmer must, by law, sell all his tobacco through the board, and the board will not sell more than the farmer's quota. Paul Van Londersele's production quota is 230,000 pounds. A plant population of 6,223 per acre will yield 2,300 pounds of tobacco per acre, so Paul plants 100 acres of tobacco — 52 acres on Dan's farm and 48 on John's. The Marketing Board also negotiates with the tobacco companies to guarantee the farmers a minimum price in the fall: in 1981, the negotiated minimum per pound was $1.52 for BL1, one of the highest grades. Barring a hailstorm or an attack of blue mould, the two Van Londersele farms will gross more than $350,000 at the auctions. Even subtracting about $2,000 an acre for production costs, it isn't hard to see why one Delhi farmer calls tobacco "the most lucrative crop a Canadian farmer can grow."

Once the tobacco is in the field, there's not much to do except weed two or three times, add more fertilizer and some pesticide and hope that it doesn't hail or that the signs of blue mould — yellow-brown splotches on the leaves, undersides marked by blue-grey spores like something found on last month's cheese — don't appear. In 1979, about 30 percent of the Ontario crop — an estimated $90 million worth — was lost to blue mould, a fungus of the same family that causes potato failure. (There are those who maintain that the Irish potato famine of the mid-19th century was started in North America and shipped to Ireland with a load of tobacco.)

As the plant approaches maturity, the leaves become broad and tough. Toward the last week in July, it grows to shoulder height and develops a flowery head. When three-quarters of the field is waving white, bell-shaped flowers, the tops are broken off; once the field is topped, it is time to start priming.

Priming is carried out in a number of stages, or "passes." On the first pass, the primers go along the rows taking off the three bottom leaves (called "lugs," or "sand leaves") of the tobacco plant. These are usually poorer in quality and cure out to a lower grade because they're not as ripe. On the next pass, they take the next three leaves, and so on, until the plant is a naked pole that looks like a five-foot Brussels sprout stalk without any Brussels sprouts on it. In 1981, there were 23 leaves on a plant — usually there are 18. The bumper crop will help make up for two bad years in a row: the blue mould of 1979 and the late frost that hit on June 17, 1980.

Sitting on a self-propelled, skeletal contraption that looks like a moon walker, five primers go along five rows breaking off the leaves with their hands and packing them in canvas bags about the size of pillowcases.

At the end of each row, these bundles are loaded into "boats" — nowadays usually a pickup truck — and taken to the tying table beside whatever kiln is being filled that day. The table gang takes the leaves out of the bags and sews them together by their stalks, then drapes them over four-foot wooden laths. This sewing used to be done by hand; now the leaves are fed through large industrial sewing machines with the laths already threaded through them, about 100 leaves per lath. The laths are passed along a conveyor belt, through the sewing machine and up into the open window of the kiln, where the kiln hanger hangs them between slotted rafters or tiers. Each kiln holds 1,250 sticks.

When the kiln is full, it's sealed shut and the curer takes over. On the farm that Dan oversees, Paul Van Londersele is the curer. The object of curing is to turn the green tobacco to gold — or to degrees of gold ranging from lemon to orange — and to dry it so that it will stay golden and burn well in cigarettes. Each kiln is equipped with a gas furnace at the bottom and a chimney, or flue (hence "flue-cured" tobacco), up one side: as hot air fills the top of the kiln, it pushes cold air down to the furnace, until the kiln is a uniform 180 degrees F, at which temperature it remains for six to eight days (eight for the sand leaves, six for the top leaves). When the tobacco is completely cured, it is unloaded into gigantic elephant wagons and transported to the pack-barn, where it is stored until it's ready to be stripped — sorted roughly into one of five or six grades and baled into 55-pound bundles, ready to be sent to the Marketing Board for auction.

The Marketing Board usually opens in October, and auctioning continues until mid-April. When the tobacco is purchased, it is sent for stemming and storage to a plant similar to the Benson & Hedges "stemmery" in Delhi — the $1 million plant built by Imperial Leaf in 1929 and purchased by Benson & Hedges in 1972. At the stemmery, the lamina (or leafy part of the leaf) is separated from the stem, and both lamina and stem are stored in cases for 18 months before being sent on to one of the two Benson & Hedges manufactories — in Brampton, Ontario, and Montreal — to be blended and made into cigarettes or exported to England.

The blend of a particular brand of cigarette is the manufacturer's secret. All four Canadian manufacturers use only Canadian-grown, flue-cured, Virginia tobacco, so the blend of different grades is the only thing that makes one brand different from another. As there are 64 different grades, and some of the stems have to be put back into the blend in order to ensure even burning, the formulas of different brands vary enormously. Last year, Benson & Hedges manufactured 7.5 billion cigarettes under 80 different brand names. With only 11 percent of the market, Benson & Hedges is the smallest of the four major Canadian manufacturers.

The Diplomat's owner is a soft-spoken, amiable Korean named Steve Hong, who stands behind the stainless-steel bar in the taproom with a vague, private smile, as if there is really someplace more important he wants to be but he's too damned polite to go there. Ten years ago, Steve, his wife Sue and Steve's mother left Korea, where Steve had managed the bar in his father's small hotel. They arrived in Canada by a route that took them through France, West Germany and Holland. Before they moved to Delhi, they were in the hotel business in Toronto. As their two sons approached school age, Steve and Sue began to look around for a small hotel in a small town, where they felt the boys would be able to grow up feeling part of a community. Three years ago, they found the Diplomat.

One of the first things Steve did was hire a headwaiter to help him run the place — Raymond Peloquin, a tall, intense Quebecker who had been coming to Delhi to work tobacco for the past five summers but who, like Steve, was looking for something more permanent. Steve and his family live in a small apartment behind the bar; Raymond has converted Room 1 upstairs into a comfortable bachelor apartment. Between them, they run a very tight ship. There is no lobby to the hotel, no front desk. The front door is always locked. The only way to get upstairs is by passing through the taproom, and even then, you have to get a key from Raymond.

By 7 o'clock, when it's time for Miss Carol's second demonstration of exotic dancing at the Diplomat, the taproom is three-quarters full with a mixture of locals and migrants, most of whom sit at tables close to the stage. Miss Carol is from Toronto, where she's rumoured to be living with a chapter of the Hell's Angels. For the week she's at the Diplomat, she lives upstairs in Room 4. A tall, thin, wispy blonde with big eyes and small breasts, she looks more like a Woolco mannequin than a biker's moll, but she has a pleasant smile and seems to enjoy her work. Dressed in a plaid shirt, denim cutoffs and spike heels, she unrolls a length of shag carpet at the centre of the stage, then walks over to the jukebox to select the four songs that will make up her set. Some of the local boys pick up their chairs and place them along one wall of the stage area and sit down, holding their beers between their legs. Carol smiles at them. The music starts.

Most of the migrants have moved to the other end of the room, near the bar, the shuffleboard and the pool table, on which a seemingly never-ending game of high-low is in progress. They pay little attention to what's happening on the stage. This worries Steve. "The French guys don't like it," he says. "They see enough of it at home. What they want is a good rock group." Someone suggests getting in a French-Canadian singer, a *chanteur* like the ones in the *boîtes à chansons* in Old Montreal. "Nah," says Steve. "That would alienate the locals. I have to make a living the rest of the year too, you know. Everybody likes rock."

Carol is spinning around on her spike heels to the deep bass emanating from the jukebox, while two of the local boys ride their chairs around the stage like horses, yip-yipping and waving their beers like stetsons. Carol looks shocked and begins to unbutton her blouse. When she stops spinning, her blouse is off and the front of her denim cutoffs is open. Then she lies down on the shag carpet and begins to slide the cutoffs down over her hips, smiling up at the boys on the stage between her raised knees. A middle-aged couple at an advantageous table near the front sip draft beer and watch impassively. The whooping and whistling almost drown out the music.

"She should be wearing a G-string," says Steve, looking anxiously around the tables. Last Monday, two plainclothes OPP officers had come in and sat by the stage trying to look inconspicuous. Fortunately, because of a mix-up with her Toronto agent, Carol hadn't shown up in Delhi until the following morning. One of the plainclothesmen had bought some marijuana from one of the migrants and then arrested him. Raymond was outraged. "Yvan told the guy he didn't have any, and the guy says, so get some, I'll give you $50, bring it out to the car. They took him into Tillsonburg and charged him with trafficking and gave him a $5,000 bail." Yvan, who is sitting across the table, looks contrite. He'd come up with $500 and been released until his trial in November.

Raymond feels responsible for the migrants. He worries about the strain between the French workers and the local population that arises from the clash of work ethics. The migrants call him their ambassador from Quebec in Ontario. His room upstairs has a phone and a private bath, a desk, a television with cable, a small refrigerator usually full of Molson's Light, his own carpet on the floor and a bright red blanket on the single bed. On a small table beside the bed are a few popular French novels and a book of crossword puzzles in English. On the wall above the desk, a cork bulletin board is covered with little slips of paper, most of them IOUs. Some of the IOUs go back five years. Room 1 is right on the corner: one window looks south along Main Street toward the Benson & Hedges plant (where Raymond worked one winter before coming to work with Steve). He calls the room his office.

Of the 30,000 seasonal tobacco workers who work in Ontario each year, about half find jobs through either the Canada Farm Labour Pool or the Canada Employment Centre. The rest are hired directly by farmers who drive their pickups into town and approach groups of migrants hanging about for the purpose. There are problems with this method on both sides. A farmer who doesn't hire through the labour pool doesn't have to provide a wage-agreement form for the worker. He has no way of knowing whether a worker intends to stay for the entire harvest, and the worker doesn't know whether the farmer pays regularly or whether the accommodations are clean.

A better method has evolved: the farmer goes into the Diplomat for a beer and casually mentions to Raymond that he's looking for two primers or a kiln hanger, and on his way back to the bar, Raymond passes the word on to a group sitting near the pool table. Immediately, five migrants are swarming around the farmer's table, and after some obligatory haggling, he tells two of them to be outside the Diplomat tomorrow morning at 5 o'clock. He'll pick them up in his truck. The farmer knows that Raymond approves of the workers, and the workers know that Raymond approves of the farmer.

"If a farmer comes in himself after the harvest has started," says Raymond, "and it's someone I don't know, I start to think there's something wrong. His gang has quit on him, that's the first thing I think. He's a slave driver, or maybe he was drunk when he was planting and the rows are all crooked, or else there are a lot of hills on his farm and the primers have to get out and push the machine. So then I don't recommend him. But if a French guy comes in, say a kiln hanger or a primer, and he says he needs another guy on his gang, then I know the farmer's okay, some of his crew quit because they were lazy or inexperienced. It happens."

It happens too often, according to some of the farmers. The harvest has to begin in early August and must be completed by first frost in mid-September. Keeping good crews until all the tobacco is in is a farmer's chief worry, and to make sure his crew stays with him, a farmer will usually hold back part of a worker's pay, usually $5 a kiln, and give it to him as a "bonus" at the end of the harvest. Raymond thinks the bonus system is unfair. He feels that if the workers had a union, some of these injustices in the system could be ironed out. But even if the migrants were interested in organizing, farmworkers and domestic servants are excluded from Ontario's Labour Relations Act, which gives all other workers the right to belong to a union. If a farmworker tries to join or form a union, he can be legally fired.

This summer, organizers from the Canadian Farmworkers Union (CFU) have been trying to drum up interest in the Delhi area; rumours were out that some were even posing as migrant workers in order to infiltrate the farms. Raymond finds this a little underhanded, but when it's announced that the CFU will be holding a meeting in the Legion Hall, he urges everyone to go.

Few Delhi farmers realize it, but they are participating in a tobacco-growing tradition that extends back nearly 1,000 years. For the past 300 years, tobacco growing has been accompanied by a second tradition: strained relations between French and English. In 1615, Samuel de Champlain noted that the Indians of the Lake Erie area were, like their cousins the Petuns farther north, "another savage nation that produces a large amount of tobacco. This is called the Neutral Nation. They number 4,000 warriors and dwell westwards of the Entonhonorons [Iroquois]."

This Band was called the Neutrals because they allied themselves neither with the Hurons to the north nor with the Iroquois to the southeast (across the Niagara River in the present state of New York). The Neutrals were a trading nation: they exchanged tobacco with the Algonquins for furs and porcupine quillwork and with the Hurons for corn. Excavations in 1950 in Norfolk County near Delhi produced trade artifacts from as far away as the Gulf of Mexico; several clay pipes found in the dig have linked the Neutrals with the so-called Glen Meyer Indians who lived in the same area from 1000 to 1300 A.D.

In 1626-1627, a Recollet priest, Father Joseph de La Roche Daillon, wintered among the Neutrals, whose territory stretched from Niagara Falls to the Detroit River and from Lake Erie as far north as the present site of London. Their population had by then increased to

12,000, and they lived in 26 villages; the principal one was situated in what is today Southwold Township, Elgin County, near St. Thomas, Ontario. Their chief was named Souharissen.

As a trading nation, the Neutrals were probably wise to dissociate themselves from the wars between the Hurons and the Iroquois, but when these wars became entangled with the greater conflict between the French and the English, the days of the Neutrals were numbered. The English supported the Iroquois and gave them rifles; the French backed the Hurons but trusted them with nothing stronger than whisky. The decision not to arm the Hurons led ultimately to the fall of New France in 1759; it led more directly to the destruction of the Neutrals in 1651.

In 1645, Iroquois warriors crossed the Niagara River and raided Huronia; in 1649, Father Jean de Brébeuf was captured and tortured; by 1651, the Iroquois, with the full support of the English, had systematically slaughtered 15,000 Petuns, 12,000 Hurons and 12,000 Neutrals. Only a handful escaped; these banded together and fled south, where they eventually changed their tribal name to the Wyandots. In 1842, the U.S. government gave them a grant of land in Kansas, and in 1892, they were moved en masse to Oklahoma, where they remain today. Their total population now is 850.

In Canada, there are few reminders of their existence: some clay pipes in the Tobacco Museum in Delhi; the Southwold Earthworks in Elgin County; and a rustproof metal statue of Chief Souharissen, one of six cast in England and shipped to North America in the early 1800s, which now stands on Talbot Street in St. Thomas. This statue, five feet tall and weighing 300 pounds, is the original cigar-store Indian.

By the first week in August, most of the Quebec migrants have found jobs, one way or another, and are living on the farms in bunkhouses provided by the farmers. But there are usually a few hundred who haven't found work yet or have given up trying altogether. They hang around the Delhi Cenotaph — a small park on King Street with a war memorial in the centre, low bushes around the perimeter and four green picnic tables donated by the Delhi Kinsmen. If they have any money, they walk aimlessly up and down King Street (they never venture onto Main Street, the exclusive preserve of the Delhi residents) until the Diplomat opens at noon.

When it isn't raining, some of the unemployed migrants lie about in their sleeping bags at a place called the Island, actually a sort of isthmus formed by a sudden loop in Big Creek about half a mile west of town. The local children, especially the girls, have been brought up on horror stories about the Island, stories in which drugs, orgies, drunken gang fights, even knifings play a significant role. Local police and the OPP patrol the Island regularly after the harvest begins, breaking up groups and sometimes marching them in single file down the highway until they're two or three miles from town. Most of them find their way back by nightfall, but the exercise is thought to be good for them. Besides, a string of foot-weary drifters is a less serious threat to civil order than a centralized group of unemployed labourers.

This theory was formed in 1966, when a partial crop failure caused by a hailstorm swelled the ranks of unemployed migrants to about 800. By mid-August, they were hungry and bored. "I had to read them the Riot Act," recalls Mayor Sayeau, a short, middle-aged man with a soft voice that tends to trail away between sentences. He leans back in his swivel chair and gazes through the door of his office. "I think I was the second person in Canada who ever read it. In those days, we used to put up big tents for them down by Big Creek, a little farther along and across the bridge. Well, they'd get restless, so we decided the best thing to do was to keep them moving, spread them out a bit. It happened this way: twice each day, we'd take sandwiches down to them, because they didn't have any money for food. Then they demanded a hot meal at night. Can you imagine that? And the OPP gave in to them, brought them down hot suppers! Then one morning, they said they wanted bacon and eggs! They started marching into town in crowds, demonstrating. Father Lannigan from Langton had been going down there and working with them, and even he was disgusted at this. That's when I read them the Riot Act."

Since then, says Sayeau, "people in town have been against the French," but there hasn't been much trouble. Most of the workers these days, he believes, are students on summer vacation. They come to Delhi to work a bit and have a good time. "We need these people," he says. "Tobacco is our commodity, and we have to put up with them. Ninety percent of them are only as bad as you treat them."

A few nights earlier in the Cenotaph, a long line of workers had formed near the bushes in the southwest corner. A young pimp stood at the head of the line taking $5 from each person who passed him and entered the bushes — about one every two or three minutes. After a while, an OPP patrol car pulled up, and the line scattered. The pimp and his girl—a thin, young kid with long, curly hair, her clothes held tight against her chest—made a dash for a car and drove off in a diminuendo of scattered gravel. The cops didn't bother giving chase. They sat down on one of the benches and smoked cigarettes.

Mayor Sayeau chuckles and shakes his head. "There used to be prostitutes come right into town every harvest. They set themselves up in trailers across the street from the Diplomat; used to see them trailers rocking all night. We left 'em alone. We figured if there were a few pros around, the boys would leave our own girls alone."

One of the few Delhi residents who have much to do with the migrants is Deno Gettas. Deno and his father Stan own the Discount Store just up the road from the Diplomat. Deno's a tall, fortyish man with an aquiline nose, greying hair like coarse steel wool and a bushy moustache that's more salt than pepper. He seems to be always laughing, passing out cigarettes, buying rounds, learning a bit of French here and there. His wide smile reveals large, even teeth. The little finger of his left hand is permanently bent. Every morning at 8 o'clock, he opens the store and minds it until his father, who is going on 80, shows up around 10:00. Then Deno is on his own until 4:00, when he takes over again until the last customer leaves, usually around 9:00. Between noon and 4:00, he can be found just about anywhere: on his boat, which he keeps in the marina at Long Point—a spit of sand on Lake Erie— or in his apartment on King Street above the submarine-sandwich shop or at the south end of the shuffleboard in the Diplomat.

By the time Carol has rolled up her bit of carpet and disappeared upstairs, the taproom is so busy that Raymond can't slow down for a minute. During the harvest season, he averages about $500 a week. That figure goes way down when the migrants leave, so he can't afford to waste time now. Deno helps out by taking a beer case from table to table, collecting empties. A few people are dancing in the area beside the stage; one migrant is standing bent over, with his long, straight hair brushing back and forth along the floor in time to a song on the jukebox.

"I've lived here all my life," a man at the next table says three times. "And let me tell you, this little town makes Peyton Place look like Disneyland." He leans back and assumes a conspiratorial look. "How many liquor outlets do you think there are in this little town? Eh? How many would you guess?" I guess six: the Diplomat, the Arrowhead Motel, the Golden Leaf Restaurant, a few clubs. "Hah, no — 17!" he says triumphantly, draining a glass of beer. "Including the LCBO and the beer store. Did you know my wife kicked me out of the house? Have to live in a motel. Costs me 60 bucks a week, and where'm I supposed to eat? Eh? I've lived in Delhi all my life. I could tell you a few things about this place, yes, sir, that would curl your hair."

Pierre, meanwhile, is describing a fight he saw last week between a stripper — evidently not Carol — and the wife of one of the locals, who had called out something uncomplimentary during one of the shows. Hélène comes over to the table — she's been playing pool most of the night — and says there's a party at Deno's after closing time.

At 1:30, most of the locals have gone home. Steve locks the doors, pulls the plug on the jukebox and breaks out three bottles of Canadian champagne. "It's my birthday," he says. Sue brings glasses, and we all drink to Steve's health. Raymond drinks his from behind the bar, refusing to join the table because one of the locals sitting with us had thrown a beer bottle at him earlier that night. I tell Steve about the fellow who's lived in Delhi all his life. Steve, who's a member of the Lions Club and who sponsors a kids' T-ball team, shakes his head sadly and puts down his glass.

"You know," he says, "I'm thinking of selling this place. Before I came here, I never knew the things that went on in an average Canadian small town. Sisters having their brothers' babies, fathers-in-law sleeping with their daughters-in-law. I was shocked. I was disgusted. They do things here that we don't even have *words* for in Korea. If someone called me one of those names, I would kill him."

When the champagne is gone, Steve produces some Scotch. Those who have to drive home have a few more beers to sober up, and those who don't head off to Deno's apartment. It's reached by a flight of narrow, brown-painted stairs leading to a landing full of pale green washing machines and spin-dryers. The door opens off the landing onto an expanse of deep white pile. Hélène, who is leading the way, makes everyone take off their shoes. In the living room, two couples occupy the sofa. Facing them, a three-tiered stereo system takes up almost the whole wall, its flanking speakers doubling as occasional tables piled with ashtrays and glasses. Through a set of French doors between the sofa and the stereo is the master bedroom. The bedroom is dark except for the blue-white glow of a television set.

In the kitchen, Hélène, who has a job on a farm near Scotland, Ontario, is mixing a pitcherful of orange juice, vodka, brandy and Southern Comfort. It looks like something that might have been squeezed out of a boil. Raymond takes a professional sip.

"Too much orange juice," he says.

"What do you call that?" he's asked.

"I call it a Slow Comfortable Screw." Hélène pours Deno's drink into a huge brandy snifter, the kind that holds about a quart and is sold only in joke shops. Deno goes off to the living room to watch Raymond and Daniel play chess.

Hélène has been working since early June, planting, then hoeing and now priming. She has a deep, golden tan and tiny blue-and-white beads braided into her hair, which is long and black and shiny. She says she is getting tired of tobacco and is thinking of going out West. Deno has a friend who has a friend who is starting up a taxi business in Fort McMurray — she calls it "Fort Make Money" — and she's trying to talk a girlfriend into driving out there with her.

"Do you know where is Fort Make Money?" she asks. I tell her it's in Alberta. "In the south?" No, up north. She shrugs. She doesn't like the North very much. Last week, she had a few days off because of rain, so she went for a drive and ended up in Sudbury. "It was awful," she says. "Not very beautiful."

By dawn, the party has thinned out to a half-dozen unshakables. The bathroom window looks across Main Street to the Diplomat; every second-floor window glows a dirty yellow through the morning mist, like a huge ship at anchor. The streetlights go out, and a long, grey tractor-trailer with BURFORD FERTILIZER stencilled on its tarpaulin grinds its way from the corner up the steep grade toward Tillsonburg.

In the living room, Raymond and Daniel are lying on their stomachs, still playing chess, still drinking Slow Comfortable Screws. Daniel has to meet Joe Guitar at the Mountain Dew sign in an hour, and Raymond is working the evening shift at the Diplomat. Across King Street, a few migrants have already taken up their positions at the picnic tables in the park, waiting for a farmer who might drive by looking for a fresh crew of primers.

Automation is one solution to the labour problem. Morris Mertens takes a different approach. His farm, in Teeterville, is too far from Delhi (about 11 miles) to attract local students. He has put in bulk kilns, but instead of hiring Canadians, he subscribes to the offshore programme. Since 1974, all his primers have been from Barbados. "They're steady, dependable. They come up here to work. They don't party all night, they don't go out with hangovers in the morning, they don't fight with each other, they're up at 5:00 sharp every morning and just raring to go. I've never had a problem with them."

The five Barbadians who work for Mertens came up on July 23 and moved into their own trailer on the Mertens farm, beside the greenhouse and a few yards from the pump. Scattered about in the tall grass near their trailer are a few empty beer bottles, a plastic dishpan full of tar-stained work gloves and an old weather-beaten cricket bat.

Mertens drives them into town every Friday night after supper. "They do their shopping, cash their cheques, and I go back in to pick them up at 10 o'clock. Some farmers only let them stay in town for an hour a week, but I figure they treat me right, so I treat them right." As long as they have work, they can stay in Canada and send money home to their families. When there's no work for them, they're shipped back to Barbados.

Some farmers provide meals for their workers, but the Barbadians prefer to cook for themselves. "Every night, they cook up a big meal," says Mertens, "their own food. Sometimes it makes me sick just to look at it. They get a big pot and fill it up with vegetables — potatoes, corn, rice, whatever they can get up here — and they have five big bowls, and they fill 'em up and cover 'em with a piece of meat, and that's their dinner. Each one of them eats as much as we have for the whole family, and they eat the same thing night after night. No bread, no butter. One day, I asked them, 'Don't you ever eat bread?' And they said, 'Not with food.'"

One of the problems with offshore labour, says Mayor Sayeau, is that Barbadians don't like coming up for early planting in the spring. A lot of them won't come up until harvest, he says. It's too cold. "I remember driving past one of our orchards one spring, just south of Delhi — we have some beautiful apple orchards in this region, used to be known for them — and I looked up, I'll never forget this as long as I live, and there were these coloured boys pruning the trees, sitting up in the branches. It was cold, and you know these coloured boys can't take the cold. Well, there was one little fella up in a tree, pruning, and he had on a tuque pulled way down over his head and his collar up and a scarf around his neck, and all you could see of him was his little round black face. He looked cold. Well, I looked up at him in this bare tree, and I said, 'What the hell is that?' It looked like a monkey. I thought maybe one of them got left up there from last year."

The Delhi branch of the Royal Canadian Legion is a low, squat, military-looking building with a wood-panelled foyer, a large main gathering room and a kitchen separated from the larger room by a grey tile counter and a folding wooden screen. The hall has a comfortable smell, like a church hall, redolent of bingos, euchre parties, casino nights. Canadian and Ontario flags form a patriotic V behind a long head table facing two solid blocks of metal stacking chairs. Above the flags, a banner has been stuck to the wall with thumbtacks: "The Canadian Farmworkers Union" in yellow felt letters on a red background and, below that, a circular crest with the words "Unite and Fight."

Seated at the table under the banner are four speakers: Wayne Pierce, president of the Simcoe and District Labour Council; Monty Davidson, a staff member of the Ontario Federation of Labour's health and safety training centre; Eric del Junco, a law student who also chairs the CFU's legal research committee; and Judy Cavanagh, from the national CFU office in Vancouver. The hall fills up with farmers, farmers' wives, farmers' daughters — but no migrant workers. Where are the migrants?

The meeting begins with a reading of a telegram from Dennis McDermott, president of the Canadian Labour Congress: "We salute the efforts of the Canadian Farmworkers Union to persuade tobacco growers to pay decent wages and provide safe working conditions for the men and women who harvest the crops in southwestern Ontario. . . . Exploitation is the rule for wage workers in agriculture. Some farm workers, particularly those who move into a region just for the harvest, then move on, live in 'shelters' that farm operators probably would consider unfit for horses or cattle."

There are mild snorts of protest from the audience. The one migrant worker in the hall, an English Quebecker named Rick, still hasn't found a job, and for the past three nights, he's been sleeping under the stars on the Island. Last night's rain had run down a gully and flowed into his sleeping bag, and in the afternoon, he had hitchhiked in sodden clothes into Simcoe to collect a $20 welfare cheque. Before the meeting, he'd been buying rounds at the Diplomat. Right now, any shelter, even one unfit for horses or cattle, would look good to Rick. And the farmers know, of course, that their bunkhouses are clean, well-lighted places. So far, the CFU's experience has been with the 1,100 East Indian fruit pickers in British Columbia, most of whom had been living in appalling conditions until they were organized into the first CFU local in 1980. There's a message from the president of the Ontario Federation of Labour that outlines the benefits of trade unionism and ends, "Yours in solidarity, Cliff Pilkey." Then the first speaker is introduced.

Wayne Pierce gives a thumbnail history of the labour movement from the 18th century to the present. Strikes are not always bad things, he concludes. Sometimes, strikers have legitimate grievances. For example, the first strike in North America was by a group of journeyman printers in New York in 1776, who struck for a nine-hour workday.

"Nine hours?" calls out someone in the audience. "Tobacco workers here work six to eight hours a day, tops. Me and my wife are out there 12 hours a day."

The mediator stands up quickly. "There will be time for a panel discussion after the speakers have finished," she says. "We have an agenda to get through."

The next speaker is Monty Davidson, a kindly, middle-aged man with an apologetic smile. He looks like David Lewis. Before standing up, he lights a cigarette and sets it in an ashtray beside his notes. He then proceeds to list the harmful effects of Diazinon, one of the 12 pesticides used by tobacco farmers. "Headaches, fatigue, blurred vision, nausea, diarrhea, stomach cramps, all symptoms that might be thought to be caused by flu. Later, the infected person might complain that he can't walk, that he twitches, that he's developing myosis and infarction, symptoms commonly associated with pneumonia—"

"Sounds like a hangover to me," someone shouts. Everyone laughs. Davidson smiles.

"Eventually, he succumbs to unconsciousness and seizures." Davidson takes a long drag on his cigarette, then puts it back in the ashtray. "Tobacco farmers use far more pesticides than anyone else in the agricultural industry: Orthene, Ripcord, Ambush, C-10, C-8, dylox, organophosphates. And that's not even considering the likelihood of nicotine poisoning. Tobacco workers get *covered* in raw nicotine, and it only takes a slight scratch in the skin to admit that deadly poison into the bloodstream. Insomnia, headaches, vomiting, running eyes and eventually death. And I'm talking about things that are a health hazard to the farmer and his family too."

Davidson sits down. The crowd is quiet. He's a decent man, but what does he want the farmers to do? They can't stop using pesticides — even if they gave up tobacco and started growing tomatoes, they'd have to use pesticides.

Eric del Junco, the next speaker, is a young, slim, casually dressed law student. He addresses the audience in a matter-of-fact way that impresses the farmers. Agriculture, he tells them, is the third most dangerous occupation in Canada, after logging and mining. The life expectancy of farmworkers is 49 years, compared with the national average of 70. The infant-mortality rate in agricultural families is 150 percent above normal. The incidence of pneumonia is 200 percent above normal. Tobacco farmers have 24 percent more injuries than any other kind of farmer.

"Despite these facts," says del Junco, "farmworkers are excluded from the laws governing paid breaks, minimum wage and overtime. The Occupational Health and Safety Act of 1978 allows workers to refuse work that's dangerous to their health, but it says clearly that it does not apply to inmates of correctional institutions, patients in mental institutions, domestic servants and workers employed in agriculture. You could spray your fields with Diazinon, a chemical that's been banned in the United States, and tell your workers to go out there before the chemical has even settled, and if they refuse, you can fire them. The Ontario Labour Relations Act, which guarantees all workers the right to collective bargaining, specifically excludes persons employed in agriculture, hunting and trapping. Ontario and Alberta are the only two provinces in Canada that continue to deny farmworkers these basic rights."

The meeting is thrown open to discussion, but there are few questions. The farmers know that the workers are not interested in forming a union, that all they have to do is be polite and show concern and nothing will come of the CFU. Their stance might be described as passive resistance.

Back at the Diplomat, every table is surrounded by a dozen drinkers. Raymond and two other waiters are carrying trays of beer at a rate reminiscent of the sorcerer's apprentice scene in *Fantasia*.

"How'd the meeting go?" Raymond asks, jingling the coins in his black leather apron. Rick gives him a brief account, and Raymond shakes his head. "It's got to come someday," he says. "These guys won't take shit forever."

"They should have had the meeting in French."

"They should have held it down on the Island," Raymond says.

At the mention of the Island, Rick shivers and looks glum. A few minutes later, two women from the meeting come over and sit down. Judy Cavanagh has short, black, curly hair and a sharp, earnest face. The other organizer introduces herself as Sandi Roy. Before getting involved in the CFU, she lived in Toronto and worked as a waitress. She has spent most of the summer living in a trailer in Simcoe, going out each day to ring the doorbells of seasonal workers who live in the area year-round, doing odd jobs in the winter or collecting unemployment insurance.

Before the CFU was ratified, says Judy, East Indian workers in the Fraser Valley were living in filthy hovels, paying 40 percent of their wages to labour contractors who were also East Indian. Last summer, three East Indian children drowned in a gravel pit while both parents were out in the fields. Another day, a baby drowned when it fell off a cot into a bucket of drinking water in a workers' shack that had no indoor plumbing.

"That's really sad," Rick says. "But what's it got to do with picking tobacco in Ontario?"

"Not much," Judy admits. "Actually, tobacco workers have it pretty good. They're well paid, their bunkhouses are usually inspected by the health department." She looks tired and discouraged. "But the bonus system is unfair, and they should have the right to belong to a union." She sighs, sips her beer and shakes her head sadly: "I guess the days of *The Grapes of Wrath* are over."

Wallace Stegner

The Question Mark in the Circle

An ordinary road map of the United States, one that for courtesy's sake includes the first hundred miles on the Canadian side of the line, will show two roads, graded but not paved, reaching up into western Saskatchewan to link U.S. 2 with Canada 1, the Trans-Canada Highway. One of these little roads leads from Havre, on the Milk River, to Maple Creek; the other from Malta, also on the Milk, to Swift Current. The first, perhaps 120 miles long, has no towns on it big enough to show on a map of this scale. The second, 50 miles longer, has two, neither of which would be worth comment except that one of them, Val Marie, is the site of one of the few remaining prairie dog towns anywhere. The rest of that country is notable primarily for its weather, which is violent and prolonged; its emptiness, which is almost frighteningly total; and its wind, which blows all the time in a way to stiffen your hair and rattle the eyes in your head.

This is no safety valve for the population explosion, no prize in a latter-day land rush. It has had its land rush and recovered. If you owned it, you might be able to sell certain parts of it at a few dollars an acre; many parts you couldn't give away. Not many cars raise dust along its lonely roads — it is country people do not much want to cross, much less visit. But that block of country between the Milk River and the main line of the Canadian Pacific and between approximately the Saskatchewan-Alberta line and Wood Mountain is the place where I spent my childhood. It is also the place where the Plains, as an ecology, as a native Indian culture and as a process of white settlement, came to their climax and their end. Viewed personally and historically, that almost featureless prairie glows with more colour than it reveals to the appalled and misdirected tourist. As memory, as experience, those Plains are unforgettable; as history, they have the lurid explosiveness of a prairie fire, quickly dangerous, swiftly over.

I have sometimes been tempted to believe that I grew up on a gun-toting frontier. This temptation I trace to a stagecoach ride in the spring of 1914 and to a cowpuncher named Buck Murphy.

The stagecoach ran from Gull Lake, Saskatchewan, on the main line of the Canadian Pacific, to the town I shall call Whitemud, 60 miles southwest in the valley of the Whitemud or Frenchman River. The grade from Moose Jaw already reached to Whitemud, and steel was being laid, but no trains were yet running when the stage brought in my mother, my brother and myself, plus a red-faced cowpuncher with a painful deference to ladies and a great affection for little children. I rode the 60 miles on Buck Murphy's lap, half-anaesthetized by his whisky breath, and during the ride, I confounded both my mother and Murphy by fishing from under his coat a six-shooter half as big as I was.

A little later, Murphy was shot and killed by a Mountie in the streets of Shaunavon, up the line. As I heard later, the Mountie was scared and trigger-happy and would have been in real trouble for an un-Mountielike killing if Murphy had not been carrying a gun. But instead of visualizing it as it probably was — Murphy coming down the street in a buckboard, the Mountie on the corner, bad blood between them, a suspicious move, a shot, a scared team, a crowd collecting — I have been led by a lifetime of horse opera to imagine that death in standard walk-down detail. For years, growing up in more civilized places, I got a comfortable sense of status out of recalling that in my youth,

I had been a friend of badmen and an eyewitness to gunfights in wide streets between false-fronted saloons. Not even the streets and saloons, now that I test them, were authentic, for I don't think I was ever in Shaunavon in my boyhood, and I could not have reconstructed an image from Whitemud's streets because at the time of Murphy's death, Whitemud didn't have any. It hardly even had houses: we ourselves were living in a derailed dining car.

Actually, Murphy was an amiable, drunken, sentimental, perhaps dishonest and generally harmless Montana cowboy like dozens of others. He may have been in Canada for reasons that would have interested Montana sheriffs, but more likely not; and if he had been, so were plenty of others who never thought of themselves as badmen. The Cypress Hills had always made a comfortable retiring place just a good day's ride north of the line. Murphy would have carried a six-shooter mainly for reasons of brag; he would have worn it inside his coat, because Canadian law forbade the carrying of sidearms. When Montana cattle outfits worked across the line, they learned to leave their guns in their bedrolls. In the American West, men came before law; but in Saskatchewan, the law was there before settlers, before even cattlemen, and not merely law but law enforcement. It was not characteristic that Buck Murphy should die in a gunfight, but if he had to die by violence, it was entirely characteristic that he should be shot by a policeman.

The first settlement in the Cypress Hills country was a village of Métis winterers; the second was a short-lived Hudson's Bay Company post on Chimney Coulee; the third was the Mounted Police headquarters at Fort Walsh; the fourth was a Mountie outpost erected on the site of the burned Hudson's Bay Company buildings to keep an eye on Sitting Bull and other Indians who congregated in that country in alarming numbers after the big troubles of the 1870s. The Mountie post on Chimney Coulee, later moved down onto the river, was the predecessor of the town of Whitemud. The overgrown foundation stones of its cabins remind a historian why there were no Boot Hills along the Frenchman. The place was too well policed.

So as I have learned more, I have had to give up the illusion of a romantic gun-toting past, and it is hardly glamour that brings me back, a middle-aged pilgrim, to the village I last saw in 1920. Neither do I come back with the expectation of returning to a childhood wonderland—or I don't think I do. By most estimates, including most of the estimates of memory, Saskatchewan can be a pretty depressing country.

The Frenchman, a river more American than Canadian, since it flows into the Milk and thence into the Missouri, has changed its name since my time to conform with American maps. We always called it the Whitemud, from the stratum of pure white kaolin exposed along its valley. Whitemud or Frenchman, the river is important in my memory, for it conditioned and contained the town. But memory, though vivid, is imprecise, without sure dimensions, and it is as much to test memory against adult observation as for any other reason that I return. What I remember are low bars overgrown with wild roses, cutbank bends, secret paths through the willows, fords across the shallows, swallows in the clay banks, days of indolence and adventure where space was as flexible as the mind's cunning and where time did not exist. That was at the heart of it: the sunken and sanctuary river valley. Out around, stretching in all directions from the benches to become coextensive with the disc of the world, went the uninterrupted prairie.

The geologist who surveyed southern Saskatchewan in the 1870s called it one of the most desolate and forbidding regions on Earth. I can remember plenty of times when it seemed so to me and my family. Yet as I poke the car tentatively eastward into it from Medicine Hat, returning to my childhood through a green June, I look for desolation and can find none.

The plain spreads southward below the Trans-Canada Highway, an ocean of wind-troubled grass and grain. It has its remembered textures: winter wheat heavily headed, scoured and shadowed as if schools of fish move in it; spring wheat with its young seed-rows as precise as combings in a boy's wet hair; grey-brown summer fallow with the weeds disced under; and grass, the marvellous curly prairie wool tight to the Earth's skin, straining the wind as the wheat does but in its own way, secretly.

Prairie wool blue-green, spring wheat bright as new lawn, winter wheat grey-green at rest and slaty when the wind flaws it, roadside primroses as shy as prairie flowers are supposed to be and as gentle to the eye as when, in my boyhood, we used to call them wild tulips and, by their coming, date the beginning of summer.

On that monotonous surface with its occasional shiplike farm, its atolls of shelterbelt trees, its level ring of horizon, there is little to interrupt the eye. Roads run straight between parallel lines of fence until they intersect the circle of the horizon. It is a landscape of circles, radii, perspective exercises — a country of geometry.

Across its empty miles pours the pushing and shouldering wind, a thing you tighten into as a trout tightens into fast water. It is a grassy, clean, exciting wind, with the smell of distance in it, and in its search for whatever it is looking for, it turns over every wheat blade and head, every pale primrose, even the ground-hugging grass. It blows yellow-headed blackbirds and hawks and prairie sparrows around the air and ruffles the short tails of meadowlarks on fenceposts. In collaboration with the light, it makes lovely and changeful what might otherwise be characterless.

It is a long way from characterless — "overpowering" would be a better word. For over the segmented circle of earth is domed the biggest sky anywhere, which on days like this sheds down on range and wheat and summer fallow a light to set a painter wild, a light pure, glareless and transparent. The horizon a dozen miles away is as clean a line as the nearest fence. There is no haze, neither the woolly grey of humid countries nor the blue atmosphere of the mountain West. Across the immense sky move navies of cumuli, fair-weather clouds, their bottoms as even as if they had scraped themselves flat against the flat earth.

The drama of this landscape is in the sky, pouring with light and always moving. The earth is passive. And yet the beauty I am struck by, both as present fact and as revived memory, is a fusion: this sky would not be so spectacular without this earth to change and glow and darken under it. And whatever the sky may do, however the earth is shaken or darkened, the Euclidean perfection abides. The very scale, the hugeness of simple forms, emphasizes stability. It is not hills and mountains which we should call eternal. Nature abhors an elevation as much as it abhors a vacuum; a hill is no sooner elevated than the forces of erosion begin tearing it down. These prairies are quiescent, close to static; looked at for any length of time, they begin to impose their awful perfection on the observer's mind. Eternity is a peneplain.

In a wet spring such as this, there is almost as much sky on the ground as in the air. The country is dotted with sloughs; every depression is full of water; the roadside ditches are canals. Grass and wheat grow to the water's edge and under it; they seem to grow right under the edges of the sky. In deep sloughs, tules have rooted, and every such pond is dignified with mating mallards and the dark little automata that glide after them as if on strings.

The nesting mallards move in my memory too, pulling after them shadowy, long-forgotten images. The picture of a drake standing on his head with his curly tailfeathers sticking up from a sheet of wind-flawed slough is tangled in my remembering senses with the feel of the grassy edge under my bare feet, the smell of mud, the push of the traveller wind, the weight of the sun, the look of the sky with its level-floored clouds made for the penetration of miraculous Beanstalks.

Desolate? Forbidding? There was never a country that in its good moments was more beautiful. Even in drought or dust storm or blizzard, it is the reverse of monotonous, once you have submitted to it with all the senses. You don't get out of the wind but learn to squint against it. You don't escape sky and sun but wear them in your eyeballs and on your back. You become acutely aware of yourself. The world is very large, the sky even larger, and you are very small. But also the world is flat, empty, nearly abstract, and in its flatness, you are a challenging upright thing, as sudden as an exclamation mark, as enigmatic as a question mark.

It is a country to breed mystical people, egocentric people, perhaps poetic people. But not humble ones. At noon, the total sun pours on your single head; at sunrise or sunset, you throw a shadow a hundred yards long. It was not prairie dwellers who invented the indifferent universe or impotent man. Puny you may feel there and vulnerable but not unnoticed. This is a land to mark the sparrow's fall.

Our homestead lay south of here, right on the Saskatchewan-Montana border — a place so ambiguous in its affiliations that we felt as uncertain as the drainage about which way to flow. It would be no more than 30 or 40 miles out of my way now, and yet I do not turn south to try to find it, and I know very well why. I am afraid to. In the Dust Bowl years, all that country was returned to range by the Provincial Farm Rehabilitation Administration. I can imagine myself bumping across burnouts and cactus clumps, scanning the de-humanized waste for some mark — shack or wind-leaned chicken coop, wagon ruts or abandoned harrow with its teeth full of Russian thistle — to reassure me that people did once live there. Worse, I can imagine actually finding the flat on which our house stood, the coulee that angled up the pasture, the dam behind which the spring thaw created our "rezavoy" — locating the place and standing in it ringed by emptiness and silence, while the wind fingered my face and whispered to itself like an old blind woman and a burrowing owl, flustered by the unfamiliar visitor, bowed from the dirt mound of its doorstep, saying, "Who? Who?"

I do not want that. I don't want to find, as I know I will if I go down there, that we have vanished without trace like a boat sunk in midocean. I don't want our shack to be gone, as I know it is; I would not enjoy hunting the ground around it for broken crockery and rusty nails and bits of glass. I don't want to know that our protective pasture fence has been pulled down to let the prairie in or that our field, which stopped at the line and so defined a sort of identity and difference, now flows southward into Montana without a break as restored grass and burnouts. Once, standing alone under the bell-jar sky gave me the strongest feeling of personal singularity I shall ever have. That was because it was all new, we were taking hold of it to make it ours. But to return, hunting relics, to go down there armed only with memory and find every trace of our passage wiped away — that would be to reduce my family, myself, the hard effort of years, to solipsism, to make us as fictive as a dream.

If I say to the owl, "Your great-grandfather lived in my house and could turn his head clear around and look out between his shoulder blades," I know he will bow, being polite, and then turn *his* head clear around and look out between his shoulder blades and, seeing only unbroken grass, will cough and say, "What house? Whose?" I know the very way the wind will ruffle his feathers as he turns; I can hear the dry silence that will resume as soon as he stops speaking. With the clarity of hallucination, I can see my mother's weathered, rueful, half-laughing face and hear the exact tone, between regretful and indomitable, in which she says the words with which she always met misfortune or failure: "Well," she will say, "better luck next time!"

I had much better let it alone. The town is safer. I turn south only far enough to come up onto the South Bench, and then I follow a dirt road eastward so as to enter Whitemud from the old familiar direction. That much I will risk.

It is a far more prosperous country than I remember, for I return at the crest of a wet cycle. The farms that used to jut bleakly from the prairie are bedded in cottonwoods and yellow-flowering caragana. Here and there, the horizontal land is broken by a new verticality more portentous than windmills or elevators — the derricks of oil rigs. Farther north, prosperity rides on the uranium boom. Here, it rides on wheat and oil. But though the country is no longer wild, this section within reach of town is even emptier, more thinly lived in, than in our time. Oil crews create no new towns and do not enlarge the old ones more than briefly. Even if they hit oil, they erect a Christmas tree on the well and go away. As for wheat, fewer and fewer farmers produce more and more of it.

To us, a half-section was a farm. With modern machinery, a man by himself can plough, seed and harvest 1,000 or 1,200 acres. The average Saskatchewan farm is at least a section; two sections or even more are not uncommon. And that is the good land, not the submarginal land such as ours which has been put back to grass. Even such a duchy of a farm is only a part-time job. A man can seed 100 acres a day. Once the crop is in, there is little to do until harvest. Then a week or two on the combine, a week or two of hauling, a week or two of working the summer fallow and planting winter wheat, and he is all done until May.

This is a strange sort of farming, with its dangers of soil exhaustion, drought and wind erosion and with highly specialized conditions. Only about half of the farmhouses on the prairie are lived in anymore, and some of those are lived in only part-time, by farmers who spend all but the crop season in town, as we did. Many a farmer, miles from town, has no farmhouse at all but commutes to work in a pickup. There is a growing class of trailer farmers, suitcase farmers, many of them from the United States, who camp for three or four months beside the field and return to Minneapolis or Bismarck when the crop is in.

Hence the look of extensive cultivation and at the same time the emptiness. We see few horses, few cattle. Saskatchewan farmers could go a long way toward supplying the world's bread, but they are less subsistence farmers than we were in 1915. They live in towns that have the essential form and function of mediaeval towns or New England country towns or Mormon villages in irrigated land: clusters of dwellings surrounded by the cultivated fields. But here, the fields are a mile or two miles square and may be 40 miles from the home of the man who works them.

So it is still quiet earth, big sky. Human intrusions seem as abrupt as the elevators that leap out of the plain to announce every little hamlet and keep it memorable for a few miles. The countryside and the smaller villages empty gradually into the larger centres; in the process of slow adaptation to the terms the land sets, the small towns get smaller, the larger ones larger. Whitemud, based strategically on railroad and river, is one of the ones that will last.

In the fall, it was always a moment of pure excitement, after a whole day on the trail, to come to the rim of the South Bench. More likely than not, I would be riding with my mother in the wagon while my father had my brother with him in the Ford. The horses would be plodding with their noses nearly to their knees, the colt would be dropping tiredly behind. We would be choked with dust, cranky and headachy with heat, our joints loosened with 50 miles of jolting. Then miraculously, the land fell away below us; I would lift my head from my mother's lap and push aside the straw hat that had been protecting my face from the glare, and there below, looped in its green coils of river, snug and protected in its sanctuary valley, lay town.

The land falls away below me now, the suddenness of my childhood town is the old familiar surprise. But I stop, looking, for adult perception has in 10 seconds clarified a childhood error. I have always thought of the Whitemud as running its whole course in a deeply sunken valley. Instead, I see that the river has cut deeply only through the uplift of the hills, that off to the southeast, out on the prairie, it crawls disconsolately flat across the land. It is a lesson in how peculiarly limited a child's sight is: he sees only what he can see. Only later does he learn to link what he sees with what he already knows or has imagined or heard or read and so come to make perception serve inference. During my childhood, I kept hearing about the Cypress Hills and knew that they were somewhere nearby. Now, I see that I grew up in them. Without destroying the intense familiarity, the flooding recognition of the moment, that grown-up understanding throws things a little out of line, and so it is with mixed feelings of intimacy and strangeness that I start down the dugway grade. Things look the same, surprisingly the same, and yet obscurely different. I tick them off, easing watchfully back into the past.

There is the Frenchman's stone barn, westward up the river valley a couple of miles. It looks exactly as it did when we used to go through the farmyard in wagon or buckboard and see the startled kids disappearing around every corner and peeking out at us from hayloft door and cowshed after we passed. Probably they were Métis, half-breeds; to us, who had never heard the word Métis, they were simply Frenchmen, part of the vague and unknown past that had given our river one of its names. I bless them for their permanence and creep on past the cemetery, somewhat larger and somewhat better kept than I remember it but without disconcerting changes. Down below me is the dam, with its wide lake behind it. It takes me a minute to recollect that by the time we left Whitemud, Pop Martin's dam had long since washed out. This is a new one, therefore, but in approximately the old place. So far, so good.

The road I bump along is still a dirt road, and it runs where it used to run, but the wildcat oil derrick that used to be visible from the turn at the foot of the grade is not there any longer. I note, coming in toward the edge of town, that the river has changed its course somewhat, swinging closer to the southern hills and pinching the road space. I see a black iron bridge, new, that evidently leads some new road off into the willow bottoms westward, toward the old Carpenter ranch. I cannot see the river, masked in willows and alders, and anyway, my attention is taken by the town ahead of me, which all at once reveals one element of the obscure strangeness that has been making me watchful. Trees.

My town used to be as bare as a picked bone, with no tree anywhere around it larger than a 10-foot willow or alder. Now, it is a grove. My memory gropes uneasily, trying to establish itself among 50-foot cottonwoods, lilac and honeysuckle hedges and flower gardens. Searched for, plenty of familiarities are there: the Pastime Theatre, identical with the one that sits across Main Street from the firehouse in my mind; the lumberyard where we used to get cloth caps advertising De Laval Cream Separators; two or three hardware stores (a prairie wheat town specializes in hardware stores), though each one now has a lot full of farm machinery next to it; the hotel, just as it was rebuilt after the fire; the bank, now remodelled into the post office; the Presbyterian church, now United; and the *Leader* office and the square brick prison of the school, now with three smaller prisons added to it. These are old acquaintances that I can check against their replicas in my head and take satisfaction from. But among them are the evidences of Progress — hospital, Masonic Lodge, at least one new elevator, a big Quonsetlike skating rink — and all tree-shaded, altered and distorted and made vaguely disturbing by greenery. In the old days, we all used to try to grow trees, transplanting them from the Hills or getting them free with any two-dollar purchase from one of the stores, but they always dried up and died. To me, who came expecting a dusty hamlet, the change is charming, but memory has been fixed by time as photographs fix the faces of the dead, and this reality is dreamlike. I cannot find myself or my family or my companions in it.

My progress up Main Street, as wide and empty and dusty as I remember it, has taken me to another iron bridge across the eastern loop of the river, where the flume of Martin's irrigation ditch used to cross, and from the bridge, I get a good view of the river. It is disappointing, a quiet creek 20 yards wide, the colour of strong tea, its banks a tangle of willow and wild rose. How could adventure ever have inhabited those willows — or wonder or fear or the other remembered emotions? Was it along here I shot at the lynx with my brother's .25-.20? And out of what log (there is no possibility of a log in these brakes, but I distinctly remember a log) did my bullet knock chips just under the lynx's bobtail?

A muddy little stream, a village grown unfamiliar with time and trees. I turn around and retrace my way up Main Street and park and have a Coke in the confectionery store. It is run by a Greek, as it used to be, but whether the same Greek or another, I would not know. He does not recognize me, nor I him. Only the smell of his place is familiar, syrupy with old delights, as if the ghost of my first banana split had come close to breathe on me. Still in search of something or someone to make the town fully real to me, I get the telephone book off its nail by the wall telephone and run through it, sitting at the counter. There are no more than 70 or 80 names in the Whitemud section. I look for Huffman — none. Bickerton — none. Fetter — none. Orullian — none. Stenhouse — none. Young — one, but not by a first name I remember. There are a few names I do remember — Harold Jones and William Christenson and Nels Sieverud and Jules LaPlante. (That last one startles me. I always thought his name was Jewell.) But all of the names I recognize are those of old-timers, pioneers of the town. Not a name that I went to school with, not a single person who would have shared as a contemporary my own experience of this town in its earliest years, when the river still ran clear and beaver swam in it in the evenings. Who in town remembers Phil Lott, who used to run coyotes with wolfhounds out on the South Bench? Who remembers in the way I do the day he drove up before Leaf's store in his democrat wagon and unloaded from it two dead hounds and the lynx that had killed them when they caught him unwarily exposed out on the flats? Who remembers in *my* way that angry and disgusted scene and shares my recollection of the stiff, half-disembowelled bodies of the hounds and the bloody grin of the lynx? Who feels it or felt it, as I did and do, as a parable, a moral lesson for the pursuer to respect the pursued?

Because it is not shared, the memory seems fictitious, and so do other memories: the blizzard of 1916 that marooned us in the schoolhouse for a night and a day; the time the ice went out and brought both Martin's dam and the CPR bridge in kindling to our doors; the games of fox-and-geese in the untracked snow of a field that is now a grove; the nights of skating with a great fire leaping from the river ice and reflecting red from the cutbanks. I have used those memories for years as if they really happened, have made stories and novels of them. Now, they seem uncorroborated and delusive. Some of the pioneers still in the telephone book would remember, but pioneers' memories are no good to me. Pioneers would remember the making of the town; to me, it was made, complete, timeless. A pioneer's child is what I need now, and in this town, the pioneers' children did not stay but went on, generally to bigger places farther west, where there was more opportunity.

Sitting in the sticky-smelling, nostalgic air of the Greek's confectionery store, I am afflicted with the sense of how many whom I have known are dead and how little evidence I have that I myself have lived what I remember. It is not quite the same feeling I imagined when I contemplated driving out to the homestead. That would have been absolute denial. This, with its tantalizing glimpses, its hints and survivals, is not denial but only doubt. There is enough left to disturb me, but not to satisfy me. So I will go a little closer. I will walk on down into the west bend and take a look at our house.

In the strange forest of the schoolyard, the boys are friendly, and their universal air of health, openness and curiosity reassures me. This is still a good town to be a boy in. To see a couple of them on the prowl with air rifles (in my time, we would have been carrying .22s or shotguns, but we would have been of the same tribe) forces me to readjust my disappointed estimate of the scrub growth. When one is four feet high, 10-foot willows are a sufficient cover and 10 acres are a wilderness.

By now, circling and more than half unwilling, I have come into the west end of town, have passed Corky Jones's house (put off till later that meeting) and the open field beside Downs's where we used to play run-sheep-run in the evenings, and I stand facing the four-gabled white frame house that my father built. It ought to be explosive with nostalgias and bright with recollections, for this is where we lived for five or six of my most impressionable years, where we all nearly died with the flu in 1918, where my grandmother "went crazy" and had to be taken away by a Mountie to the provincial asylum because she took to standing silently in the door of the room where my brother and I slept — just hovered there for heaven knows how long before someone discovered her watching and listening in the dark. I try to remember my grandmother's face and cannot; only her stale old-woman's smell after she became incontinent. I can summon up other smells too — it is the smells that seem to have stayed with me: baking paint and hot tin and lignite smoke behind the parlour heater; frying scrapple, which we called headcheese, on chilly fall mornings after the slaughtering was done; the rich, thick odour of doughnuts frying in a kettle of boiling lard (I always got to eat the "holes"). With effort, I can bring back Christmases, birthdays, Sunday-school parties in that house, and I have not forgotten the licking I got when, aged about 6, I was caught playing with my father's loaded .30-.30 that hung above the mantel just under the Rosa Bonheur painting of three white horses in a storm. After that licking, I lay out behind the chopping block all one afternoon watching my big, dark, heavy father as he worked at one thing and another, and all the time I lay there, I kept aiming an empty cartridge case at him and dreaming murder.

Even the dreams of murder, which were bright enough at the time, have faded; he is long dead and, if not forgiven, at least propitiated. My mother, too, who saved me from him so many times and once missed saving me when he clouted me with a chunk of stove wood and knocked me over the woodbox and broke my collarbone: she, too, has faded. Standing there looking at the house where our lives entangled themselves in one another, I am infuriated that of that episode, I remember less her love and protection and anger than my father's inept contrition. And walking all around the house trying to pump up recollection, I notice principally that the old barn is gone. What I see, though less changed than the town in general, still has power to disturb me; it is all dreamlike, less real than memory, less convincing than the recollected odours.

Whoever lives in the house now is a tidy housekeeper; the yard is neat, the porch swept. The corner where I used to pasture my broken-legged colt is a bed of flowers, the yard where we hopefully watered our baby spruces is a lawn enclosed by a green hedge. The old well with the hand pump is still in the side yard. For an instant, my teeth are on edge with the memory of the dry screech of that pump before a dipperful of priming water took hold, and an instant later, I feel the old stitch in my side from an even earlier time, the time when we still carried water from the river, and I dipped a bucket down into the hole in the ice and toted it, staggering and with the other arm stuck stiffly out, up the dugway to the kitchen door.

Those instants of memory are persuasive. I wonder if I should knock on the door and ask the housewife to let me look around, go upstairs to our old room in the west gable, examine the ceiling to see if the stains from the fire department's chemicals are still there. My brother and I used to lie in bed and imagine scenes and faces among the blotches, giving ourselves inadvertent Rorschach tests. I have a vivid memory, too, of the night the stains were made, when we came out into the hard cold from the Pastime Theatre and heard the firehouse bell going and saw the volunteer fire department already on the run and followed them up the ditch toward the glow of the fire, wondering whose house, until we got close, and it was ours.

It is there, and yet it does not flow as it should; it is all a pumping operation. I half suspect that I am remembering not what happened but something I have written. I find that I am as unwilling to go inside that house as I was to try to find the old homestead in its ocean of grass. All the people who once shared the house with me are dead; strangers would have effaced or made doubtful the things that might restore them in my mind.

Behind our house, there used to be a footbridge across the river, used by the Carpenters and others who lived in the bottoms and by summer swimmers from town. I pass by the opaque and troubling house to the cutbank. The twin shanties that through all the town's life have served as men's and women's bathhouses are still there. In winter, we used to hang our frozen beef in one of them. I remember iron evenings when I went out with a lantern and sawed and haggled steaks from a rocklike hindquarter. But it is still an academic exercise; I only remember it, I do not feel the numb fingers and the fear that used to move just beyond the lantern's glow.

Then I walk to the cutbank edge and look down, and in one step, the past comes closer than it has yet been. There is the grey curving cutbank, not much lower than I remember it when we dug cave holes in it or tunnelled down its drifted cliff on our sleds. The bar is there at the inner curve of the bend, and kids are wallowing in a quicksandy mudhole and shrieking on an otter slide. They chase each other into the river and change magically from black to white. The water has its old quiet; its whirlpools spin lazily into deep water. On the footbridge, nearly exactly where it used to be, two little girls lie staring down into the water a foot below their noses. Probably they are watching suckers that lie just as quietly against the bottom. In my time, we used to snare them from the bridge with nooses of copper wire.

It is with me all at once, what I came hoping to reestablish, an ancient, unbearable recognition, and it comes partly from the children and the footbridge and the river's quiet curve but much more from the smell. For here, pungent and pervasive, is the smell that has always meant my childhood. I have never smelled it anywhere else, and it is as evocative as Proust's madeleine and tea.

But what is it? Somehow, I have always associated it with the bathhouse, with wet bathing suits and damp board benches, heaps of clothing, perhaps even the seldom-rinsed corners where desperate boys had made water. I go into the men's bathhouse, and the smell is there, but it does not seem to come from any single thing. The whole air smells of it, outside as well as in. Perhaps it is the river water or the mud or something about the float and footbridge. It is the way the old burlap-tipped diving board used to smell; it used to remain in the head after a sinus-flooding dive.

I pick up a handful of mud and sniff it. I step over the little girls and bend my nose to the wet rail of the bridge. I stand above the water and sniff. On the other side, I strip leaves off wild rose and dogwood. Nothing doing. And yet, all around me is that odour that I have not smelled since I was 11 but have never forgotten — have *dreamed*, more than once. Then I pull myself up the bank by a grey-leaved bush, and I have it. The tantalizing and ambiguous and wholly native smell is no more than the shrub we called wolf willow, now blooming with small yellow flowers.

It is wolf willow — and not the town or anyone in it — that brings me home. For a few minutes, with a handful of leaves to my nose, I look across at the clay bank and the hills beyond where the river loops back on itself, enclosing the old sports and picnic ground, and the present and all the years between are shed like a boy's clothes dumped on the bathhouse bench. The perspective is what it used to be, the dimensions are restored, the senses are as clear as if they had not been battered with sensation for 40 alien years. And the queer adult compulsion to return to one's beginnings is assuaged. A contact has been made, a mystery touched. For the moment, reality is made exactly equivalent with memory, and a hunger is satisfied. The sensuous little savage that I once was is still intact inside me.

Later, looking from the North Bench hills across my restored town,

I can see the river where it shallows and crawls southeastward across the prairie toward the Milk, the Missouri and the Gulf, and I toy with the notion that a man is like the river or the clouds, that he can be constantly moving and yet steadily renewed. The sensuous little savage, at any rate, has not been rubbed away or dissolved; he is as solid a part of me as my skeleton.

And he has a fixed and suitably arrogant relationship with his universe, a relationship geometrical and symbolic. From his centre of sensation and question and memory and challenge, the circle of the world is measured, and in that respect, the years of experience I have loaded upon my savage have not altered him. Lying on a hillside where I once sprawled among the crocuses, watching the town herd and snaring May's emerging gophers, I feel how the world still reduces me to a point and then measures itself from me. Perhaps the meadowlark singing from a fencepost — a meadowlark whose dialect I recognize — feels the same way. All points on the circumference are equidistant from him; in him, all radii begin; all diameters run through him; if he moves, a new geometry creates itself around him.

No wonder he sings. It is a good country that can make anyone feel so.

And it is a fact that once I have, so to speak, recovered myself as I used to be, I can look at the town, whose childhood was exactly contemporary with my own, with more understanding. It turns out to have been a special sort of town — special not only to me, in that it provided the indispensable sanctuary to match the prairie's exposure, but special in its belated concentration of Plains history. The successive stages of the Plains frontier flowed like a pageant through these Hills, and there are men still alive who remember almost the whole of it. My own recollections cover only a fragment; and yet it strikes me that this is *my* history. My disjunct, uprooted, cellular family was more typical than otherwise on the frontier. But more than we knew, we had our place in a human movement. What this town and its surrounding prairie grew from — and what they grew into — is the record of my tribe. If I am native to anything, I am native to this.

Don Gayton

Deeper Into Prairie

Wind sifts over an undulating, directionless sea of hills, a rare block of original prairie. The outright greens of spring have given way to mid-summer blue-greens, yellows and browns. Here, on top of one of the higher hills, is a circle of stones, with a firepit still visible in the centre. Anthropologist John Dormaar found two tepee ring sizes on the prairies: a smaller one that predates the arrival of the horse and a large one that came after. This looks to be one of the large ones.

Surely there were practical reasons why Plains Indians made their camps on hilltops like this one. The movements of people and game could be seen from a distance, stronger winds would keep the mosquitoes down, and so on. But there may also have been spiritual reasons for exposing oneself to a great sweep of distance. A culture that needed dream beds may have also needed this calm and oceanic view.

Prairie can be so large and featureless from this perspective that it ceases to be a landscape at all. It becomes tangible only at a microscopic, hands-and-knees level. From a distance, prairie is an abstract. Clouds fill in, as does the mind.

Underneath this tepee ring is a soilscape, with strata of deposition, lenses of gravel and columns of solonetz. An opaque mirror of the sky, soil also contains random shapes and elegant bands of colour. Both sky and soilscapes are random and change unpredictably.

Those who study the soils of this country make direct connections between their medium and the sky when they dig test holes. Sunlight is necessary to fully appraise soil colours, so in the morning, the soil surveyor stands to the southeast as he digs a test hole, keeping the sun over his shoulder, and he slowly shifts around to the southwest as the day wears on. The reward for hours of shovel work is the unexpectedly rich blacks of litter, the browns of organic staining and the mineral yellows.

Colour in soil has such a profound meaning that it forms the basis of the four great taxonomic groups of western Canadian soil science: the browns, dark browns, blacks and greys. Hans Jenny, the famous soil-classification expert, took a year off late in his career to study colour through the medium of painting. Prairie potters seek out these subtle colours of earth in clays from places like Eastend, Lethbridge and Wood Mountain.

Then there are the sands. There is something special about sandy soils. They blow; they reach phenomenally high surface temperatures; they hold virtually no water and fewer nutrients. Yet sands support the most diverse native plant communities on the prairies. The desert sands of the southwestern United States and Mexico support the most diverse plant communities of North America.

There is a little elevator town, Ernfold, that sits on shallow, gravelly soil on the CPR main line between Moose Jaw and Swift Current. The remarkable thing about Ernfold, visible from miles away, is the single row of blue spruce. Towering over the prairie, the tallest trees in the whole region, the mature and majestic spruces follow the CP tracks on either side of Ernfold.

Like Tom Sukanen's landlocked ship at Beechy, they are anomalies on the landscape. Legend has it that the trees were planted back in the 'teens by a local railroad section hand. No one is there to care for them now, section crews having left Ernfold long ago. But the spruces are content. They were planted along a high, sandy ridge and got a helping hand through the seedling stage. That was all the trees needed. Even though they may never reproduce, life to a full term is assured. They might even outlive Ernfold.

Sandy soils seem to be the only prairie soils that permit a healthy growth of conifers. The heavier loams and clay loams common to the area may heave and buckle in the spring, refuse to allow hardening off in the fall, create oxygen shortages around the roots or allow the pH to rise too high for conifers. No one really knows the reason. But fir, spruce, pine, larch and cedar, so sought after by both urban and rural landscapers, frequently die protracted, lingering deaths on the prairies, unless they are in sand.

Soil of any kind is a curious and difficult medium. It is scientifically and economically important, like space or the oceans. It can be approached through physics, chemistry, geography, microbiology, geology or, rarely, art. But soil is opaque and agonizingly random. You begin to see the reasons why soil science is not a familiar discipline and why it is well known for attracting unique and difficult personalities.

Soil was once thought to be nonliving matter. Now, we know that nearly every characteristic of soil is affected by living organisms. Nostoc, for example, is an insignificant-looking blackish algae crust frequently seen on bare patches of soil. It has been found to contribute to the soil nitrogen economy by fixing atmospheric nitrogen.

Then there are the huge and rapidly cycling populations of soil microorganisms that break down plant litter. Live bacteria, dead bacteria, fungi, microbial waste products and free enzymes of microbial origin are components of nearly all soils. A common rule of thumb is that each gram of agricultural soil will contain roughly 1 billion separate microorganisms.

One microbiologist, trying desperately to get around the problem of opacity while estimating the size of soil microbial populations, hit on an indirect but revelatory method. He took the biological energy compound adenosine triphosphate (ATP) as an analogue of live soil microbial biomass. ATP is a good measure, since it is present in all living organisms and breaks down rapidly after death. Fireflies also use ATP to run their tiny phosphorescent lanterns. The microbiologist leached ATP from a soil sample and added it to an extract of firefly tails. The amount of phosphorescence produced was a measure of the size of the soil microbial population: the greater the glow, the more microbes present in the soil. This is a bioassay in the truest sense of the word, developed by a scientist who was thinking right at the level of the organism.

Occasionally, these microbes manifest themselves. The wanderer of prairie might stumble onto a puffball, a curious leathery sphere the size of a large egg. At some obscure signal, miles and miles of underground fungal threads will join to form this curious reproductive structure (the Spanish name for it means "witch's fart"). Once the puffball breaks open, wind will carry its spores for miles.

Other soil dwellers make their mark. The classic prairie chernozems — the most highly developed of all the grassland soils — can become literally saturated with the introduced earthworm. Researchers are divided on the value of this immigrant from the Old World: earthworms aerate soils effectively with their tunnels, but they break down huge quantities of stable organic matter and convert it to less stable forms. Viruses, springtails and nematodes are also part of the prairie-soil bestiary.

The tallgrass prairies that once grew on these chernozems are history. When early explorers wrote home about stirrup-high grasses, they were talking about the bluestems of the tallgrass prairie that covered the eastern Dakotas, reaching up across the southern borders of Manitoba and Saskatchewan. Modern students of plant ecology often have difficulty with the concept of tallgrass prairie, because there is simply none of it left. The prodigious fertility of the chernozem underneath was its undoing.

Beneath this tepee ring is another scape, the prehistoric one: scattered thinly across this land are dinosaur beds, medicine wheels, fossilized trees, ancient kill sites, glacial flutings and strange concretions, artifacts of a past so distant that memory no longer has a place. Deduction and imagination thus become powerful tools.

A certain response to the prairie grass and wind and stars once inspired the construction of elaborate stone medicine wheels, such as the one at Moose Mountain, Saskatchewan. To the builders, it was clear, then, why the long strings of rock needed to radiate from the centre cairn at precise angles, why the wheels faced the sky and to whom they spoke. Some archaeologists speculate that medicine wheels were used for astronomical observations, to help mark the course of the seasons. Others feel they were more ceremonial in nature. No one knows for sure. Momentarily clearing the mind of the conventional, expected realities and standing among the modern grass and wind and stars, one might see the reasons for the medicine wheels become clear again.

The stones of my tepee ring weather quietly. There were once thousands of rings, wheels, pictographs and boulder effigies on the prairies; now, we are left with a few hundred at most. The rest were victims of our continuing need to consume land.

These stone structures are a mute reminder of a shifting but metastable occupation of this land that goes back some 10,000 years and may someday be found to go back 50,000 years to the late Pleistocene. This period, the era before the present one, created the prairie landscape and set the basic terms for human use of it. There was a time during that era when humans coexisted with sabre-toothed tiger, mastodon and superbison. The late Pleistocene history of the prairies is foggy and obscure. Yet there may be landscape lessons behind that fog that would have great meaning for today.

The Cree, the Blackfoot, the Sioux, the Sarcee, the Gros Ventre, the Saulteaux, the Assiniboine and the Métis cultures were all nearly extinguished by European colonization of the Canadian prairies. That colonization process was certainly less brutal than an earlier one in the United States, but the net effect was much the same. The colonial society, with its overwhelming sense of cultural superiority, effectively denied the histories of these aboriginal cultures, rendering them all but invisible. But bits and pieces of those histories do come to light, and two very significant fragments are from the region of Wood Mountain, Saskatchewan.

Sitting Bull and his band lived in the hills just south of Wood Mountain from 1876 to 1881. They came seeking refuge after their unprecedented rout of the U.S. Cavalry at Little Bighorn. To the credit of the Dominion government of the day, they were allowed to stay, safe from military reprisals. But time, the death of the buffalo herds and hunger took their toll. Dominion officials allowed the Sioux to enter but never offered Canadian citizenship or material assistance, for fear of angering the Americans. One Canadian, Major James Walsh of the North West Mounted Police, took a personal interest in the well-being of the Sioux. However, when word of this got back to Ottawa, Walsh was quickly transferred away from Wood Mountain.

Sitting Bull watched his band slowly disintegrate from hunger, disease and internal strife and finally gave in to the persistent demands for his return to American soil. He knew full well what would happen once he went back and resigned himself to it. In 1890, he was murdered by reservation officials in Standing Rock, North Dakota. That was the end of an era.

A few of Sitting Bull's younger generals refused to return and stayed on at Wood Mountain. Long Dog, one of the chief's most trusted associates, is buried there. Andrew Ferguson, a Sioux rancher from Wood Mountain, showed me the grave site, an isolated bluff on the reserve. There is a simple metal marker and a rough wooden fence. There is no mowed lawn, just the native stipas and wheatgrasses.

That tiny graveyard at Wood Mountain links us to another luminary in North American aboriginal history. Many historians feel that Chief Joseph was the greatest military mind the continent ever produced, better than either Sitting Bull or Robert E. Lee.

Joseph's crime was an attempt to return to the eastern Oregon hill country that was taken from his people, the Nez Percé. The U.S. Cavalry went after the band, and in what was probably the first recorded example of guerrilla warfare, Joseph and his people alternately eluded the troops and struck them unexpectedly. The action lasted for most of 1879 and ranged through Oregon, Idaho and Montana. But the inevitable end could be postponed only so long, Joseph knew, as did Sitting Bull before him. After an agonizing powwow in eastern Montana, Joseph gave himself up. The authorities resettled Joseph and his followers in Nespelem, a dreary community in northeastern Washington, cruelly close to their beloved Wallowa country. Joseph wrapped himself in his blanket and waited to die.

But a few of his people did not. Living on leather and exhaustion, they slipped across the Medicine Line into Saskatchewan, becoming part of the ethnic mix that is Wood Mountain. One of the immigrants was White Bird. Another small metal plate marks his resting place in that legendary graveyard.

The wind across this hilltop is a steady pressure, combing through the grass and the tepee ring. This is the wind that blows empty grain bins into the coulees and turns snow into polished marble. In the old days, it carried mosquitoes away from hilltop Indian encampments. Now, in dry years, it carries away the summer fallow. In prairie cities, still imperfectly tuned to their environment, it tips over park benches and destroys young garden transplants. Lethbridge, on the dry prairies of southeastern Alberta, has an average windspeed of 12 miles per hour day and night, winter and summer. It is a fact of this bioregion, like winter, grasshoppers and the CPR.

Tepee rings, dream beds, buffalo jumps, turtle effigies. Marks on the land: myths. These things are not found on farmland, only on the dwindled remnants of native prairie, along with the burrowing owl, the crocus and the horned toad. The symbols and essences of our natural bioregion are slowly being traded off in our dubious quest to be the world's breadbasket. Somehow, we must find room for both the natural essences and the wheat. They need each other.

George Galt

The Wheat Farm

The woman, who ran a wheat farm with her husband, drove through the Qu'Appelle Valley and along the Fishing Lakes to Fort Qu'Appelle, where she stopped for groceries. Green hills rose around the lakes, and the water was clear blue. Turning west, we found prairie again: not the sheer flatlands you saw from the train window but gentle rolls and dips. Ducks paddled in the green sloughs. The farms were vast ploughed rectangles. Infrequently, we passed a house and barn or a row of seed bins. In the dusty town of Abernethy, dirt roads and wooden buildings, we stopped for the mail, then travelled four miles south to the Lyster farms. The woman, her husband and their two daughters lived in a small frame house that had been built as a Methodist parsonage in a town called Kenlis. It had been moved to the Lyster property in 1926.

"You didn't waste wood in those days," she explained. "Every board had to be hauled across the prairie from the rail line." Her name was Pat. She had married Bryan Lyster, whose family had worked these farms for over a century. Before that, the land had been unploughed prairie.

"I think Bryan's out seeding lentils," she said. I walked down the long straight driveway to the public road. The land was dry, and the road, graded but unpaved, threw up spirals of dust when a car passed. The smooth fields looked to me like one big farm, acres of ploughed land but no people. I came to a coulee, a gash in the prairie deep and wide where bushes and trees grew. The air was dancing with mosquitoes. If you looked into the middle distance, you could see a thick screen of them, like rain.

The two girls and their mother and I ate stewed lentils from last year's crop. She talked about her work as a part-time remedial teacher for a blind student. Then we were silent. A bird sang out in the yard. I asked about the winter.

"I was storm-stayed twice this year," she said. "Then you get so you don't want to go anywhere in the snow. And that's not a good feeling."

I said I found it quiet.

"Do you think so? I don't notice anymore." She had met her husband at university in the East. They had lived in cities, but he had wanted to return to the family farm. She had moved often as a child. Her father had worked in the armed forces.

"Farm life has given me a kind of stability I never had."

In the guest room, she showed me a history book on the Abernethy area. I read that Bryan's great-grandfather, Edwin Lyster, had been born near Melbourne, in Quebec's Eastern Townships. Edwin had come west in 1879 through Chicago and St. Paul. The Canadian Pacific had not then reached Indian Head. In 1888, Bryan's grandfather Chester was born at Kenlis, near Abernethy. He had taken over the family farm in 1929; Bryan's father had done the same about 20 years later. Marion, Bryan's mother, had taught in the local primary school. The book said that Marion had first arrived in Abernethy on a rainy evening in the fall of 1942. Enquiring at Quong's Café, she had been directed to the people who boarded the teachers. Quong's Café. *Juss' about every taow i' Sascashawhan have one Chinese family.*

The next morning, Pat drove me out to the field where her husband was at work. I had asked to watch some planting, and he had smiled. "I think of rice paddies when I think of planting. It's seeding here. We put seeds into the ground."

He waved me over to the tractor. At 9 o'clock, he had already seeded for several hours. Using the good weather, he was working from before dawn to after dark. We continued to drag the seeder and discs around the field in bigger and bigger circles. He was not given to idle chat. I asked what he thought about, up in the cab all day. He had to watch the discs, he said, and monitor the seed. "I'm hopping in and out a lot, to refill seed or fertilizer. When it's going well, I have my classical music." A tape deck had been installed in the cab.

We stopped at his blue-and-red three-ton truck, parked in the field near the road. From the truck, we blew grain into the five boxes of the seeder, using a wide, pliable plastic pipe. It was like holding a fat fire hose. Several loaves of bread were spilled on the ground when we had finished. "I'm doing Glenlea this morning," he said. "A utility wheat." Slapping mosquitoes, we climbed back up to the cab. In half an hour, the field was done. We emptied the seed that remained in the boxes into burlap sacks and swung them onto the small pickup truck. The last of the grain, he sucked out of the seeder with a portable car vacuum cleaner.

He said we were going to move to another field. "And do canary seed." But first, he needed to buy more fertilizer.

Rumbling in the half-ton on the road to Abernethy, we passed his house and dipped sharply into the green coulee. "This is where our wildlife lives. Deer, foxes, rabbits, raccoons." In a few minutes, we were back up on the dry flats. Some fields showed the unploughed buff stubble of the previous fall. Others had been turned over. A truck and a seeding machine stood in a distant field. Otherwise, the country looked empty, except in the direction of Abernethy, where a small collection of low buildings was spread around the two elevators. SASKATCHEWAN POOL was painted in big letters on one, UGG on the other. They made a strong vertical statement, both defying and reinforcing the flatness of the earth. And more than anything here, they proclaimed the presence of humanity, though not in the same way as the spires of rural Quebec. The elevators did not dominate their landscape. Like lighthouses, they survived and performed a task, but any sense of control they conveyed was illusory. Prairie farmland, like the ocean, could be badly disturbed by erratic weather. The elevators stood against the wind and rain and snow, separating man from nature while making an accommodation between the two. With its little birdhouse superstructure for a head, the elevator assumed an organic humanesque shape, an announcement that the far-reaching emptiness was populated. I found as much visual pleasure in their simple lines and graceful proportions as in any hand-carved Quebec barn or gingerbread Ontario farmhouse.

We turned into the fertilizer yard, where he kept an account. Parked under the conveyor belt, he pulled his shovel out of the cab and strapped a dust mask over his face. The ash-coloured chemical flowed onto the floor of the truck, making a grey cone. He shovelled hard at the pile, spreading it across the fertilizer compartment. On the other side of the divider was a larger area for seed. The fertilizer left a cloud of fine, parching dust. Above, through the broad sky, floated tufts of cirrus cloud.

On the way back, we stopped at the old Lyster homestead. He shared a row of cone-capped metal seed bins there with his father, who still occupied the 19th-century farmhouse. Bryan emptied the remaining Glenlea grain, and we wheeled the 40-foot gas-powered auger to a canary-seed bin. "This machine is super-dangerous. It's a foot-remover," he cautioned. We shoved one end of the auger into the seed and started the motor. He stood at the back of the bin shovelling grain toward the churning metal bit. Into the back of the truck spiralled a rain of golden kernels.

Over lunch, he told me his fields all had surnames. "But a field doesn't take your name until you die. Or until you sell it." He worked five quarter-sections (800 acres), acquired over the 10 years he had been farming. Later, he would have his father's three. Work and family appeared to be the totality of his world. An experienced journalist, he wrote articles in the winter for a farm magazine, *Country Guide*. I looked through a recent issue in which his article "Watch Out for Cutworms" had appeared.

In the afternoon, I had agreed to speak at a school. Pat and I drove to the town of Balcarres, where she commuted several times a week to teach her blind student. I was introduced to Myrtle Love, who taught 10- and 11-year-olds. Myrtle said a few words to her class, and then I spoke. She had unfurled a wall map over the blackboard. I remembered the Canada I had known at the age of 10, this same paper abstraction: at the top, a lot of ink-blot islands and one that looked like an upside-down dog's skeleton, but a smooth line along the bottom border. And below the border, just three letters — U.S.A. — on white space that did not belong to us and about which we did not have to learn, though draining it of colour and expunging the dots of its cities seemed even then like risky bravado.

Myrtle Love's pupils asked why I was crossing the country. I said I had wanted to make the map real for myself and I had found a publisher who would advance me some money. They wanted to know how I remembered what I saw. "What do you think of Canada?" one child asked. "Which is your favourite part?" queried another. I said Canada was different from South America, where I had last travelled. But after the talk, wandering down the dusty main street, I found echoes of Peru. The buildings of Balcarres were low, many with false fronts. In the dark restaurant where I sat for a cup of tea, Indians lounged in the booths, dressed shabbily, idle and poor, reminiscent of a South American scene. And back out in the street, mosquitoes swarmed.

"Excuse me, sir, you do a survey on my building?" enquired the Balcarres Chinaman nervously. (Peru as well, I remembered, had a large Chinese population from its railway-building years.) I closed my notebook and shook my head. "My place almost the town centre. Lottery tickets. Video. Liquor. Everything you want." He rushed back into the store, but business looked slow, even with the government liquor franchise.

In the late afternoon, Pat dropped me at the Motherwell homestead, about halfway on the dirt road between Abernethy and the Lyster farms. W.R. Motherwell had been provincial minister of agriculture from 1905 to 1918 and federal minister during the '20s. His property had been declared a national historic site. I walked through a hedge into the quiet 19th-century scene. A couple in period costume were hoeing the large vegetable garden. At the end of the path, I came to a building with didactic displays on prairie settlement and the scientific farming methods Motherwell encouraged. Like many of the pioneers in this part of Saskatchewan, he had come from Ontario. As much as they could, they had brought Ontario with them. "The Ontarians," said the writing in one display, "believed that hard work, Christian living and individual enterprise were the only sure roads to success and prosperity. Men were to be masculine and self-reliant; women, the supportive 'fairer sex.' " On another panel were enlarged photographs of an old train. The text read: "A unique method Motherwell used to inform the province's farmers was the Better Farming Train. It travelled the province in the summers of 1914 to 1918, 18 cars long, filled with exhibits on all aspects of western farming. Thousands of men, women and children visited the train, attending lectures and demonstrations."

Outside, I was greeted by another young woman in period costume. The long smock and high boots looked uncomfortable in the heat. She had blond hair pinned at the back and a Nordic face with large blue eyes. We walked alone onto the back lawn. It was early in the season — there were no other visitors. She began talking about Motherwell in a voice that sounded rehearsed but genuine. I found myself mildly interested in the dead farmer but distracted by my guide's blue eyes. She spoke of the design of this place: the shelterbelts that Motherwell had planted around the farmstead; the Ontario barn behind us with its double-pitched gambrel roof; the lawn-tennis court; the dugout where snow collected in winter, providing water for the house and garden. Motherwell had come from the town of Perth, where stone was favoured as a building material. He had brought this taste in architecture with him and had erected a cut-fieldstone dwelling that could have been lifted off any residential street in his hometown. I knew Perth. There was a dreamlike sensation in seeing a piece of it here on the dry prairie: a turn-of-the-century Italianate stone house — immaculately restored — the green lawns, the tree lines, the genteel ornamental garden. There was nothing like it for hundreds of miles. A breeze ruffled the smock of the blue-eyed woman. She did not mind the mosquitoes and seemed content to be living in someone else's clothes. She was a traveller. After the summer season, the house would close, and she would return to Greece.

Inside, we went through the kitchen, the study, up the back stairs to the servants' quarters and into the room where Motherwell slept. The house suffered from a dark Victorian interior, but standing by the bed, you could see out the window far across the prairie: light, the broad sky, space. She led me down the front stairway into the living room, where we looked at the Indian beadwork Motherwell's wife had collected.

"Indians have come to look at the site," she said. "But they don't always like to see their things here. Some say Indian artifacts don't belong in this house."

I set out on the dirt road to the Lyster property. Before the coulee, a man in work clothes stopped his car and offered a lift. It was a few minutes to six. He was on his way to the fields. "I'll be out there till midnight," he said.

After supper, Pat and I visited an older woman on a neighbouring farm. "Yes, I knew him," she said of Motherwell. "And her too. She was just right for a politician's wife. She knew how to do it. But I'll tell you something. Quite a few in this area were against what they did with the house. It's the Eastern government, you see, coming in and spending all that money. Waste and interference, that's how many here saw it."

Heather Robertson

Miami

Miami, Manitoba, is a respectable town, a tiny cluster of white gingerbread houses 70 miles southwest of Winnipeg on a minor highway that comes to a dead end 100 miles farther west. A big billboard that says "EAT — at Bird's ESSO" and, farther down the road, a red Coca-Cola sign that indicates May's Lunch and Texaco station are the only spots of colour, thrown out like fishhooks to catch the odd traveller. Bird's is just the local garage, a white shed rising out of the mud with a heap of ancient cars and wagons piled up behind and, off to one side, a grubby hamburger stand owned by a former Miami policeman who was fired for drinking in the pub in his uniform. Bird has gone into Renault cars on the side; three shiny red-and-yellow bugs are lined up along the highway. He's done a good business among the retired farmers in town, who still like to drive downtown even though the village is only five blocks long and three blocks wide. Everybody drives to work in Miami. A car is a flag signalling where you are. Without a car in a small town, you're invisible.

May's Lunch is up for sale. No sign is posted, but May's husband Roy hands out illustrated brochures to all the customers. May and Roy Dave have had the coffee shop and gas pumps for 15 years, and they're ready to retire. "Yes! Business is growing and becoming too much for us!" says the brochure. It's not very convincing. You can sit in May's cozy plywood diner for an hour before a car will turn in. The business is mostly local men stopping in for a Coke or coffee or a plate of french fries. Along with the food, May and Roy provide a running commentary on every event, great or small, that has happened in Miami in the last 50 years, complete with analysis, opinion and brief character sketches of all the people involved. May's is one of the key gossip centres in Miami, because they get the news from the outside first. Truckers roost in for lunch like carrier pigeons, bringing the latest tidbits from Swan Lake or Brandon, and the grapevine of telephone linemen and construction crews carries news up and down the highway all day. In their smiling, polite way, May and Roy discreetly pump all strangers as to where they're from, where they're going and what they're doing in Miami. In a small village where very little ever happens, people are news and a stranger is an event. The diner is a tiny homemade building with half a dozen stools at the counter and little Arborite tables. A sign on the wall says: "No Cheques Please!" Roy and May live 20 feet away in a small white cottage with a hand pump over the well outside. They're asking $35,000 for the diner, the house, a garage, an empty machine shed, two antique gas pumps and two acres of land.

South of the highway, the land rolls away in lush folds and ripples, a quilt of coal-black earth with patches of acid green that change slowly to yellow in August. Every year, the pattern is a little different. Wild grass by the road waves like hair in the wind; the ditches are full of dandelions and thistles as big as bushes. In the glare of noon, the light is so pure that the leaves on every tree two miles away are as clear and sharp as the blade of grass at my feet. It's the light of Italian painters in those tiny crystal landscapes that stretch away to infinity in perfect miniaturized clarity. Five miles away, the fields dissolve to water, an undulating mirage in which the farmsteads with their windbreaks float like islands in a stream. In spring, the blue flax blooms like patches of fallen sky, and the air is full of the sweet smell of lilacs and freshly cut grass. At night, the highway reeks with the perfume of squashed skunks, and fat bugs plop against the windshield. The darkness is thick with the sound and smell of growing. Summer is a miracle. The bare, frozen earth turns green overnight as the crops pop out of the ground with an almost audible "sproing," like bedsprings; they grow and ripen, ready for harvest, in 10 weeks. Summer on the prairie is passionate and selfish, a desperate grab for warmth and life.

Miami's two white grain elevators stick out against the green backdrop of trees along Tobacco Creek, which borders the town to the north. There used to be more elevators, people say, but they were torn down long ago, leaving vacant patches of tall grass by the CNR tracks. Miami's population is a little less than 400. People have come and gone, but the town has remained the same since it was built in 1889, when the CNR came through. Miami still has only one main street, a long gravel road running parallel to the railway, with all the shops facing the tracks like soldiers standing at attention. Like all prairie towns, Miami was designed for the convenience of the railway. Main Street is exactly as long as the average freight train. Goods were unloaded from the train into vacant lots or sheds next to the tracks and then lugged across the street to the stores. Ideally, the position of the boxcar carrying a storekeeper's merchandise would perfectly match the location of his store on the street. Too cheap to pay the drayman, most merchants carried their own stuff or hired the local barflies for the price of a glass of whisky or a plug of chewing tobacco. It was in the merchants' interest to snuggle up as close to the tracks as they could. They could not, however, build on the side of the street the tracks were on, because that land was owned by the railway.

Miami's tallest building is the two-storey Grandview Hotel at the west end of town near the CNR station. The Grandview used to be three storeys, but it has shrunk with the commercial traffic. The tiny old rooms are neat and clean; most of them have been closed off and turned into a residence for the owner, who makes his living from tending bar in the beer parlour downstairs. The rest of Miami's single row of shops are small frame buildings, some with false fronts, some little more than sheds. It's hard to tell them apart, because except for the Bank of Commerce, which is dull yellow, they're all painted white with maroon trim, and some don't bother with signs. There's no need to, because there's only one of everything in Miami — one bakery, one meat market, one hardware store, one church — and everybody knows where they are. Most of the signs are hand-painted wooden boards, worn and weathered, but all the proprietors are known by name anyway — Vern's Café, Moorey's store, Westaway's drugstore — and most of them have been there forever. The street, which for a reason everyone has forgotten is called Norton Avenue, has seen one or two coats of asphalt, but the mud has quickly taken over again, pitching and heaving against the frail buildings in great waves. At night, only the cheap neon sign over the Grandview Hotel is illuminated, and half the letters are burned out. Three or four dim streetlights are spotted along the entire length of the street. The wind hums through the wires and through the tinsel Christmas decorations left up from last year. Even the new buildings look old. The stores do not share common walls; a tiny gap of two or three feet is left between stores and screened from the street by a white picket fence. Intended as protection against fire, the gaps fill up with weeds and scrap paper and give the main street a snaggletoothed look. Because few of the stores have basements, they quickly lean and sag, each little box tilting at a slightly different angle. Every store has venetian blinds. In the afternoons, when the blinds are drawn against the sun, they look closed, gone out of business. It's a shock to open a door and find a man, snug as a snail in the gloom, ready to sell you a roast or a cheese or a pair of Stanfield's jockey shorts.

Miami is a neat, clean town. Everybody says that. They've been saying it since 1909, when the school yearbook stated, "Nowhere would one find a neater or a cleaner town." The people are very proud of the town. The streets are wide and level, covered with fine gravel and shaded by large, stately trees. The boulevards, like the lawns, are neatly mowed. There are no weeds in Miami. The old brick houses with their verandahs and carved cornices and weather vanes are well kept, trim and shiny with white paint; their tidy lawns are enclosed by little iron or picket fences. Almost every house has a nameplate by the front door — A.C. Orchard, A. Moreton, J. Murray — which is odd for such a tiny village, where everybody knows everybody else and the houses don't bother with numbers. "The hardware dealer got in a big stock of nameplates about 1955," says J. Murray, scratching his head. "I guess they were all the thing then." The names are different, but all the plates are the same. Some shabbier houses are hidden discreetly behind a screen of trees or sleep beneath a tangle of ancient hawthorn hedge. The houses are decaying like old wedding cakes, but they still look elegant, picturesque. There are no shacks in Miami. People here have good taste. Pink plastic flamingos, which are very big in Plum Coulee, do not walk Miami gardens.

Miami is proud of the countless awards it has won from the Manitoba Good Roads Association for being the best-kept village in the province. Its crowning triumph is the Miami Citizens' Park, a sliver of land near the tracks where the CNR section house used to be. The park was built by the retired municipal reeve, Lorne Kennedy, who lives across the street. Mr. Kennedy's own yard is clipped and trimmed and weeded and filled with a whole population of painted wooden gnomes and a stone wishing well. When he ran out of space in his own yard, Mr. Kennedy moved across the road to the vacant lot. With money provided by the village, he installed a cookhouse and a picnic table, built a shuffleboard court and a horseshoe pitch and ran up a Canadian flag. He collected and painted a lot of litter barrels, put in a Men and Ladies and erected an ornamental steel windmill he'd found on a farm. There's a wooden box in the park provided with a guest book, and there's another wooden box with a padlock for donations. Everything is shiny with paint and neat as a pin. The name of the park is spelled out in round whitewashed stones set in a bed of red and white petunias.

Every day, Mr. Kennedy can be found in his park, a thin, stooped woodland deity, clipping, watering, weeding, digging, picking up scraps of paper and keeping a hopeful eye out for tourists. The park has caused a terrible feud between Mr. Kennedy and his neighbour, Mr. Dundas. Mr. Dundas's yard is also spick-and-span, but unadorned. Fearful that the ever-multiplying horde of gnomes would spread across the road to the park, he accused Mr. Kennedy of "junking it up." Mr. Kennedy keeps close count of the number of campers and trailers that stop in the park and greets each new catch with the glee of a fisherman who has just reeled in a whopper.

"It's a nice quiet town," says Mr. Kennedy. "Our little village might not have any future, but that's what's at a premium now, a quiet place to live. I'm not in favour of getting industry in. They pay the lowest wages, and when the time comes, they lay all the people off, and then they're on relief."

Mr. Kennedy, a farmer, was elected reeve in 1956 by two votes over the incumbent; he was considered a radical and a screwball because he wanted concrete bridges. "We were still in the horse-and-buggy days. One councillor had been on for 21 years. He was a nice fellow and needed the money; we couldn't get him out. He got in every time through the sympathy vote." Mr. Kennedy was defeated in turn in 1962 by a group of younger men who thought he was holding back progress. "Retired people pay their bills, and there's no problems," says Mr. Kennedy. "You got to have a place to live your lives out."

Miami streets are free of litter, thanks mainly to the unpaid efforts of a tall, dignified gentleman in a gold-braided cap who wanders about relentlessly pursuing gum wrappers and odd bottles. "He thinks," snorts the druggist's wife, "that he's the FBI." There are no junkyards piled high with rusty tractors, no gutted cars in the high grass along the ditches, no stray dogs. No dogs. The silence makes itself felt first in Miami. The silence and the stillness. The sidewalks are deserted winter and summer. No one sits on his front porch or rakes his lawn, no children zip around on tricycles, no teenagers bomb down the main streets in souped-up cars. No one shouts or cries or laughs except in the schoolyard at recess. If you look at the houses, you see there are curtains in the windows and plants on the sills. They are occupied. But where are all the people? Inside. Knock on any door, and it will yield a woman doing the wash, an old man watching television, a covey of matrons printing name tags for a convention. Life in Miami is intense, but it all takes place inside. There is something indecent, unrespectable, almost dangerous about sitting outside exposing oneself to the sharp eyes behind the flickering lace curtains.

The cemetery is the first thing you notice about Miami. It's on a little rise off the highway just as you come into town. Cemeteries are guidebooks to prairie towns. A glance tells whether the residents are Catholic or Protestant: Catholics prefer marble angels and flowery inscriptions; Protestants, plain black granite. Names are a clue to race and ethnic prestige; older Anglo-Saxon tombstones frequently state the birthplace in Britain or Ontario, others do not. There are no Jews or Orientals; they have their own burying grounds. The cemetery indicates a community's wealth, social structure and taste and its respect for death and tradition. Miami's respect for its ancestors is elaborate enough to be Egyptian.

The graveyard is not, as in most rural communities, a patch of ragged prairie sod or even mowed city grass: it's a garden. The grass has been carefully exterminated. Each grave is a rectangle of black soil sprinkled with sand inside a neat concrete curb, planted with peonies, caragana, juniper, ornamental cedars, geraniums and petunias. The graves are connected by dirt and gravel paths and shaded by large spruce trees, which sough in the wind. In June, when the peonies are in bloom, the cemetery is filled with their odour of sweet putrefaction. The cemetery has the symmetry and restraint of formal gardens at Versailles; the dead, in Miami, are cultivated.

The largest tombstone, a carved pile of pink granite, belongs to Miami's patriarch, William Thompson. The inscriptions indicate that the Thompson family has, through tragedy and spinsterhood, virtually died out, a fate which overtakes an astonishing number of pioneer families who achieve instant and extraordinary success on the frontier. There is a whiff of witchcraft about it, as if they had been silently and sullenly hated to death. All the other gravestones decrease in size and cost according to the social prominence of the people lying underneath. Most are plain black granite cut to an identical pattern. There is, as everywhere, a special corner for orphaned men, veterans of the two wars, who are buried by the Legion with simple grey markers. There is one grave, a Mennonite's, outside the fence in the grass. Miami has a lot of widows; dozens of graves have only a man's name on the stone, which indicates that these widows have money, since in poorer areas, it is now fashionable to engrave the stone with both names at once, a sort of two-for-the-price-of-one arrangement, and to leave only the date blank for the survivor.

The remarkable thing about Miami is the astonishing old age to which many of the residents manage to survive. According to the markers, some of the first children born in Miami lived to celebrate Manitoba's centennial in 1970. Obviously, if they could endure the frontier, they were indestructible. Miami is still full of old people; longevity is now the norm. These old people are not vegetables locked up in geriatric centres; they're tough, strong-willed and independent. The Struldbrugs have formed Miami's personality and determined its destiny. Their influence in the community is decisive.

The village of Miami began to grow in 1889 after the railway had decreed that a station would be built across the dirt road from Billy Thompson's farm. By the time the first steam engine thundered into town, more than a dozen buildings had risen out of the ground and the platform was crowded with cheering businessmen. The train brought loads of lumber; soon, the prairie was echoing to the *tack tack* of hammers as the town was thrown up — first a grain elevator, then the Grandview Hotel, a blacksmith, a butcher, Angers' livery barn, Collins and Munroe general store and a harness shop.

The Methodists and the Presbyterians engaged in a frantic race to see who would have the first church in Miami. They finished in a dead heat. The Methodists, however, were embarrassed by being unable to afford a permanent minister and were forced to rely on the services of the itinerant preacher; a permanent minister, who required a manse and a salary of $525 a year, was a tremendous achievement and a prize coveted by every rural congregation.

Everything was up to date in Miami. The buildings smelled of fresh lumber and varnish; they were trim and bright with white paint and big plate-glass windows shaded by awnings on summer afternoons. Ambitious merchants built their shops two storeys high, and the family lived upstairs over the store. Lesser men, unable to afford so large a structure, put up false fronts on their humble shacks to make a single storey look as if it were two and lived in back. The shops were all built to an identical plan — long, narrow, rectangular boxes stretching back from the street, dark except for two windows in front, the size of which indicated the affluence of the proprietor. They were all built jam up against the road and opened directly onto the wooden sidewalk. No money was wasted on lawns, fences or steps. The design was a deliberate stratagem to save taxes, since a store could be assessed only on its narrow frontage. Wooden signs as wide as the shop announced the name of the owner and the type of business in plain block letters; the only other decoration was a little carving over the windows and a fancy cornice across the top like a fringe of hair. The stores had an attractive, humanoid look — the door in the middle like a mouth and the two windows across the top like eyes whose expression changed daily, depending on the hang of the lace curtains and the degree that the sash, like an eyelid, was open. The grandest building of all was the Grandview Hotel, three storeys high, with a view of the Pembina Hills from the top floor and a splendid carved-oak bar.

By 1901, Miami had a newspaper, an offshoot of a little printing company that specialized in printing names on grain bags. The carpenter, T.W. Stubbs, also ran a furniture and undertaking business, and upstairs, he operated a photo studio. In 1912, he sold out to the harness maker, who added shoe and harness repair to the list. His wife, who had a sewing machine, did the work on binder canvases, awnings, fur coats, gloves and shrouds. It was common, and not considered greedy, for businessmen to maximize their income by picking up three or four jobs. The baker baked bread in a big brick oven behind his confectionery store, which specialized in fruit, soft drinks and ice cream; he was also a painter and decorator and an occasional butcher. The Massey Harris agent, Sandy Kerr, sold real estate and insurance; he also bought grain, owned a creamery and looked after the affairs of the municipality from a little office in the agency. In addition, he repaired all the Massey Harris machinery that he sold and apparently financed many sales out of his own pocket, since a 1908 advertisement declared that Mr. Kerr had "money to loan." Sandy rented out a cubbyhole in the Massey Harris building to the lawyer, and the doctor worked out of the drugstore, where he had an office upstairs. The drugstore had the telephone exchange. The doctor didn't miss a trick either; he advertised himself in Gothic script as:

A.L. Shanks
M.D. C.M.
Physician
Surgeon and Coroner
Issuer of Marriage Licences

The doctor, however, had competition from the midwife, a Mrs. Cole, who had trained at the Leicester Borough Asylum in England. Mrs. Cole took in sewing and pregnant women. The women boarded in her house for a few days before and after the baby was born; Mrs. Cole delivered the baby and called in the doctor if there was any emergency. The service was designed primarily for women living on isolated farms, who were cut off from medical assistance. Mrs. Cole was in such great demand that a small stone hospital was built beside her house in 1921, built and equipped entirely by public subscription. More than 1,000 babies were born in the Miami Cottage Hospital before it was closed in 1956 for lack of patients.

Although the village had only about 300 people, it was busy and hustling. Farm wagons pulled by big Clydesdales stamping their hairy feet at the hitching posts lined the main street in front of the bank and the elevators, smart buggies zipped between the livery barn at one end of town and the drugstore at the other, and gay blades rode bicycles when it didn't rain. The first car arrived in 1904; there were seven by 1911, the year the wooden sidewalks were replaced with concrete. Miami had a policeman (the owner of the livery barn) and a little red two-cell jail with bars on the windows to contain the Saturday-night rowdies. Crime was so minimal in Miami that the jail was soon moved to the fairgrounds, where it was used as an office for the caretaker.

Money was made quickly and spent even more quickly. The farmers enriched the businessmen who, in turn, spent the money on turning Miami into a miniature version of rural Ontario. They built houses of brick, three storeys high, with gabled roofs and leaded stained-glass windows and neat lawns out front surrounded by iron fences. Stone was scarce, so the most elegant houses were built of concrete blocks manufactured in the cement plant up in the hills, each block carefully shaped to look like cut stone. They were decorated with shutters, ornately carved white wooden verandahs and little wrought-iron railings around the captain's walk on the roof. Maple, ash and elm trees were dug from the creeks and ditches and planted in the yards; corseted ladies in silk and taffeta gowns served afternoon tea on the grass. The train brought mysterious treasures from eastern factories, and wealth and social status were measured in luxuries: Miami soon acquired a jeweller, who specialized in watches and eyeglasses, a dressmaker, a tailor and a Chinese laundry, and the general store featured "twenty-century suits" ready-made from Toronto. Banquets of seven and eight courses featured venison, oysters and half a dozen different kinds of wine. Several meat markets offered fresh sausages every day and fish in season; but the gastronomic sensation was Ferris' Ice Cream Parlour, where homemade ice cream was served at dainty wrought-iron tables. Mr. Ferris also advertised 30 different kinds of chocolates and cut hair on the side. Beautiful picture postcards of Miami were available at Westaway's drugstore, and the printer did a brisk business in calling cards and engraved invitations, which the dozen members of the social elite exchanged with solemn civility.

The culture of Ontario was imported along with its trappings. Dozens of clubs, lodges and fraternal societies sprang up as barricades against anarchy. The most formidable was the Royal Templars of Temperance, mobilized in 1895 by the doctor, the druggist and the undertaker's wife, who rounded up all the children into a Band of Hope, which sang temperance songs in the Odd Fellows' Hall but had no noticeable effect on the amount of liquor consumed in the Grandview Hotel bar, where the men drank standing up, apparently on the theory that when they'd had enough, they'd fall down. Everybody, of course, belonged to all the organizations. Shut up in their concrete houses with their heavy oak panelling and flowered wallpaper, served on linen and silver by farm girls disguised as cooks and housemaids, they tried to forget that they were stuck out on the bald prairie in a shack town engaged in a desperate and sometimes ludicrous struggle to make ends meet. Civilization, lovingly dismantled and imported on the train, was a truculent and feeble transplant. Cement houses were cold as death, dust blackened the lace curtains, and tea parties were spoiled by blackflies and grasshoppers. Savings vanished in swindles and bad gambles; businesses dissolved into bankruptcy. The vulgarity of the prairie was irrepressible.

Only three of Billy Thompson's eight children lived to see the end of the century. Men maimed themselves with axes and were mangled in farm machinery. Children died of diphtheria and women of tuberculosis. People aged quickly; the men went bald, and their deep, sunken eyes peered sternly out of craggy faces burned mahogany by the sun and wind. Their wives weathered, their jaws set square and determined and their hair pulled severely back into a bun. Nobody smiled in the early photographs, because their teeth had usually rotted and fallen out. Billy Thompson's little cemetery filled up quickly. It was a great achievement to be old.

As the centre of social gravity shifted to the town and the pastoral values of husbandry and hard work fell into disrepute, Uncle Billy leased his farm and moved about from daughter to daughter, an old man with a long white beard, carrying all his belongings in a grain sack on which was printed in large letters: WILLIAM THOMPSON — MAYOR OF MIAMI. He had wanted the village to be named after him, but it was named instead for a tribe of American Indians by a party of disgruntled surveyors who complained that there were already too many towns in the Northwest with the same English name. Local residents pronounce it with a drawl — Mahamuh. It's a trick, a code which identifies strangers and sets them apart.

A stranger is standing behind the worn wooden counter among the old-fashioned pill bottles at the back of Westaway's drugstore. A retired druggist from Winnipeg, he is responsible for tending the store while Jack Westaway is away on vacation. "I have written a song in honour of Manitoba," he says. He rummages in back and eventually produces a child's scribbler, the kind with a sheaf of wheat on the cover. He opens it and begins to sing in a tuneless singsong tenor as he conducts with his right arm:

Fresh bread, fresh bread!
Manitoba, Manitoba!
Love, love, love
Fresh bread, fresh bread, et cetera

The song was rejected in the competition for the official Manitoba centennial song.

"What do you think?" he asks.

Fresh bread?

"Of course!" he says. "That's what prairie towns are all about, the smell of fresh bread coming from the bakery early in the morning as you walk to work. It means everything—life, food, home. You don't smell it in the city.

"This is a great little town," he says, leaning close, "a fabulous town. Think of the potential of that name! Miami! Why, you could develop it into a real resort, just like the other Miami. Somebody with a few bucks could build big hotels with swimming pools, campsites, trailer parks . . ." He waves his arm around. "Build ski runs in the winter, snowmobile trails through the hills. Boy, with a little imagination, you could really cash in on the name of this place! It's a natural!"

Miami never made it to being a real town or even a real village. It's an unincorporated village, governed by a three-man committee with an annual budget of $9,000. They're really caretakers, who dole out money for streetlights, sidewalk repairs, gravel and culverts. Miami is a farmers' town; it has never achieved an existence or identity separate from the agricultural community. The town is a convenience for the farmers, a place to shop, a place to retire; when they're through with it, Miami will vanish as quickly as it came. Most townspeople understand that.

The population of the entire Municipality of Thompson, of which Miami is a part, is only a little more than 1,000 and shrinking steadily. Miami reached its peak in population and prosperity shortly after the turn of the century; once all the land was taken up, the tide turned. The exodus began to run the other way in 1914, as trains gathered up all the young men they had brought West only 5 or 10 years earlier and carried them back to boats headed for Europe. Hardest hit by the war exodus were the patriotic Anglo-Saxon areas like Miami.

It was funny how the economic booms, which had brought young people to the West, took only the young people away. Young men returning from World War II found themselves displaced by the combine, so they went to the cities to work in factories that built combines. Generation after generation, the young people grew up and left. As the farms increased in size, the town shrank. It lost its newspaper, photographer, undertaker, ice-cream parlour, Chinese laundry, lawyer and movie theatre. The doctor now comes only three afternoons a week from a nearby town. Roy Compton closed his John Deere farm-machinery agency in 1951. "If we'd have kept on," he says, "we would have been the same as the rest — a big 'For Sale' sign outside saying we're broke."

The people are mystified by Miami's decay. It is seen as a conspiracy, and it is blamed on an undefined, amorphous "They," a powerful bogey-man who reveals himself, under pressure, to be anything from the Prime Minister to kids with long hair. Survival is not a necessity for Miami, it's a matter of pride. Criticism of the town is taken personally. Any suggestion that Miami may be slipping or stagnant is interpreted as a slur, a deliberate insult to everyone who lives there. The residents react with fierce, defensive rage, a torrent of vituperation against socialism, abortion, pollution and all the other urban vices that are killing small towns. "Discipline!" shouts a bleary farmer, holding forth in the Grandview Hotel pub about the difficulties of finding kids to work for $1.50 an hour. "We need to bring back discipline! Those kids need to know who's boss. Those lazy bums can make more on welfare than they can working!" He stares defiantly at his cronies, who nod in agreement. "This welfare is such a racket; why, it's just Communism! We're goin' right over the top; it's Russia all the way!" The farmer lowers his voice and looks around conspiratorially. "Honest John," he whispers. "He would help us. If we could bring back Honest John." The other farmers all nod again and, taking a big swig of beer in memory of Honest John, savour their political exile.

The spiral of extinction begins slowly, imperceptibly, and ends quickly. A few businesses close down, the tax base shrinks, and a greater financial burden is borne by the residential property. When people begin to complain about high taxes, services are curtailed; then the town begins to look crummy, and people move away. Miami is hanging on the edge of the final precipice. "We have 50 homes with one widow in each of them," sighs Jim Murray, the municipal secretary. The village has no bicycle licences, no animal licences, no business licences — or no building permits. "We're so pleased if anyone wants to build here that we don't restrict them," says Mr. Murray. There is one new building in town, the credit union, and one new house, the credit union manager's. Miami has sewers but no waterworks; each house has a well and a cistern. The abundance of water that made Miami such a good place to settle in in 1889 has probably destroyed it. "Towns without water installed waterworks years ago, because they had to," says Mr. Murray. "Water attracts industry. They've got development now, and we don't." Without industry, Miami can't afford waterworks. Like a princess in a fairy tale, Miami makes herself beautiful in the hope that someday, a prince will gallop by and bless her with wealth and eternal life.

Community business in Miami is measured by the meetings — the less business, the longer the meeting. The Thompson municipal council meets all day. There's always lots of correspondence and delegations but no spectators. It's considered in bad taste in small towns to attend meetings. The councillors are embarrassed by having to speak in public, and they resent the implication that they are not doing their job. The minutes of the meeting are given to the local newspaper correspondents, who write up a short summary for the weekly papers. This way, the public knows only what the council wants them to know. Incompetence and corruption are allowed to persist for decades before anyone finds out enough to do something about it. Few people even know that council meetings are open to the public, and the length of the meetings is enough to discourage all but the most stubborn spectators. Of course, if the public attended, the meetings would be much shorter.

The six farmers arrive all clean-shaven and dressed up, their hair slicked down and their red faces scrubbed shiny. The older ones wear suits and ties; only their earth-stained fingers and the heavy black boots below their pant legs give them away. Sometimes, a strip of long john appears between the cuff and boot top. One of them carries a shiny black attaché case, which he snaps open and shut with great authority. The younger men wear their newest and cleanest jeans and windbreakers. They roar up in their pickup trucks in a cloud of dust, beaming, pregnant with civic responsibility. The meeting begins with a jovial exchange of dirty stories and the choicest gossip. Everyone has heard it already, but they enjoy telling it again.

The handyman appears to report that the fire engine leaks and his new low-bed truck is too long to turn the corner onto Main Street. A debate follows on whether to widen Main Street or shorten the truck. It's decided to shorten the truck.

A culvert salesman is next. "How are we fixed for culverts?" asks Rudy, looking solemnly around the big oak table. No culverts today, thanks.

The postmaster appears to complain about the broken sidewalk in front of the post office. The widows are giving him hell. Council promises an official inspection. Another man stomps in to complain that the boulevard in front of his house has not been mowed. This precipitates a heated discussion on the handyman's laziness, complete with councillors' eyewitness accounts of precise times and places they have seen him sitting around. One of the councillors says he'll mow the lawn himself for only a nominal fee.

The handyman reappears to complain that he is being paid only $1.75 an hour while a new man has been hired at $1.90 an hour. The councillors purse their lips and go all steely-eyed, muttering to themselves about greed and extravagance. The council believes in getting the most for its money. The town foreman is paid $5,000 a year; his titles include caretaker of cemeteries, sewage engineer, water-tank caretaker, fire chief, fire-hall caretaker and caretaker of Miami and Rosebank disposal grounds.

A letter is read from a lawyer on behalf of a Mr. Warsaba, who is going to sue the municipality because a bridge was washed out somewhere in the hills in a flash flood and Mr. Warsaba sailed over the edge of the bank in his car and landed in the mud on the creek bottom. Several hours later, his wife found him and dug him out, but before he could pull his car out, a second car sailed over and landed on top of it. Mr. Warsaba is claiming $450 damages for the total destruction of his car. Council has a big laugh.

The delicate question of the Miami police force is raised. Two policemen were hired in the summer of 1970, after the school principal complained that some boys had thrown beer bottles at his house and squealed their tires on the boulevard in front of his property.

"We just took a couple of the worst hell-raisers and made them the town police," smiles Sid Cox, a member of the village committee. "It sure stopped the trouble."

The Miami police had only been on the job a month at the time of the great hole mystery. "What do you do?" I asked one of them, whose ears stuck straight out on either side of his big blue hat. He grinned and blushed. "Try to look busy," he said. At first, the police took themselves very seriously. They patrolled the empty highway in front of town and caught farmers speeding down Main Street in their pickup trucks; they nabbed a few housewives making illegal U-turns and lay in wait for drunken teenagers outside the school dances. Looking snappy in their brand-new blue uniforms, which were just a little too large, they swaggered into Vern's Café every morning for coffee, stamping their feet hard on the floor to make their shoes sound like RCMP boots and fingering the revolvers in their belts as they cast a suspicious eye over the crowd of cheerful farmers. They were paid $200 a month each and worked out of an office in the basement of the municipal building behind the men's washroom. It was, in fact, part of the men's washroom.

A year later, one of them was caught drinking on duty. He was fired and got a job bartending in Morden, a town 15 miles south. His buddy quit in sympathy and joined the Morden police force. His loss was a severe economic blow to Miami, because he owned the Miami police car, a blue station wagon with a detachable red light on top and a cot in the back, which was also the Miami ambulance. This policeman was also the television repairman and agent for Admiral appliances; his shop closed down when he left. He took his mother with him to Morden; she was the baker, so the bakery closed. His wife worked in the bank; that job fell vacant. The volunteer fire brigade was decimated, because the two policemen were its backbone. They held fire drills twice a month in the men's washroom and finished them off with a case of beer and a poker game. The loss of the local police suddenly exposed the Miami people to the financial ruthlessness of the RCMP traffic patrols, since previously, the town constables had widely publicized the location of hidden radar traps and had alerted everyone as to which nights the RCMP detachment would be away attending a wedding or a stag.

A year has passed, and Miami remains without police. "We've been real lucky," grins Rudy Hink. "It's been quiet. It saves us $5,000 a year."

By noon, the little council chamber is rank with sweat. Yet all these issues are essentially trivial. The council has only one overriding concern — roads. Roads are an obsession. Most of the municipal budget of $76,000 goes for road maintenance and snow removal. The topic of roads brings the councillors to life; hands waving and nostrils flaring, they can happily discuss gravel, culverts and machinery for hours and days. They are connoisseurs of gravel, authorities on its cost and quality, experts on the precise day of the year on which it must be applied. The purchase of a new road grader can consume months of weighty deliberation. Like all farmers, municipal councillors are machinery freaks; each purchase is entered into only after the utmost investigation and the most subtle negotiations. All of the councillors go along to Winnipeg to inspect the road grader. They can charge $1.50 an hour and 10 cents a mile for inspection tours, which usually include a rollicking afternoon in a Winnipeg pub featuring topless go-go dancers. The councillors do a lot of inspecting, but they are paid only $600 a year. (The reeve gets $1,200.) Local farmers conscientiously bring every rut, pothole and blocked culvert to their attention. The better the roads, of course, the easier it is for farmers to bypass Miami and drive to other towns.

Although they will quickly plunk down $50,000 for a new piece of machinery, council will not approve even a tiny amount of welfare without a howl of protest. Excluding an annual grant of $3,400 to the nearby hospital, the municipality's health and welfare budget is $5,600 a year. Every cent of it is begrudged. Although the administration of welfare is handled by the provincial government, which pays the total cost of transients and 40 percent for residents, welfare is regarded by each councillor as a personal affront and an appalling drain on the community resources. Discussion of welfare consumes about as much time as roads. The municipality has two families receiving assistance — a musician in town, who plays with a rock band, and a colony of hippies in a shack in the hills.

The meeting resolves itself into a leisurely gabfest, a communal chewing of the fat which is conducted with decorum and politeness. Everyone is allowed to talk as long and as often as he likes, while the rest listen in respectful silence. Great weight is placed on personal observation and anecdote. Every picayune detail is raised, every matter examined from all possible angles; there's no rush, no urgency, no railroading. No grievance, no expenditure is too small for consideration. The delicate matter of the silver tray is raised last. Ralph "Mac" Nast, the town barber, who has served on the village committee for 15 years, has been forced to retire because of failing health. Council has purchased a silver tray for him in Westaway's drugstore. Jim Murray produces the bill. "He quoted us $24 plus $6 for the engraving," says Rudy Hink, clearing his throat. "The bill comes to $52." There is an angry silence around the table. "Jeez," says one councillor, "I said we should have got it in Winnipeg." Rudy Hink pulls the tray out of its box of tissue paper. It's elaborately engraved with Mr. Nast's name and his years on the council. He looks at it. "Well," he shrugs, "I guess we can't take it back."

Mr. Nast and his wife, who have been waiting outside, are ushered in. The councillors stand up and look very red and shy. Rudy Hink makes a short speech and thrusts the tray at Mr. Nast. The councillors applaud. Mr. Nast, trying to look cool and nonchalant, blushes and gazes down at the ground.

"We're like a wheel with spokes in it and everybody does his share and I done mine," he blurts out. Jim Murray takes flash pictures of Rudy Hink handing the tray to Mr. Nast. There is an awkward silence; people shuffle their feet. No one can think of anything to say.

"Mac," one of the councillors suddenly booms out, "whenever I think of sewage in this town, I think of you. You know more about every pipe in Miami than anyone else I can think of."

Mr. Nast shakes hands all around. Then he puts the tray under his arm, and as he limps out, he is wiping the tears from his eyes.

Mac Nast's barbershop is spotlessly clean and empty except for the old barber chair, a Coke cooler and a small table littered with Superman comics. The little building looks 100 years old. "I built it myself," says Mac, "in 1948."

Miami's downtown has been swept by fire and many of the first buildings destroyed, but their style has been carefully reproduced. Rural prairie architecture is not a holdover but a unique, deliberate and distinct tradition. It's homemade and unprofessional, a plain, functional style which, like the log cabin, evolved out of the strictures of land and weather and the aesthetic sensibilities of the community. Prairie cities try to look like Toronto, but small towns try to look like the Old West. They are conservative; their repudiation of the progress symbolized by steel and glass indicates not only respect for the past but the pride of people who like to make things themselves, with their own hands. They also suggest decent poverty. It takes money to buy culture, and Miami hasn't had that kind of money since the turn of the century. The buildings are plainer than they used to be. The fancy cornices have been stripped away, the hardwood floors have been covered with tile, the fronts are faced with stucco and cheap fibreglass. All the Victorian gewgaws imported from Ontario have been gradually jettisoned like so much excess baggage. The buildings look pasted together, transitory.

Although Miami has been in existence for almost 85 years, it looks as helter-skelter and impermanent as it did in its first decade of life.

"It used to be that you cut people's hair as to what suited them best," mutters Mac. "Now, you get nothing but complaints. Parents complain about long hair on the kids. They make you feel you don't know nothing about cutting hair. Everyone's dissatisfied." Mac used to have a poolroom in back, but he closed it down a few years ago, sold his house and moved into the back of the barbershop. He's lucky to make $75 a week cutting hair and selling pop and tobacco. "If I was to start today, I wouldn't go into a small town," he says. "But I'm too old to take training. I'll just hang on."

Hanging on is what most merchants are doing. The younger ones scramble. The young man who runs the new pool hall has gone into lawn chairs, fishing rods and suede handbags, and his window is plastered with signs advertising sunglasses, air freshener, cigarette lighters, watch straps and pocketknives. Carr's Hardware around the corner is an odds-and-sods place, a small store that specializes in galvanized pails, baseball bats, teapots, barn spray, warble powder, potato dust and fishing licences, a place you go to pick up a new rake or a couple of nails when you run out. Carr's prices are high, but profits are small, so in 1970, he went into snowmobiles. In one year, Mr. Carr sold 120 snowmobiles, more than any other Moto-Ski dealer in Manitoba. He didn't actually sell them; he traded them for wheat, barley and cattle, giving the farmer a price just below market value. "Carr's got a whole herd of cattle," says a farmer, pointing down the highway to the pasture behind Carr's house. Carr made enough money to expand into campers and trailers, which he displays in his front yard. His hardware store is up for sale.

The meat market next door gets a steady trade from the widows and schoolteachers in town. The butcher offers a small selection of roasts and chops in a glass case. Buying is an intensely personal experience, a contest of will and ideology with the beefy butcher, who has very strong and vocal opinions on every topic. Once in the door, you are obliged to buy something. To walk out without a purchase is an insult.

Shopping in Miami is a stately procession, a royal progress down the street, an adventure fraught with dangers and discoveries. You say hello to everyone, and everyone says hello to you. Each encounter comes freighted with information about weddings, pregnancies and sickness and offers the opportunity, through a chance remark or observation, to change the social course of the community. Notices of meetings are posted in the entrances to the grocery stores and cafés, and a welter of little handprinted signs pasted to windows advertise everything from baseball bats to the next meeting of the Slim and Trim Club. A trip down Main Street makes you *au courant* of all the latest events. Minuscule changes are noted and commented upon — an empty beer bottle on the step of the Grandview Hotel, a strange car, Elsie Hink's new hairdo. The excitement comes from chance. Although the people are always the same, the kaleidoscope changes slightly every day. As Sid Cox says, "There's always something doin'." Shocking and traumatic events are so rare that even the tiniest interruption in the smooth flow of time is treated as an occurrence of immense magnitude. Small towns are anthropocentric. People revolve in fixed orbits like stars and planets, each one convinced that he is the sun of the universe. The immediate galaxy is the local community; distant cities and foreign countries take on the quality of mysterious and hostile outer space, reachable only after several million light-years of travel. What happens out there is interesting but beyond control. This pleasurable sensation of personal significance is reinforced by all the rituals of the community and by the decorum of trade.

The centre of trade in Miami is Leathers' General Store, which is in the very middle of the main street. "I have fed five generations," beams Mr. Leathers. The store is a work of art. With the exception of electric lights and venetian blinds, it is preserved exactly as it must have been the day Mr. Leathers started work in 1916. Stanfield's are stacked high on old wooden counters next to tidy piles of stiff blue jeans and striped overalls; shoe boxes are piled up to the ceiling so that Mr. Leathers has to scramble up a ladder if anyone wants an odd size. The only concession to fashion is a shelf of red-and-purple polka-dot caps, which are all the rage among farmers this summer. Racks of bright jelly beans and striped humbugs are placed tantalizingly on the oak counter, worn hollow by thousands of hands. Behind the counter, shelves and shelves of neatly stacked tins rise up to the ceiling; bananas, oranges, cake mixes and cookies are arranged on the countertop, and onions are in cardboard boxes on the floor. The store is dark with old wood and jammed full with goods, but everything, including round, bald Mr. Leathers, is clean and neat as a pin. The clock is stopped at 10 to 4.

Mr. Leathers does all the shopping himself. The store is too crowded to roam around in, and only Mr. Leathers knows where everything is. He waits on each customer personally, patiently, with courtly politeness, going off to find each item individually, one at a time. He walked back and forth behind the counter so much that he eventually wore right through the oiled hardwood floor and had to have it replaced. One by one, he stacks the items on the counter and adds the cost on the adding machine.

Shopping at Leathers' can take hours. It's a social occasion, a meeting of minds and a reaffirmation of existence. The vulgar and impatient can always shop down the street at the Co-op, a bright and shiny supermarket which is teetering on the verge of bankruptcy. Mr. Leathers does a comfortable business. The store and his house were paid off long ago; he spends nothing on improvements or advertising; taxes are almost nil. When he dies, his store will vanish.

Business in Miami is family business, handed down from father to son. The name of the store is the name of the owner; only in a small town is it still possible to open the door of Leathers' store or Moorey's grocery or Westaway's drugstore and be waited on by Mr. Leathers, Mrs. Moorey and Mr. Westaway in person. Jack Westaway was a successful druggist in Kapuskasing, Ontario; he came home to Miami to take over the family business when his father died in 1942. It was the natural thing to do. Westaway's is a child's garden of delights, a wild chaotic confusion of hair spray, oven mitts, rat poison and *True Confessions* magazines. You can get anything you want in Westaway's drugstore, including famous Westaway's Stomach Powder, a home remedy with fans as far away as Vancouver. Being the only drugstore in a small town full of old people is profitable, but Mr. Westaway carries on a sideline. The Miami liquor store is located in a dark corner of Westaway's drugstore between the hair colour and the pills. A sign in the window announces that it is open from 11 a.m. to 12 noon and from 1 p.m. to 6 p.m. and CLOSED ALL DAY MONDAY. Everything in Miami is closed all day Monday to give the merchants a rest after Saturday-night shopping until 10 p.m. Most of the merchants spend Monday in Winnipeg, shopping.

"It cost me $4,000 to buy the liquor to set up," beams Mr. Westaway. The bottles are hidden away in a little cupboard; a few dusty specimens are displayed along the top, and you make your selection from a list posted on the wall. The selection is quite broad. "Rye mostly," says Mr. Westaway. "I don't sell much wine. It's big for wine around Swan Lake — Indian reserve, you know." He speaks enviously of the druggist in Swan Lake. Mr. Westaway buys his liquor directly from the provincial government in $1,500 lots; he makes a profit of 10 percent on every sale. The rural liquor trade is not restricted to druggists: down the road, the furniture dealer has the booze.

Progress is catching up to Mr. Westaway. "They told me I have to tear down the wall to *show* the liquor," he says in a shocked voice. "And the next licence holder will have to put it in the *window!*"

He scampers in to get the bottle and wraps it up quickly in white paper with a big "Rexall" stamped across it in blue ink.

The ice of the Miami arena is bathed in soft blue light. The lobby is crowded with parents peering through the big windows screened with heavy wire mesh. The bolder mothers and fathers make their way to the wooden benches on both sides of the darkened arena, where they huddle together with woollen blankets over their knees. It's March. The ice is getting soft. The Miami Figure Skating Club's ice carnival is the last event of the winter.

One after the other, sometimes alone, sometimes in groups of three or six, the girls trot out onto the ice to perform to music played over the loudspeaker. Even the littlest girls, who fall down a lot, go through elaborate routines dressed up as pigs and bears and mice, ankling along lickety-split to *Talk to the Animals*. There's just enough time for them to rush off and change costumes before they're back in the *Wizard of Oz*. Every number requires a whole new set of matching outfits — witches, dwarfs, flappers, showgirls, señoritas — plus specialty jobs like the Tin Man. The costumes are dazzling, not just skating dresses with a few ribbons tacked on or stuff rummaged up around the house but brand-new satin and chiffon outfits complete with hats and bows and stage makeup. The carnival goes on and on. There are 26 numbers on the programme, and every girl appears in two or three. The skating deteriorates as the girls get older and fatter. Miami's little girls are very well fed, with big behinds and thick legs, but they make up in perseverance what they lack in grace. Five of the soloists, each more elaborately dressed and clumsier than the last, have the same last name. Miami has its share of skating mothers.

Mothers are what the Miami carnival is really all about. The mothers plan the programme, drive the girls to practice and design and sew all the costumes. The carnival is spectacular, a triumph of organization for the mothers. The mothers, of course, say they're doing it for their daughters, but there is an overtone of competition, fierce, vicar-

Heather Robertson

ious satisfaction in their daughters' success as a measure of their own social prestige.

Miami kids are always in uniform. There aren't any kids on the street playing kick-the-can or making mud pies in the ditches. Kids are hard to find, because they're all in the same place somewhere playing baseball or hockey in green-and-white Miami sweaters or going to a Scout or CGIT or 4-H calf club meeting. Miami is jock country. The village claims to be the sports centre of southern Manitoba, and great victories are recalled dating back to 1933 or 1906 in leagues which most people have never heard about. The town's reputation rests, however, on sports that were played by men. (Old photographs of hockey and lacrosse teams show bankers, carpenters and morticians with handlebar moustaches, bulging biceps and chests puffed out proudly beneath their striped jerseys, grouped stiffly around a silver cup.) When the West was young, sports were a good excuse for a party and a general booze-up. Now, the kids provide all the entertainment in the community, conscripting their parents as audience. There is nothing left for the adults to do except drink. Even dances have faded away. There are only one or two a year in the Miami area, and they all have cabaret licences. Because of the liquor, people can't bring their kids. "It used to be that everyone went," says a farmer who used to play sax in the community orchestra, "and you'd dance with everybody. Now, people go with a little group and dance with them. You don't get to see anybody else. A lot of people won't dance until they've had three or four beers. That's what people like; they like to drink."

The dictatorship of the peewees is accepted without question. Miami believes in discipline. The strategy is to keep the children too busy to get into mischief. "The kids," comments one grandmother, "are played out. They come back to school on Monday dead beat. Some of them fall asleep on the desk." The routine exhausts the parents as well, but many of them welcome the busyness and boredom. They escape into childhood. The children only appear to be in control. It's the adults who impose and enforce the routine. The children are enslaved by their parents' nostalgia.

"The kids are still in the '50s," says a teacher. "There's a big emphasis on drinking, roaring around in cars, good times, you know, yuk it up. The pool-hall culture. Hanging around."

Miami kids are clean, tidy and well behaved. "There's no peace kids around here," grunts a Legion member with satisfaction. A few kids hang out in the pool hall, but the pool hall is clean and tidy too. I feel a little sorry for the knot of boys lounging around the door. Their hair is short, their clothes are pressed, and their faces are clean-shaven; they have a puzzled, rather pathetic, James Dean look. Life is frozen in 1956. The feeling is oppressive.

"We were a dead bunch," admits a man who grew up near Miami in the '50s. "I didn't even start drinking beer until I was in grade 12, and I was considered wild."

"There's a real in group of girls who run things, who consider themselves 'queens,'" says the teacher. "They're socially active, always the leaders. They feel they're a little more attractive, better dressed; they have a greater sense of their own competence. They're in the minority, but there's more of them in Miami than in other communities. You could call them the nicey-nice girls.

"A strange thing about Miami is the lack of high school girls who get pregnant. There seems to be less screwing around going on. If a girl was willing to get laid, she could really pick and choose . . . there's no population of grubby girls. No gang. The guys don't have a ladies' auxiliary to their gangs. Gangs have to hang around the chocolate shop, and you can't do that in Miami."

The kids' only escape from parental surveillance is on the highway. A car is a necessity for rural kids. A car is liberty and love, a dark secret place where they can be alone with each other. They live in cars because it's the only private place they have. Equipped with a radio, a heater and booze, a car is a little home on wheels, an instant escape. The kids' conventional dress and manner is a disguise; conformity protects them from scrutiny and allows them, in the privacy of their cars, an intense, sexy and joyous personal liberation. Clustered in hidden ravines by the creek, the car radio on for entertainment, they can say "fuck" all they like, drink warm beer from the trunk and enjoy the exquisite pleasure of necking in the tall grass. If somebody has a little dope, they'll smoke it in the dark, but a better high is to bomb down a gravel road drunk as a skunk at 90 miles an hour with the soft sweet-clover night rushing in the windows. Every now and then, a kid rolls the car and breaks his neck. "It's sort of like the Vietnam War," says the teacher. "You get to expect a daily number of napalmings, you learn to expect a certain number of deaths. Parents don't attach the blame anywhere. It's an act of God." Parents establish scholarships in their dead sons' names. They exert no pressure on the RCMP to police reckless driving more vigorously. In fact, parents are angry and humiliated when their children are arrested for speeding and drunk driving, especially if the trial is written up in the local paper. Death is accepted as a natural part of being young.

"Saturday night is the big time," says a young man. "When you're younger, you go to a movie. All the kids sit in the back row in the theatre. There's always lots of mooching and smooching in the back. When you get older, you drink. Kids start to drink about 16. Drinking just takes over. If you're a big strapping farm boy, you gotta prove that you can be a big drinker. The big fellows, they gotta drink like crazy! It's the real thing on the weekend. You go to the next town, and you drink like a son of a bitch.

"Parents look down on drinking. The kids have to hide it. I remember one mother saying, 'My Margaret is a good girl.' Christ, she drank like a fish. Everybody drinks like crazy at dances. Cops set up roadblocks to every goddamned dance. You send a scout car through. He'll go without beer, and he'll phone if he hits a roadblock: 'Look out for those cocksucking cops!' You always go in bunches. The car is always crowded. If there's any screwing, it's on the grass or in the backseat of the car. If a girl gets pregnant, she'll vanish. Suddenly. Oh, there's lots of accidents. I've been in an accident. Most kids wind up in court by the time they're 21.

"There's two kinds of kids: the sissies and the bad boys. The bad boys drink and smoke. I started smoking at 11. Everybody does. And you swear like a bastard. Parents don't really object. Swearing is a part of life. The church doesn't have any hold on us. Fuck the church. There's a lot of driving around just for something to do. If I've gone over a road once, I've gone over it a hundred times. You get bored. Sure, you get bored. That's why most younger kids play hockey. What the hell else is there to do?

"Quite a few kids drop out of school, go to work on construction, driving a truck. Everybody wants to get a job. It doesn't matter that much what kind of job. Once you're out of school, you're a man. You can do everything a man does, screw and drink and everything. Your friends can be 17 or 37. You're accepted in the workaday world. You're not young anymore."

The old ladies are gathered in a little white bungalow opposite the school. The furniture has been shoved out of the living room to make space for the quilting frame, which takes up just about the whole room. It's a widow's house, full of dark oak curlicue furniture and those obese, overstuffed, maroon plush chesterfield sets that everybody in Canada owned in the '40s. The chesterfield and armchair have a white lace doily on the back and one on each arm. The small windows are piled high with houseplants. All the widows in Miami peer out through a screen of luxuriant foliage; healthy houseplants are a source of great pride and social prestige, although one lady, Mrs. Marshall (who is also the champion quilt maker), is by far the best houseplant grower; her house is a miniature rainforest. The plants give a restful, murky, undersea quality to the house.

The ladies are seated around the quilting frame, three or four to a side, each in her appointed place. The quilt is spread out taut on the frame, a huge pink-and-white trampoline destined to be a wedding present for a local girl. A baroque pattern of swirls and whorls has been traced on in pencil; the ladies stitch it in with fine white thread. They stitch quickly, methodically, relentlessly, scarcely glancing at the material. Their wrinkled, liver-spotted hands move delicately over the surface, like moths; when they come to the end of a thread, they snip it off neatly with a pair of tiny, sharp sewing scissors. Stitch stitch snip stitch snip stitch stitch. The rhythm of their needles keeps pace with the flicker of their tongues, as they spin the web of life, measure it and snip it off. They are the Fates, these white old ladies with hair nets and goggle glasses like the bottoms of pop bottles; Miami's reputations rest in their withered, ruthless fingers. They rule Miami like a cartel of aged queens, setting the standards in dress, conduct and moral behaviour; their decision, once given, is absolute. News is heard here long before it gets to Vern's; it is mulled over, evaluated and passed along, complete with the quilting bee's editorial opinion. Their judgements are reached quickly, since their standards have remained unchanged for 50 years.

"We have a nice lunch and a little gossip," beams one of the matriarchs.

"Oh, yes," pipes another, "if we didn't come here, we'd miss all the news!"

"Sometimes, the men say it's just . . ." The first woman trails off, not wanting to use a word like dirt or muck.

"Well, I think that when my husband goes to his card games, they're worse than we are," booms the second lady, who speaks very loudly because she is deaf. Several of the women are quite deaf, which means that all the news has to be repeated two or three times. They can see lips moving out of the corner of their eyes and demand to be told what was said. This makes the other ladies frown and go white around the mouth.

The quilting club is sponsored by the United Church, although the ladies seem to spend more time making quilts for weddings and showers than they do for sale. Crib quilts are their specialty. "Every time somebody is having a baby, we sell a quilt to the grandmother," states the hostess with satisfaction. The quilts are superb. They come in a galaxy of colours and any one of dozens of patterns from patchwork to appliqué; they are made with great taste and painstaking workmanship. The going price is $70; most are sold to Americans. One was hung in the Winnipeg Art Gallery. The ladies have a sharp sense of the financial value of their past; they cackle with delight at their ability to thwart American bargain hunters who want to make off with their antique furniture.

One of the ladies is left-handed and is causing a problem, because she keeps running into other people's territory on the quilt. This observation leads to an extended discussion of left-handedness and its effect on children, based on the personal experience of several of the ladies who have had or taught left-handed children. It includes a complete list of everyone in the Miami area who is left-handed.

"Both our bankers are left-handed," states one woman emphatically, as if to clinch the argument.

"Has the new banker any children?" queries another woman, not missing a stitch or raising her eyes from the quilt.

"Yes, two," pipes the hostess, looking around in triumph at being the first with the information. The other ladies look grumpy.

"Are they old enough to go to school?"

There is a general nodding of heads and a cacophony of affirmatives around the quilt. The stitching picks up speed.

"Have they moved in yet?"

"Oh, yes!" says the hostess. "They were here on Friday. They were uptown for dinner Friday night."

"*Before* Friday," crows a woman across the quilt, striking like a snake. "I saw the children playing behind the house on Friday morning. They were up before I was."

"Yes, before I was too," adds the woman next to her.

They stitch for a while in silence. Only two children. "Terry Atkinson had four, didn't he?" asks a woman. Everyone nods. "And the station agent, he's leaving. He has four too, doesn't he?" They all nod. There is no melancholy in their voices, no gloom but rather an unexpected and startling hint of satisfaction.

"Mrs. Sprott! You're on my square! Do you see where you are?" Mrs. Sprott, who wears magnifying glasses, has intruded about six inches into Mrs. Marshall's section of the quilt. Mrs. Sprott peers around, confused.

"Oh, am I?" she chortles. "Well, what's the matter?"

Mrs. Marshall sets her jaw and looks daggers. Mrs. Sprott discreetly quilts her way back out.

"Mrs. Sprott is *84*," whispers the hostess loudly. "She mows her own lawn and has *beautiful* plants. Her house is so *clean!*" Mrs. Sprott beams with pleasure. "You must see her house," the hostess continues. "It's just down the street, near the Collingwood."

"That's the old folks' home," says Mrs. Sprott condescendingly. "Our senior citizens live there."

The old people greet Miami's imminent demise with pleasure. They meticulously chronicle the progress of its decay, savouring each loss, each failure, with a small smile of triumph. "The town will die with the people who are in it," croaks an old crone, pursing her lips complacently. The old people built Miami. It is theirs. It is their right to take the community down with them. There is a casual cheerfulness about it, as if everyone has reached a secret agreement to destroy the town rather than let it fall into the hands of the enemy.

"I tell you, we're gettin' fewer and fewer," chortles the president of the Miami Legion, Branch 88, looking around at the six men in overalls gathered in the room. No one has bothered to wear his beret and medals. "Six. Is that enough to be legal?"

"Haw, haw," roar the men.

"Well, we're here," states the president, shuffling his papers. He clears his throat. "Comrades, we'll open the meeting." They scrape to their feet and bow their heads while the president reads from a little dog-eared book.

"They shall grow not old, as we that are left grow old. Age shall not weary them, nor the years condemn. At the going down of the sun and in the morning, we will remember them." The men repeat in unison:

"We will remember them." All together, they say: "Lord God of hosts, be with us yet, lest we forget, lest we forget." They stand for a minute, heads bowed, in silence.

The business is haggling over liquor accounts from the World War I banquet. "It sure was a good supper!" beams one veteran, patting his paunch. "We all got filled up that night!" The testimonial ashtray for Emil Desjarlais cost $4. "Aw, don't bother writin' everything down!" the treasurer yells at the secretary, who is labouring along in a big, round hand. "Our kitty men are all home and in good shape!" booms comrade president. Every month, the men put in 25 cents to buy cards for members in the hospital. "We've had nobody in the hospital for the last two months, so we're home free!"

Mike Hofer, boss of the Miami Hutterite Colony, is seated proudly in front of his homemade plywood desk which, since it contains all the records of the colony's $500,000 annual business transactions and the colony's only telephone, is the seat of his power. A cherubic man with a bristly brown beard and apple cheeks who, at 36, has fathered the nine children who appear at intervals to grin shyly around the door, Mr. Hofer is outspoken, garrulous, a bubbling fountain of jokes, anecdotes and strong opinions about everything. Sleek and prosperous in his sparkling-clean checked shirt and baggy, black, homespun trousers, he tilts his chair back on two legs as he talks and rests his feet on the desk, waving his bottle of Labatt's Blue the way an executive waves a cigar.

"If there's anything new in farming to make a dollar easier, we sure try!" he beams, taking a mighty swig from his beer bottle which ends only when, Adam's apple working furiously, he has drained the bottle dry. He plunks it down on the desk and gestures to his wife, a stout woman swathed in a voluminous ankle-length print dress, who immediately produces another. I am seated across the room on a wooden pew plucked from a defunct rural church, drinking dandelion wine. Yellow as piss and strong as whisky, it is, without a doubt, the best wine I have ever tasted. Mr. Hofer makes it himself according to a recipe passed along from boss man to boss man as a kind of ceremonial badge of office. Mr. Hofer also possesses the only key to the colony's wine cellar.

The Miami Hutterite Colony is a commune, a Protestant community based on Christ's teaching that his followers live in a state of material poverty and brotherly love. A small commune with only 85 people — most of them children — and 3,000 acres of land located south of Miami near the site of old Nelsonville, the colony looks much like a camp, which in fact it is, since everyone lives in identical white bunk-houses purchased cheap from a government construction camp when the colony was established in 1966. Divided into duplexes and furnished with yellow varnished wooden furniture made by the commune carpenter, the bunkhouses stick out like spokes from the simple church and communal dining hall at the hub. Mr. Hofer takes me on a tour. The spring wind is cold, and the yard is very quiet. It's siesta time, says Mr. Hofer with a big yawn. A handful of giggly girls in long dresses and kerchiefs are in school, a small one-room country school scavenged from a dead village, but nobody cares if the kids play hooky, since as far as the Hutterites are concerned, the school, which goes only to grade eight, is just a token concession to the worldly corruption of the provincial government. It's not in the centre of the community but stuck off to one side in the scrub.

We walk toward the dairy and the pig barns, past a rippling field of geese, followed by a fuzzy, frolicking puppy. I pat it. "Wanna buy the dog?" queries Mr. Hofer. No. Huge, modern and automated, the barns reveal acres of squealing piglets, endless rows of Holsteins and cacophonies of chickens. The colony produces 5,000 geese a year, 3,500 hogs and 6,000 chickens, and milk from the cows is sold to a cheese factory. The Hutterites do their own butchering, and the grain from their 3,000 acres is used for feed. Each department is in the charge of an overseer — the goose man, the pig man, the milk man, et cetera — who, like the boss himself, is elected by the adult men of the community. Farming decisions are made by a council of all the overseers, including the minister, who, with the boss, approves all major purchases. The boss takes charge of all negotiations with the outside. "We were in Winnipeg buying shoes for everybody," he moans, waving his arms in despair. "Last year, they were $9.75 a pair. This year, we had to pay $10.90." The shoes are distributed from house to house by the minister, who is also the shoe man. Everybody gets the same kind. The women make all the clothes and knit the socks on a knitting machine, but the boss goes along on their trips to buy material to make sure they don't get anything too expensive or too bright. "If women's lib gets in here, we'll lock 'em all out," he chortles. The boss pays all the bills and supervises the community bank account, which is called the Miami

Holding Company. No individual Hutterite has any money; even pension cheques and the Family Allowance are turned over to Mike.

The commune earns $1,200 a day, a gross annual income of almost $6,000 per capita, substantially more than the average independent Miami farmer makes. The frugal habits and spartan style of the Hutterites keep expenses to a minimum: radios and television are forbidden, although kids smuggle transistors around in their baggy mediaeval pockets and a fair amount of hell is raised whenever the elders are away on a buying spree. The whole colony travels around in a single International van. All money which is not invested in the farm is saved. In another 10 years, when the colony has doubled in size, the boss will be able to plunk down between $250,000 and $500,000 in cash to buy land for some of his families to set up a new Hutterite commune in Manitoba.

We head toward the dining hall for dinner. The men, curious but self-effacing, are seated on benches at long trestle tables, and the women are in the kitchen, spooning soup and vegetables out of enormous stainless-steel vats. The boss buys all the colony's food, a year's supply at a time, and supervises its preparation. His wife bustles around the kitchen. "My wife Justina, she's the chief cook and bottle washer," Mike says proudly. The food is plain but nourishing — salad and pickles, roast chicken, mixed vegetables and a lumpy glob of potatoes and flour, oozing grease, that looks like tapioca, which the boss, gobbling it down with relish, calls "little grey fellas."

The last stop after lunch is the wine cellar, a small cool room in the basement of the dining hall beyond the shelves of tinned peaches piled up to the ceiling. The boss unlocks it carefully with one of the keys on his jangling chain. The room is ringed with stained wooden kegs filled with half a dozen different kinds of wine. One of the kegs is sitting on a beautiful carved wooden table. I pat it. "Wanna buy the table?" asks Mike, his eyes flashing like cash registers. Unfortunately, he won't sell the wine.

You often see Hutterites in Winnipeg, where it looks as if every Hutterite in the province comes to town on the same day, but never in Miami. They don't shop there. They don't send their kids to the Miami school or enrol them in hockey or CGIT or Scouts. They don't vote or curl or join the Rebekahs. "For all they do for the community, they might as well have smallpox," snarls a farmer. Almost everybody, not just in Miami but throughout the prairies, hates the Hutterites. They are universally slandered, persecuted, discriminated against. "Aw, they're a crooked bunch of buggers," a respected Miami citizen tells me. "The police don't lay charges against Hutterites. They get away with everything. They steal pigs, strip cars. If they want to buy a farmer's land, they'll irritate the guy until he has to sell. I know one guy, they dumped a shit wagon right at his gate!" People gleefully spread rumours about Hutterite children stealing candies from Leathers' store or peddling the colony's weed spray door to door or their fondness for midnight visits to a bachelor farmer to get a little high on colour TV. "You set up a colony, look how many votes you'd get," scoffs Reeve Rudy Hink, "and look how many you'd lose." Although there are fewer than 10,000 Hutterites in the three Prairie Provinces out of a total population of almost 3.5 million, rural people talk about them as if they were about to take over the West. Communism works. Not only have the Hutterites survived as an autonomous culture and economy, they have grown and multiplied, working like bees with the most advanced machinery and technology yet maintaining their 400-year-old religion, antique dress and communal system. Many of the established colonies are worth more than $1 million, with $1 million in gross annual sales. The Hutterites' wealth is as obvious as their contempt for it. They are a living reproof to the independent farmer who, unwilling to admit that a Hutterite may be richer than he is, gnashes his teeth with rage and spits vituperation. He sells out and leaves the land; the Hutterites buy the land he leaves. "Pretty soon," grumbles an elderly farmer, "the Hutterites will be the only farmers left in western Canada."

Edward Hoagland

The Old Men of Telegraph Creek

The McPhees and the Others

June 10, Friday: I am staying at the Diamond C Café, "Pioneer Out-fitters, Est. 1874." It's the only lodging in town and is run by Edwin Callbreath's parents. The Anglican bishop is here for his annual visit, a stooping listener of a man; also a Kennecott survey crew, so we're jammed. In the morning, I climbed up the hill a couple of levels to the two McPhee brothers'. Alec has the best vegetable garden in town. Dan, who lives up the last flight of stairs, is something of a landlord, own-ing a shack and two houses left him by friends who have died, in lieu of money that he had loaned. Both McPhees arrived in the West about 1904 and worked on the railway that runs to Prince Rupert and on a network of government trails to the north, building a wagon bridge across the Bell-Irving River, which hasn't been bridged since. While they were doing this, they'd walk back and forth across on a cable, daredevil-style, balancing themselves with their loggers' peavies. In

1912, when they were cutting a trail in the valley of the Nass, which is only now seeing its first roads, the local Tsimshians rode out to intimidate them, circling on horseback and firing their rifles. That winter was Alec's last visit south to a city.

Dan was the first to move to Telegraph Creek, although not until 1930, when he was put in charge of the maintenance crew on the village roads. He arrived on the riverboat, looked around at the size of the town and said to the Hudson's Bay man, "If I'm here next Saturday night, I'll kiss your blessed ass." ("Been here 36 years," he laughs.) He's a lean, wry, humorous man, haggy and coltish by turns. He looks like a canny grandpa from Tobacco Road — long nose, floppy hat, black shirt and pants — and when he tells a joke, he seems to swallow it, like a shot of whisky, and feel it go down and simmer nicely. Dan always kept the security of the government job, but for the winter, he picked up a trapline on the Scud River and Yehiniko Creek from a moonshiner whom the Mounties kicked out. He used to average 30 marten a year. Martens are so dumb, he says, that if you see a marten's tracks, that marten is yours. On the wall is a picture of him behind his dog team, in a high-collared native sweater, holding the handgrips and looking abrupt and rough and ready to shout. He had a half-breed wife who died three years ago and left him lonesome and rather itchy and at loose ends. One of his several sons still lives with him, bringing the money in, while Dan cooks. As the family absorbed his attention, he traded the trapline to another Scotsman for 26 cleared acres on the Chutine, intending to farm. The Chutine was better for farming than the Scud was, just as the Scud, with its twisting sloughs, was better for trapping. Nothing came of the trade, however, since Dan remained the road foreman and his wife ran a small hotel in town; not for the Scotsman, either, who drowned the next year in his new territory while cranking his motor. That was the way it usually happened. The outboard would stall, and the man couldn't keep hold of the oars at the same time as he cranked. The boat swung into a riffle and swamped, and the river swept him under a drift pile, where it didn't make any difference if he could swim or not.

It's hard to elicit descriptions of the other people on the Chutine. Some were wanderers, always out after gold or hunting somewhere, living from hand to mouth on what they could get at the moment. Others organized their lives as a farmer does, raising a regular schedule of vegetables, which they canned for the winter, filling the potato house with potatoes and onions and salting away a winter's supply of fish. Since there wasn't a market, of course, it couldn't expand beyond subsistence farming. If the man didn't leave, he cleared more and more land and built more and more barns with the time on his hands, until by and by, he died.

Alec McPhee is a shorter, more ebullient man. He has blue eyes, yellow-silver hair and a red, toothless mouth, and he scrunches over his crossed knees like a boy, sniffs a breath in through his nose and stares boldly out of the window to see who's going to be coming past next. When he speaks, he shakes his head and his whole body shivers delightedly, because everything that he finds to say amazes and amuses him. He was the town's gravedigger; he was the carpenter and electrician; he was the powder man on the public-works crew whose job was clearing the river of snags. So he's a fortunate man, he says, never to have blown himself up or to have caught a fever from a corpse. When he was stringing wiring to the school from the government generator near the Mountie's house, he slipped on the icy steep slope, tangled the top of his hand in the spool and, although he was wearing mittens, lost only a single finger. Explain that good luck if you can. Never having married, he has an uncared-for, jumpy air that brings him cookies and stews from the widow next door and the nurse down the hill. He's an irresistibly blithe man, an urchinlike man. Apparently, he did approach marrying an Indian girl once, but in some way or other, she banged her head on the gunwale of the boat when they were down by the Iskut and fell overboard in a rapids and drowned.

In the winter of 1932, with a responsible job in the Prince Rupert area, Alec was out prospecting along the Nass together with a friend. It wasn't the right season for prospecting, but it was their only chance. They had a dog team and were having a lark, crossing into land new to them, Damdochax Lake, Muckaboo Creek. They kept postponing returning, and since Alec's brother already had gone to live in Telegraph Creek, all of a sudden, when they noticed that they were on the Telegraph Trail, they decided to forget the ties which they had and hike to the Stikine. This they did, potting game as they went and bumming tobacco from the relay men on the line. They had so much fun and poked up so many side creeks, dawdling along, that they were at it 105 days, all told. Not until 40 miles out of Telegraph Creek did they run out of snow. They simply packed the stuff that was left on the backs of the dogs. They couldn't stop, they'd grown so attuned to moving.

After seeing how Dan was, they went right on to the Jennings River country, which is 160 or 170 miles farther north, and back again. On Level Mountain (the historic hunting ground of the Tahltans) one spring night, sitting in front of their tent, they watched every imaginable sort of game cross before them: caribou, moose, deer, black and brown bear, mountain sheep, mountain goats, like a splendid parade, as if on display.

He was in his 40s by then. This lilting, long, weightless trip was just the latest of many for him, and as handy and busy as he was about town, he kept going out. He prospected to the Big Muddy River and the Turnagain River, 150 miles to the east, a rugged country of big boulders and scrub spruce where he saw not a soul for weeks, not even a Siwash—maybe a rusted old stove in a lean-to or a rotted deadfall. He wound back by way of Cold Fish Lake and the valley of the Klappan and the high source plateau of the Iskut. Another year, in the winter, he travelled northeast a couple of hundred miles to the Rancheria River in the Yukon where there was a strike—this the teeming caribou country, so every night, he was able to shoot one and camp right beside it, gorging himself and his dogs. When he went out in the fall, in some places, he hadn't been able to find a drink of water for miles, but next April, on the return, he could hardly struggle through the very same streams which had been dry, and in every half-promising creek, a man would be gophering with a shovel and sluice, throwing up sand. It amounted to working for wages, like other work, since each creek settled into providing a set rate of pay, which then diminished gradually over the years until it wasn't enough to live on, although the gold dust on the bottom continued to sparkle.

Alec's registered trapline was in another direction entirely, down by the Boundary on the Stikine, and included the Katete to its head as well as the first seven miles of the Iskut River. For years, he averaged as many as 100 beaver a season, each worth about $30, and perhaps 50 marten ($15) and 35 mink ($20) and 2 or 3 otter ($10) and 1 or 2 fisher ($75). He'd fish through the ice for rainbows and cutthroats and Dolly Varden, besides shooting a couple of moose. Down where he was, 10 feet of snow lay on the ground by February, and the moose endured by huddling in the spring-fed sloughs alongside the river, which didn't freeze over, or else under the thickest cover of spruce. Whenever they were forced to cross between sanctuaries, they were helpless, wallowing like an overstrained snowplough, leaving a mournful, deep trench exactly the shape of their bodies, whereas he ran lightly on top on his snowshoes. The wolves travelled the open ice where the wind scoured it bare. He used to see 12 or 15 at once playing on the sandbar across from him, big ones with little ones. Eight wolves, loping tightly in a pack like a gang of sled dogs, came up the river from the direction of Wrangell one day. He thought a friend of his was arriving to visit. Dirty and shaggy, they whirled into the yard and sniffed his two bear dogs, a unique and spindly little breed about the size of a terrier, developed by the Tahltans. The wolves didn't kill them, and when he clapped his hands, they turned and ran for the opposite bank of the river and got up in the woods and howled. Another time, in the spring, a grizzly got caught in a beaver trap and so tangled up in the willows, it didn't have leverage enough to break free. The willows were waving as though in a wind. John Creyke, who was staying overnight, went down and shot the bear with nothing more redoubtable than Alec's trapline .22.

Grizzlies are the gorillas of the continent, the man-of-the-mountains, of interest to everybody, but Alec speaks of all these animals and people with equal affection and gaiety, poofing his words out, laughing, nodding, shaking his head, recrossing his legs and swinging the top one, blinking and looking boldly out of the window. He says he's seen an eagle dive on a salmon and get taken under when the salmon sounded. He says the Siwash kids will be into his yard after his radishes as soon as they're up, and he just wonders whether he's planted enough for both them and him. When he was on the lower Stikine, he might not see man, woman or child for seven months in the year, unless maybe he snuck into Wrangell. It got a bit stiff toward the end, but it was the richest territory anybody had, and when you're alone, you keep busier. It's surprising the company a bunch of sled dogs is. He had a jovial four-dog team that could pull a quarter of a ton. In difficult snow, he'd break trail ahead of them, as when they went to his overnight cabin up the Katete. Once out of the coastal belt, though, running for home on the ice, he went 70 exuberant miles with them in a day — jogging behind the sled, jumping on, jogging again and jumping on. When he trapped, he had his summers off, except for being powder man; and when he was prospecting, if he made any money, he took the winter off, except for wiring and carpentering the town. He sold his furs to the local man, but his friend Gus Adamson preferred to ship to Montreal in hopes of a better price. One particular year, the bottom fell out of the market when Gus did this, so the catch he was offered $1,500 for in town had fallen in value to $900 by the time it got East.

Dan McPhee even prospected for sturgeon in some of the lakes. Since these can go over 1,000 pounds, it wouldn't need many to set you up. The Bear Lake Indians caught one very occasionally and kept it alive as long as they could, tied in the shallows, cutting steaks off its sides. Both McPhees have a smile they reserve for such antics. Dan's is ironic and civilized, and Alec's is curious and buoyant. Tired from my visit now, they both look like small hooligans, Dan rather trembly and drawn. His word for most people I ask about is "born locally," with a pursed smile, meaning illegitimately, but his smile means mostly that he wishes that he'd had a hand.

I love the town, with its up parts and down, its steep roofs, usually tin, so that they shine. The Anglican church is bread-brown, with a leaning steeple, high, miniature windows and a needlework-chiselwork interior. The river clips by in front in a channel of 300 yards, and graceful, swaying catwalks go out for disposing of trash. The old telegraph cabins are across from the Diamond C Café, and the Catholic church, a hefty log house painted yellow, is on the highest terrace. The school is out of sight on the bluff. The Tahltan Reserve, which is called Casca after a related tribe, is behind that, higher still, and is reached least strenuously by walking a mile up the draw which Telegraph Creek cuts through the bluff. On Front Street, by the river, besides the Anglican church, the Mounties' office and a row of weathered board houses where several Indian families live who have chosen to leave the legal shelter of the reserve, are the two stores. The lofty, immaculately red-and-white one is the Hudson's Bay store, and the other belongs to the traditional private trader in competition, who right now is a young Alaskan. Each has considerable traffic, and in each, the nurse has posted a list of the children who are late for their second Salk shot. The children are rounder- and flatter-faced than the Tlingits and a redder brown. They are louder, wilder, more hammery, from being so much farther off. They treat me to the Bronx cheer as I go by, they mock my stutter and range the town, climb the rock chimneys, which go giddily hundreds of feet up the bluff, run down the paths to the thickets along the Stikine and throw stones at the birds harder than children in Wrangell would. At the same time, they're shyer and more intrigued, studying me, asking my name. They flop into soft puppy piles on the grass, listening to an older child talk. As this is a thoroughly Indian town, they're at home everywhere, like the men, who are not defensive or grudging. And the girls have a yielding daintiness, a real doe-deer quality, along with the prettiness of the Tlingits.

June 11, Saturday: Next to Dan McPhee's is Ah Clem's old house, with a long green dogsled in the yard. Snowshoes hang under the eaves, as well as a packboard, a saddle, saddlebags, salmon nets. There's an easy chair, with a hide over it, and a dog on the porch that stands up very tall, its coat like a luxury fur. Ah Clem had many jobs — cook in the hotel, rock man constructing the orderly terraces. Also he fed the dogs in the summer, when upward of 200 of them were staked on the bank of the river, howling and yapping; he cooked up a gruel of salmon and grease and potatoes twice a week. He is survived by his half-breed son, a fat, sleek-haired man more Chinese than Indian in appearance, and by his grandchildren, who look more Indian.

Gus Adamson lives next and last, beyond Ah Clem's son. Since Alec McPhee went on pension, Gus has been the river snagger. It may be an office joke somewhere in Victoria that a person still exists who keeps the deserted Stikine navigable. Gus, however, thinks about scarcely anything else, between the paperwork and his troubles with crew. They complain because, in an effort to save the government money, he feeds them on rice and tapioca instead of on fresh beef and fruit, like McPhee used to do. He has two men to help him, and they make three 2-week trips to the Boundary during the season, blowing away obstructions. The boat is an old-fashioned longboat, infinitesimal alongside the bank as we look down on it. He's a sturdy, feisty, bald bantamweight, so remarkably small that he seems to be blown up like a balloon, the way small men by a process of inversion sometimes do. He's deaf now, has dental difficulties and a bright red complexion and is missing the central part of his nose. He speaks slowly, choosing his words, and he lives in a pocket-sized, shipshape house with a large, middle-aged Indian woman.

Perhaps so I won't meet her, we sit outside in an ancient car. He feels he hasn't been authorized to talk to me about the river and doesn't want to stay with me longer than politeness demands, but he's such appealing company, with his close-to-the-vest manner, that he's hard to let go. He looks in my eyes. Deciding there's something kindred in me, he says we could talk for a month about the river if he were authorized to. He arrived in Telegraph from the Peace River in 1935. After scouting around, he affixed himself on the Dease and Stikine as a river freightman and trapped in the winter between Great and Mud glaciers and the Porcupine — or, in other words, between Alec McPhee's strip of the river and the Callbreath family's. The man there before Gus had just drowned — Jack Fowler, who had prospected to Nome and to Dawson City and had carried the mail and done other glamorous things and was living with his second wife by this time, a strong-minded squaw named Annie, although he had waited too long getting started to leave any kids behind. Gus's prize year was in the late '40s, when in a quick 25 days, he caught 62 beaver. Recently, he built a new hut on the spot to sleep in when he snags down that way. He rubs his back; he's been having an old man's ominous pains. Small ear, big hearing aid, facing me. And that's all that he'll say.

In the afternoon, John Creyke's son is married. Creyke is the best hunting guide anywhere around and would be the leading citizen if he weren't Indian; as a result, there is no leading citizen. Since I'm too timid to invite myself, I take a walk along a sandy scratch trail above the river, with flowers and pretty ground pine. A rolling game country stretches 50 miles south to about the Scud, where the mountains fist up 9,000 feet. Coming back across a grassy range, I meet a loose troop of horses, which slide out of reach like so many fish, wheeling in a flat, careful curve as if they were tied head to haunch: insouciant, bonehead horses, sinister in the face. No wild animal looks any tougher. They have the corrupt, gangster faces of mercenaries and that tight herding instinct. A roan and a white do a little kicking, and when the roan yawns, all the rest catch the yawn. Incidentally, I understand that the fat horse I saw from the plane flicking his tail was completely alone and had wintered alone from last September, so he's lucky to have survived the wolves and the snows.

Can't get over the river. The gorge emphasizes its cutting power without hiding it, but it wiggles offstage right away. This is the one place it's looked at, but after a few working curves, it's gone.

I stopped at the Wriglesworths'. They live above Alec McPhee and next to Dan, on the other side of his house from Ah Clem's son. Theirs is a nonmorganatic marriage and an unambiguous one, so it's a pleasant glimpse after the pictures I've had of the wife going home to her relatives every afternoon after cooking lunch. Mr. Wriglesworth has a rather strange, biblical face, quite like Lincoln's on top, with a forehead like a furled flag under a shock of upright hair. He looks like the prophet who walks in front of a migrating people carrying a staff and as though his face were younger underneath the skin than outside, as if the deep lines had been cut from grinning more than from anything else, grinning at the bright sun more than at friends. Mrs. Wriglesworth isn't as prepossessing. At first, she seems like any well-meaning, shrunken-down woman from a farming community who has done her best all her life and done well yet has always worried a lot and never felt that her best was worth much. She ducks in and out apologetically, serving a marvellous home-brew beer which is as sweet as cider — I can't get enough. Her hair is a frumpy dab, her mouth bends like a bobby pin. "Don't tell him that," she interrupts. "He's not interested in that." She says that she never is favoured by such an outgush of words from her husband, so why am I? But she grows on one, what with the sweet-tasting beer and the smells of supper. The nagging turns out to be not nagging but only her end of a constant byplay. He's a witty man, and he's on her whenever she sheds a tear chopping the onions. He boasts to me about a world-record "broad jump" she made years ago, after she'd brushed up against a hornet's nest. "That's quite a surprise, when you turn around and you see your wife in midair, doing fine, when you never knew before that she could jump at all, even a little ways. There she is, taking off."

She has the knack of turning a bottle cap over by pressing on it with one finger, a delicate motion, using the pad. I practise as though we had a winter of long nights ahead. She's about 10 years younger than Mr. Wriglesworth, and they married in 1934, after he had already been on the river for 10 years. They met, in fact, at Groundhog Jackson's place, near the Grand Rapids, as it is called, and they settled on the homestead which Wriglesworth had established at the mouth of the Chutine. For a while, a tentative placer-mining operation was going on some distance up a tributary of the Chutine, where he earned wages on the "grizzly," which sorts the big nuisance rocks out of the sluice. Generally, though, they lived on what they raised and what he was paid for his furs. Beans, cabbage, turnips, potatoes, carrots, peas, squash, lettuce, tomatoes: everything grew. The thriving grouse were their chickens; they let the woods raise the chickens, and they ate snowshoe rabbits and a yearly moose or two. Each moose furnished 600 pounds of meat or more. It would get a crust on the surface but would keep through the winter in the cold. In the spring, they often ate beaver, which they enjoyed. The year-round utility food was salmon belly or salmon prepared in some other way. It could be dried and smoked, each fish being split into four parts and finally folded up again into its original form. This was what they fed their dogs and was the form that the Indians used, smearing grease on the fish to soften them up before eating them and sticking them up around the campfire like so many boards. The Wriglesworths also canned salmon or slimed them with brine strong enough to blacken a potato or else kippered them, which was delicious, the fish being soaked in a liquid mix of brown sugar and smoked salt and taken out, smoked and then rested and given a second smoking. They could net such great batches of salmon from June to September that really the only limit was how many hundred pounds they wanted to do the work on. They ate the young mountain goats, too — though with an old billy, you might as well boil up a stone — and the yearling black bears, tasting of berry fields, whereas a grizzly's meat was fishy and scavengerish.

Since the Chutine ramifies into a full river system in its own right, Mr. Wriglesworth had more of a trapping territory than he could use. Because the number of men who were still active declined to a tiny group, he got Shakes Creek and Yehiniko Creek as well, both tributaries of the Stikine, both about 25 miles long. Yehiniko has a lake at its head with mineral licks and the sheep coming down, and on Shakes Creek, where Chief Shakes made his last trading trips to meet the Tahltans, he counted 80 goats in a streaming, stretched-out band. Maybe three times a year, he went to Telegraph Creek, on the ice with his dogs or in his skiff. Otherwise, the purser on the riverboat, whose name was Dar Smith, would do errands for him and pick up the mail. During these brief stops, the various cooks on the boat gave Mrs. Wriglesworth some tea and some chat, and she went down to Wrangell to have her first baby. The second was due in the winter when the boat didn't run, so they went to Vancouver for that. They had several neighbours: the Dan McPhees, of course, at one time; and the Groundhog Jacksons; and the Clearwater Jacksons, no relation, whom she liked better. There was a Monkey Jackson living in Telegraph Creek, but this Clearwater was the unfortunate Jackson who brought a boatload of domestic goats into Wrangell one time and tied them under the pier and went into a bar for a drink. When he came out, the water had risen, and they all were drowned. The closest neighbour was old Kirk, two miles up the delta of the Chutine. He was a gentleman of the old school, a bachelor with an antiquated horse and a snow-white beard, and was a remnant of the Ninety-Eight Rush and of old Jack Fowler's generation. He couldn't hunt anymore, but he had about 20 acres that he had painstakingly cleared, which has vanished in jack pine now, and he lived pretty well from his land. Twice in the beaver season when Wriglesworth was away, Edith packed her children through three feet of floodwater to him.

They were all conscientious neighbours. There were no bushwhackers, no screwballs, no suicides. I walk around and around the experience with my questions, but I can't dislodge it from its naturalness. They made berry beer from soapberries and wine from the saskatoons. The children did correspondence courses in a regular regimen so that the son has gone whole hog lately and become a computer programmer. Even the bears were good neighbours. Once when Mr. Wriglesworth had fastened his canoe to a tree, which happened to be on a bear's trail, the bear yanked it out of the water by hitting the rope with his paw and then reassumed ownership by sitting down with his back to the tree and rubbing a swatch of bark off. And once when Mr. Wriglesworth had paddled 45 miles from his cabin to the source of the river near Chutine Lake, which has V-walls and icebergs tumbling in and a truly stupendous relief, he was leaning over, punching holes in the thin coating of ice which had formed along the bank. He couldn't locate several traps; although it was only a modest little stream here, it had risen two feet overnight. But he heard the ice breaking across from him. Feeling for a trap chain, he paid no attention until he noticed a grizzly wading directly his way. When he let go of the bank to drift downstream, the bear swam toward him convergingly. After he shot it, the body floated grimly ahead of his canoe for a long while. But these were two incidents in a life's residence on the river, a continual association with game. Except for shooting stew meat and beaver with a light gun, he'd go through the year using two cartridges, one for his first moose and one for his second.

The tumbling market in furs, as well as their children's needs, ended the Wriglesworths' tenure at last. He hasn't the stories of rambles like Alec McPhee's, but he used to see 30 moose at a time up on the Chutine where a fire had burned out the evergreens and let the willow and alder grow chest-high. As the different old-timers died or retired, the huge labyrinth of the Stikine itself belonged to him. He went down 90 miles to Great Glacier, where one side of the valley is a wall of green ice and the other side is hot springs, dammed by the beaver and surrounded by vegetation as in a botanical garden. It was a kind of exotic swimming hole, the water lukewarm. The steep, slippery clay banks made a slide. You'd slide in and splash and look up at the ice.

June 12, Sunday: A cold, sunny morning like November in New York. The town still delights me, its brown bluffs and tumultuously climbing green hillside across the way and hand-hewed, eloquent cabins spotted around. Saw Mr. Wriglesworth go by, with his patriarch's head and a springy, dignified step, a pack on his back, for a prospecting trip of three days.

I spoke with Mike Williams this morning. He's a husky old Indian on Front Street. He says that John Bull takes care of him now; his knees have gone bad. He has a booming, hoarse voice, a short nose, bushy eyebrows and a wrinkling smile under his eyes. He trapped the rich Iskut and Porcupine country with Fowler before Fowler died. He and Dora, his wife, would hike down in March with their boat on the sled and live alongside Fowler's house. One year, they cleared $7,000 between them, with Mike's two brothers. Mike remembers him from back in 1908, when Fowler was already old, and yet when he died, he was starting a mink ranch, spending the day fishing and cutting up fish. He didn't drown, as Gus Adamson said, because Mike found first his snowshoes stuck in the snow, then his hat and finally Fowler himself, "croaked," face down in a bank of snow. Apparently, after falling through the ice, he'd crawled out of the river and was trying to get back to camp before he froze. One winter when he was younger, his prostate gland burst, but he toughed that out and survived. And he spent an entire year alone on the Taku watershed, a large river system to the north, where he thought he was onto some gold. When he returned, he was batty and babbling; he was handing out gifts on the trail. He gave his shirt and snowshoes and shoes away to the Indians he met and gave them his samplings of ore and his fisher skins.

Mike remembers being told by his father how, during the months of the gold rush, people slept all over town, in the streets, on the woodpiles. His grandfather owned a farm on the Scud which might be worth $$$$ today because of the copper find, except that he let it go for back taxes one time when he was poor and sick. Mike grew up a trapper and hunter and says he likes sheep meat better than goat and groundhog better than beaver. Moose is tastier and tenderer than caribou, except in the spring, because caribou pick up their summer flesh quicker. He says the supply of furs partly depended upon how plentiful the rabbits were, although the coyotes came in with the rabbits and sometimes raised Cain with the furbearers. In a pretty fair winter, he might catch 10 wolverine, 20 or 30 marten, 50 or 60 beaver, 10 to 15 mink, maybe 30 fox, 2 or 3 otter and all the squirrels he wanted, although he didn't eat squirrels like some people did. He knows that long ago, the Indians used snares for everything, before they had guns, but he's never snared. He does speak the Tahltan language, however, because his parents spoke nothing else. When the rabbits are numerous, the salmon are not, and vice versa, so this is a salmon summer coming. His nets are coiled in a washtub in the living room while he works on them. The run of kings will begin very soon. Then the sockeyes begin to arrive in July and the cohos the first of September. He says you can see them break water where a creek empties in, jumping the obstruction of the current. You set your net in an eddy alongside the main flow. In the Sheslay River, which is north on the Telegraph Trail, you get salmon so big, you can't use a knife to cut their throat, you need a hatchet.

A neighbour drops by, a brawny, sensible man with a large face who, like Mike, is a great deal friendlier to me than I remember the Skeena Tsimshians being. The cabin is comfortably high-ceilinged. The walls are pink. There's a low sofa, a vase of wax flowers, a horseshoe over the door, a few Christmas bells tacked up from last Christmas, several mirrors around, a sack of Five Roses flour in the corner and a stove made out of a metal barrel. Three decorative paper balls hanging from the centre of the ceiling seem to be lights for a moment, but of course, they aren't. The talk turns to beer — the types of home brew, the commercial Old Style which we are drinking and the Over Proof that you get in the Yukon. There's a motto on the wall from the Alaska Highway:

Winding in and winding out
Leaves my mind in serious doubt
If the dude that built this road
Was going to hell or coming out . . . .

Dry Town is upriver from Front Street and considerably higher. It's a row of shacks on a giddy shelf over the river where not many families live anymore. The roofs have acquired a right- or a left-handed lean. Gap-runged ladders rest against them, which used to be employed in getting the snow off. The shingles have warped in the shape of fish scales and are patched with pieces of rusty metal. The windows are boarded up, and when one peeps through, the interiors are heaped with chests and trunks, as if a travelling troupe had lived in them. The dozens of holes under the porches, dug by the sled dogs, add to the same atmosphere. This was where a number of Indians moved when their ancient capital town at the junction of the Tahltan River was abandoned; it was the first of a series of anxious, aimless shifts and switches for them. Some of the houses are locked and in better condition, but the only person I ran across was a bloated and addled fellow, evidently feebleminded. The one dog there played with me as Indian dogs always do, quite as any pet might, except that he never actually ventured within reach. He acts out the fooling and fun, like a charade, not undoing it by trusting himself in anyone's mitts.

Dry Town was dry by law, of course. Across the river is another cluster of houses, newer-looking because the roofs are painted bright colours and the willow tops wave animatedly in front of the windows, where the Caribou Hide Indians lived from 1949 until three years ago. A village is being founded for them at an old campsite of theirs called Eddontenajon, at the head of the Iskut River. Before 1949, they had lived in total isolation at the head of the Stikine and Finlay, 10 days on horseback from Telegraph Creek. The Caribou Hiders were mostly Sikanni, a tribe of the Athapaskan family, and when they were moved close to town, they didn't mix with the Tahltans, as the government had expected they would. The Tahltans thought them backward and slightly dumb and silly. Their missionaries were Catholic, not Anglican, and before the age of the missionaries, the Tahltans ruthlessly lorded it over them. Under threat of death, they were not allowed near the Stikine, either to fish or to trade with the Tlingits and Russians. Appropriating their furs, the Tahltans doled out traps and gunpowder to them in dribbles just sufficient to keep them from starving, so they had been eager indeed to make the long move to the legendary river of salmon, with its white man's facilities. The trouble was that the moose close around had been hunted out, though they did find plenty of salmon, and the Tahltans were not enthusiastic to have them, and their missionaries were unenthusiastic about the Anglican Tahltans. So now, they have started again from scratch.

From a distance, overgrown as it is, it looks rather gay on the other side, not transient and dusty and scuffed like Dry Town. The trail down to the landing and the trail over the mountain to Eddontenajon and Caribou Hide and the forts on the Finlay River still show. According to Alec McPhee, the Tahltans said that the Caribou Hiders spoke "broken Tahltan." They ran up debts at the store, they were the bad guys, though nobody thought them so very seriously. In Hazelton, too, I remember a small band of interior Indians lived across a river canyon from the settlement of the Tsimshians. The name of their village, Hagwilget, meant "quiet people," and so little contact was maintained between the two groups that they only knew who had the best baseball team by comparing their scores against the whites' team.

Alec McPhee has unearthed a map of Fort Wrangell from the 1890s for me, including routes to the Klondike. It's full of bold speculations, distortions and bluff. Printed notes say "smooth trail here," "very rough country." The back is overspread with an excited pencilled diary about porpoises and bluefish killed on the lower Stikine and moose sighted and prospectors seen. Miner and cartographer are equally thrilled, but unfortunately, most of the diary is illegible; a magnifying glass would be needed. It's not his own, and one hears about so many diaries in a place like this, where time has stopped still, that I guiltily let drop the matter of finding a way to preserve it.

McPhee is bolt upright in his chair, holding his crossed knees and sniffing breaths in, twitching his head. When I ask for more stories of trips, he says that they were just wonderful trips, that's all — no disasters on them. He even brought a horse to carry the grub, so that all he had to do was to saunter along and enjoy himself. He says once he found a $5 nugget which had just the shape of the long-handled shovel that he'd dug for it with. A guy from Seattle in the next tent to his cleared out one night and cleared out with the nugget as well.

Have been lying down with a sore throat part of the afternoon but talked to the Anglican reverend a little. He's a tiny, struggling man with a hard-pressed, accentuated air. Being a veteran of six years in town, he has a strong glare-squint and rather a frontier stomp to his walk. He has a grating voice and a brave, lonesome smile. He carries a Kleenex in one hand and seems to be always dandling some phlegm on his tongue, as if to prove to himself that his cough doesn't frighten him. Having got past the bishop's visit and the Creyke family's wedding, he's greatly relieved at the moment. Last night, he played piccolo until very late at the wedding dance; it was one of his successes. He eats supper in the café for company, standing in the middle of the floor to be close to everybody and darting over to his place at the counter from time to time for a brief mouthful. Usually, he speaks of himself as "we," repeating the sentence once or twice in a lower and lower murmur, like a man who forgets that he isn't alone. He's a person of pugnacious judgements which revolve around each other. He respects the Indians and resents the outer establishment of cozy bishops and clever young men from the University, such as the two schoolteachers up on the hill. He lives in a wretched, flimsy mess of a house and tells me sternly that I probably pad my books and am a hypochondriac. We retire from front-line work like this and discover we haven't even a roof over our heads, he says, so he spends every leave driving back to his parents' old house in Saskatchewan, repairing the chimney and paying the taxes, though he isn't particularly fond of the place. He takes a couple of local kids along to show them a bit of the world, but it sounds like a desperado drive, like the nurse's month in Las Vegas every fall or the riverboat cook's voyages to Samoa.

The nurse is another lorn figure, a jittery, bombastic lady who stalks the streets with the martial haste of someone with nothing to do and the eyes of the village on her, as she supposes. This is her tenth year, and she's so abusive to patients that nobody goes to see her unless in extreme situations, when she turns about and becomes first-rate. If a baby in Casca goes into convulsions, she'll order in a government plane.

I haven't neglected my landlord, who's full of lore locked away, but he's elusive. He's recuperating from an ulcer operation, so he sleeps in the afternoon and the rest of the day is underneath one of his 1930s' trucks. He also has a vintage tractor and three vintage cars which he's picked up over the years from people who were leaving town. If we do exchange a word, he's under the chassis transferring parts and I'm squatting next to the running board. Although he's not as gentle a fellow as the captain, his son, he's a milder Callbreath than the grandfather was, the forceful Callbreath of 1874. He's a lean-knit half-breed with high cheeks, walnut skin and a delicate nose — he looks like a honed Indian. His lips are so swollen from the sun that he can't adjust them into an expression. They're baked into testimonial form or a sort of art form, like the curve of a fish backbone on a beach. His wife is the kindest woman in town. People call her Aunt Eva, which embarrasses her when it's a drunk stumbling in the café. She is always at work, and she reminds me of photographs from the '30s, with her sagging dresses and her wayward, meek nose. She cooks maternally and is indulgent in her gossip; strangers pretty well put themselves in her hands. Since there have been times when her husband hasn't been expected to live, they argue whether they should stay on. He wants to be here with his motors, and she wants to move to one of the cities where her children are.

The two patron families of Telegraph Creek were the Callbreaths and the Hylands. The Hylands were businessmen. They kept a store and married white women and managed their ranches tidily, rather than hurling themselves at the occupation. But old Callbreath married a native and plunged into ranching hard. He lived downriver 14 miles, on the far side. He tried to raise chickens and cows, in spite of the rugged climate, and kept a huge, milling string of horses which Roy spent his boyhood in the midst of. It was all work and no money, cutting hay, putting up shelters, provisioning the Telegraph Trail, and he got out of it as soon as his father died. The estate was a crosshatch of debts anyway. He liked trucks, not horses, tinkering, not business.

He doesn't know what to tell me. In so much wild country, there has only been one outlaw, and his era coincided with the First War. He was from Hazelton, named Gunanoot. When we were first here, my wife taught his great-grandsons in Sunday school. Callbreath describes Gunanoot as a pleasant-looking, short, popular guy who would turn up every once in a while to outfit himself at the Hylands' store. The alarm wasn't raised until he left town. He had a space the size of Minnesota to dodge about in and did trapping in order to pay back the friends who were keeping his family fed. It was emotionally punishing, however, going on for 13 years as it did, because the Mounties weren't able to catch him. He killed a white man who had assaulted his wife and was taunting him about it. A few hours later, he shot a second man, a friend of the other white man who was trailing him, but by accident, thinking that this was the same enemy and that he had missed. He didn't kill anybody after that, though the Mounties sent out harassing expeditions. He would often drop in on a big-game party for an evening's talk and to borrow some salt, and he appeared at the various trading posts on the Dease and Finlay — he would ask the factor what he would do if Gunanoot ever showed up. Some of the hardy prospectors helped him out, as did the Nass Tsimshians. At last, after such a display of long-suffering woodsmanship and civility, his side of the story was told. The Mounties agreed through his relatives that if he would only please turn himself in, they were sure he would be acquitted. Late in life, he was bitter about these years, but he was the guru young men came to see before setting out on the Telegraph Trail. A mountain was named after him (7,250 feet, with a glacier on it) in his stronghold, right at the mythical head of the Skeena.

June 13, Monday: A dazzly morning. It's like having a second language to be at home here. I'm a different personality. In the city, I overplan, I'm a worrywart, too punctual, but I came all the way to Wrangell after having been told that the boat was booked full and with no idea whether I would find anywhere to live if I did get upriver.

You can recognize the old residents like Callbreath and John Creyke by the cluster of vehicles which have accrued to them, a sign of their having survived. Creyke lives in an empty church, a high fiefdom at the end of Dry Town. A sleepy call answered my knock. I went in. The bed compartment in the corner was surrounded by a curtain of cheesecloth, and a woman's annoyed voice told me to "Pull it back. Pull the curtain!" When I did, there they were.

Mrs. Creyke is a bulky woman who looks as wise as a gypsy medium, as Indian women who have borne 14 children frequently do. She rolled over to go to sleep again, but her husband rose. He's a vigorous 60, quiet-spoken and tall, with thriving white hair, deep-set eyes and massive ears. He's the son of an itinerant, rich Scotsman who had many liaisons during a period of residence of several years. Some Britishers came to be Indian agents and trek through the bush, some to be officerly missionaries, but this one came purely for fun. Whenever his family sent money for a ticket home, he spent it all, until they had to enlist the assistance of the Hudson's Bay.

Being polite, Creyke rubbed his face awake. He said it was lucky he lived in a church, or he wouldn't have room for these wedding parties. He put on a pair of pinstripe pants and moosehide moccasins decorated with beads, and we sat at the edge of the bluff on two logs. Being used to fancy hunting clients from the States, he was doing the favour, simple and unbuttered-up with me. But he liked the sunshine — it was as though he were washing his hair in it with his hands — and the shimmying, wriggling river below. Occasionally, he has snagged for Gus Adamson, but he doesn't like this high water; he'd just as soon stay off the river entirely. Hunting has nowhere nearly that danger; hunting and game are everyday life. Laughing, he said he was old enough to start prospecting now. You fiddle around wherever you happen to have set up your camp and see if you stumble on anything — that's what they call prospecting. In the old days, he packed for the Callbreaths and Hylands as well as the outfit that Hudson's Bay had. He took supplies to Hyland Post, which is a 14-day trip with a string of 70 or 80 horses, nine days coming back unloaded. His trapping territory was more or less the same as where he hunts now: that is, to the east along the Klastine River for the 50 miles between here and the head of the Iskut River and including Ice Mountain, a broad dominant volcanic cone of 9,000 feet; then on another 20 miles over an intervening range to the Klappan River; and all the way up the Klappan to its source at Tumeka Lake; and up the fork of the Little Klappan as well, to its source at Gunanoot Mountain, which is 200 miles from where we are. He's been south to the Nass, which is farther than that, and north to the headwaters of the Yukon and west to the International Boundary and east into the Liard River system — one of the iron men, one of the princes.

As I have before with other people, I try to get Creyke to name a favourite valley in this gigantic ocean of heaped-up land almost too enormous to comprehend — some splendid retreat. But he doesn't respond. His conception seems to be very different. His own assigned territory is twice as large as Delaware, limited though he feels it to be. He didn't huddle somewhere in a lovely valley; he travelled through; he went everywhere. There was a range of mountains for hunting caribou and another for hunting sheep — maybe still another for goats. There was a river for salmon and a river for trout. There were rivers after these rivers and ranges after these ranges, uncountable vivid valleys that were a heaving, pelagic green. Once the knack was acquired, it was nothing to go for a month or the summer, lazing along as calmly as a long-distance swimmer, and never encounter an end.

Nowadays, everybody has shot their dog team, so if a boy wants to go out in the winter for moose, he borrows Ah Clem's son's dog and Dan McPhee's dog, Mike Williams' dog and John Creyke's dog and combines them. Sheep are the glamour game, because they live high and because they're high-strung. For some reason, goats don't look up, so unless you kick a stone down on them, you can stalk them successfully by getting above. But moose are the beef of the north, because you can eat the meat day in, day out. Sheep, even caribou, after four or five meals, you lose the taste for. Since nobody is trapping wolves anymore, they kill lots of moose calves in the spring. The cow will swim to an island in the middle of a lake where the wolves aren't as likely to go, but then a bear may swim over and find the calf hidden. Creyke has about 40 head of horses, who winter well, he says. The temperature on the range drops to 30 below, but the snowfall isn't excessive. They paw down to the grass, and their bells and their habit of herding tightly spook the wolves off.

Since I rousted him out of bed and since he has given me enough of his time, he goes indoors to wake his wife and get the breakfast fire going. He stands erect as a captain of industry, and although he can't read or write, he's the cosmopolite of the town.

The Hudson's Bay clerk is a frail functionary. For most of his life, he has switched about among isolated posts such as Telegraph Creek and has grown as pallid as a cave creature. Moveless, friendless, he does without either sun or company. And the one schoolmaster I've met appears to have been completely bleached out by the long winter. He played some chess with the Catholic priest but read very little. He's a zestless young man but does like the kids. He says they have good imaginations, if little or no curiosity to learn; he hammers the stuff into them. Says the parents get drunk constantly, as though they only existed for that, and the kids sometimes are neglected for days. It's interesting that the only antlers in town belong to him. It's so virginal here that game is still meat to everyone else, not a trophy.

They're a grim bunch, some of these institutional whites — the trudging pastor, the scolding nurse with her bobbed black hair, like a neurotic nanny, and the ashen clerk. The permanent people like the McPhees are wood sprites by contrast or else witty, mischievous oracles, like Mr. Wriglesworth. They *are* wood sprites. Nothing goes on, and yet the village is carbonated; it tingles. Blithe old codgers walk down the steps from the terraces, like Rumpelstiltskin. For an old trapper to have any neighbours at all is a luxury. The resilience, the self-sufficiency, overflows.

A.J. Marion isn't particularly like that. He was a versatile hobo, a cabinetmaker and carpenter, and he left Ontario for Detroit, then Rochester, then Jamestown, Virginia, where he helped build an exposition that Teddy Roosevelt opened. A pal and he flipped to see whether they'd go to New York or St. Louis. St. Louis won. Later, they proceeded to Seattle, where they were sitting around the union hall one time when the business agent came in and said jobs were going begging in Juneau. "Where's Juneau?" Of course, they went, though, and sitting around the bunkhouse in Juneau, they heard about the Stikine. They bought eight dogs, two sleds and a ton of grub and came up on the ice in 1913 (already, he was past 30). From Telegraph Creek, they went on for 150 miles into the Cassiar Mountains. The creek which they staked was barren, but they worked so hard that World War I had been on for almost a year before they heard about it.

Marion has a horrendous reputation in town; he bites people's heads off. His house is a level below Dan McPhee's, and although his door is wide open the whole summer, he's left to his own devices by the others. I was told that the early afternoon was the time to chance him, when he would have warmed to the day but not yet heated up. I found a hard-boiled, amusing, quick-memoried man who reminds me of a circus straw boss I once knew. He opens up to a silent listener. We got out the photograph albums of moustached friends and plump, self-effacing, half-breed women. Because he was a money man too, he talks about the rich scions who arrived on the riverboat to get drunk and hunt, the Mellons, the Schlitzes. A Smithsonian collector who was a crack shot with a .22 searched for bush rats. One squeak of his lips in the right location and out popped a horde. The Museum of Natural History in New York sent a man who gathered up buck brush and leaves to go with a family of caribou, along with an artist to draw the backdrop. The artist was so talented that at a dance that was held, he could sketch a couple circling the floor and present the picture to them before they passed him again. I told him the same museum has a Tsimshian war canoe 50 feet long.

Marion is the "hard" variety of bush professional, like my Hazelton friend Jack Lee was. There is a hard variety and a mild one, such as Alec McPhee or George Engelmann in Wrangell. It's a matter of style, not of prowess. You can visualize two men gutting a deer. One of them goes at it like a soldier who is stripping a foe, and the other rather resembles a woman poking through her purse, examining what it contains, although she knows what everything is. Marion operated a fleet of canoes and scows on the Dease River to Lower Post, as well as a bunch of wagons and trucks on the tote road between Telegraph Creek and Dease Lake. The Stikine then was a conduit to a vast interior area, before the Alaska Highway. Indians poled and paddled for him, and he managed a Hudson's Bay post on the lake, buying $18,000 to $20,000 worth of furs every year. Altogether, counting the take of the independents and the other Bay posts, $175,000 in furs used to leave Telegraph Creek in the spring. A village grew up around his cabin, and the small strike on Gold Pan Creek in 1924 provided a lucrative flurry for the traders like him, the pack-train men and the river men. For the miners, however, rushing into the country and paying through the nose, it was a dead loss. They found just another stream with a glittering name and too much gravel and too little gold. The village Marion started is a blank now, except for a single old Indian lady, a Mrs. Asp, who has chosen to stay by her husband's grave. Somehow or other, she kills a moose every year and scratches up a potato patch. She can only be reached by boat, and she is said to be past talking to, if indeed she is still alive. Nobody really seems to know.

His own wife is dead. His children's vacations are marked on the calendar, and he is waiting impatiently. As busy as they are with their families, maybe none of them will be able to come. It's a lonely wait, obviously — no telephone service — and he talks about quitting the Stikine. Except for the Anglican reverend, he's the loneliest man in town and the only person for whom becoming elderly is an ordeal. He has a sarcastic mouth, used to getting things done, and piercing blue eyes, bushy white eyebrows, a purple nose, which he rubs, and an energetic voice, and he sits here reading an old *Maclean's* magazine for the seventeenth time. He says he bought a ranch on Shakes Creek for his kids, built an oil house for fuel and a mouse-proofed grub house, both on the river, with the ranch house set back, which the bears have ripped through several times now. But nobody took the idea up; it's all gone to scrub and jack pine. He wears clean engineer's clothes, a railroad man's cap and little springs wrapped around his arms to hold up his sleeves. His stove and floor are polished to shine. He tells me about the spring cleaning he held — had a native girl in and supervised.

Edith Iglauer
from

Fishing With John

The next morning, we were up at six and fishing back and forth between Pearl and Watch rocks in wild surf, with many gulls following our boat. The fishing was wonderful; John caught four huge springs while I sat on the deck beside the fish box and watched. We were coming once again south-southwest, around behind the breakers at Pearl Rocks. The sun was high in the sky, and its rays shone straight down into the water.

Something felt different. The *MoreKelp* was surging forward, and the rumbling of the Gardner engine took on a heavier note. We're going too fast, I thought — much too fast for trolling. I leaned over the side to see why. Jagged peaks in the water below us were so clear that I gasped. Just then, the Gardner seemed to die; my heart stopped. Terrified by the stillness, I looked up just in time to see all the fishing lines drop straight down into the tide boiling over the rock piles into which we were heading. What was wrong with the Gardner? Why had it stopped in this awful place? I stared at John. His face had that intensity that it got whenever he was fishing dangerously. He had one hand on the wheel while he looked over the side at his lines. The amazing thing, I thought, was: we are going to pile up on the rocks, and John doesn't seem to care. He straightened up again, looking — it was hard to believe — blissfully happy.

The quiet — so very quiet — lasted an eternity. The boat swayed, pushed by the swirling currents, and I thought: Here we go!

Was that sound the Gardner speeding up? Yes! I could hear the engine's rumble over the roar of the surf. Thank God! I was standing up now, clasping the chain rail, staring at the breaker, expecting to crash. I looked around at John. He was grinning as he made a slow turn to starboard, into quieter water. I looked up at the port pole tip; its spring was moving violently. We must have caught a fish. He shouted, "Did that scare you? Hold tight. We're going to do it again!" And he did; and once again after that. Each time, the sound of the Gardner was reduced to a whisper. Each time, I found it hard to breathe until I heard it start to grumble again.

"That's it. The tide has changed again," he said finally. We continued north along the west coast of Calvert Island while, for the second time that morning, he was washing gorgeous huge springs, all mildcure, that he had caught. I sat down on the edge of the fish box and said, "Please. Please explain to me what you were doing, so I don't die of fright the next time the engine nearly stops in the middle of fishing so close to rocks. I thought we were in real trouble."

"I can only make this manoeuvre if the tide is right, on the flood for Pearl Rocks, when the sun is shining right down into the water and I can see those horrible bloody peaks clearly," he said and laughed. "It's hair-raising all right, but I catch my biggest springs when the tide eddies behind the rocks like that. What I did: I turned and headed for two landmark peaks with the sounder showing 12 fathoms, and I kept opening up and opening up the poor old Gardner until we were going six knots, putting on that speed to keep the gear up," he explained. "Then I suddenly throttled the engine down to dead slow so the gear could go straight to the bottom and hang behind the rock, where the fish were lying in the eddy. From their point of vision, the lines are surging forward like living food, and the springs start up and follow the lures and strike at them. It's a way of getting lines down into holes and

243

crevasses, and a wonderful trick, as long as the motor is dependable. Otherwise, you're on the rocks, and the gear is tangled and full of junk." He leaned over and patted my hand, which was gripping the guy wires. "You have to know what you're doing," he said. "So far, the Gardner has been good to me."

John had been predicting a southeasterly gale ever since I washed the windows, and now, the sky was overcast. "Fishermen are like farmers — always looking at the sky in relation to the land to see the speed and direction the clouds are moving from," he said. "We watch them all the time for any change. You can see the top clouds going like hell, and that means it's blowing upstairs and eventually going to come down. If you see a black streak coming along fast — sometimes as fast as 35 miles an hour — go find someplace to hide. I watch the weather *all* the time."

He threw out the gear again at a place called Dublin Point with the remark, "We sometimes get a spring here." He caught another 12 salmon — a mixture of smaller springs and coho. The sky was filled with threatening black clouds, so we ran into a good harbour.

Early the next morning, we heard on the radio that the fishing strike had started. For once, we actually sat down to a leisurely breakfast of scrambled eggs, bacon, toast and coffee, before we went through Hakai Passage to Namu. I was washing dishes when an enormous ground-swell sent the frying pan on the counter crashing to the floor. Meanwhile, John was heating water in the pail on the stove to wash down the hatch after he delivered his fish. "I don't like B.C. Packers, but I certainly am grateful for Namu, because it has helped so much to keep the fleet fishing," he said. "If you have to have something fixed, like a radio or a winch, they'll have you in and out in a day there, rather than several days to a week someplace else. It's a far better and cheaper spot to be broken down, with a machine shop at the float. Namu has many quiet floats and a few horrible lights, while Hardy is now a *blaze* of mercury gelo lights. I sure do like Port Hardy best for selling my fish. Both the Hardy and Namu plants are union, but Seafood Products at Port Hardy is a small company and a lovely atmosphere, plus a good employee situation. On the other hand, there's no logging at Namu, no road and no winter population; also no appalling marine traffic jams. It's easy and convenient to work out of Namu, and social life is a blank compared to Port Hardy, which means that for me, it is 100 percent less exhausting because there's *room*. There's no choice to shop, a lousy company store and no liquor store, but there's *room!*"

We arrived at Namu at 10:30 a.m. to sell the fish we had caught before the strike. We were the second-to-last boat in. The whole fleet must be here, I thought; I had never seen so many fishing boats tied up in one place, five and six deep. The tops of the trollers' upright paired poles made a fine design of thin vertical lines above float after float; the air was thick with them. In among the trollers, which I would naturally notice first, I slowly began to pick out massive drums with nets wrapped around them and high curved decks of towering seiners. Even though I disliked seiners, because they swept up all the fish in whatever area they set their nets, in my pre-*MoreKelp* days, they were my idea of what fishing vessels should look like. I loved the majesty of their lines and size. They were so big that they dwarfed neighbouring gill-netters, whose smaller drums were like toys beside them.

John got his southeasterly gale as we were turning to go to the cannery. The clouds opened, and rain streamed down on us as we tied up at the unloading dock — a wall of concrete from where I stood. A wire ladder was swinging from the top; it could not have threatened me more if it had been a grizzly bear. A head appeared above it over the side of the dock, and a young Chinese shore worker called down to John, "Do you want me to put your name down on the board for the lineup? You'll be number 11."

John shouted back, "Yes, thanks." As he pulled off his wet Stanfield's and hung it over the stove, he said to me, "We wouldn't be able to fish anyway in this weather."

We sat down in the pilothouse to await our turn to unload, and a large black bird arrived outside on the gunwale and stared at us. John took a wooden whistle from the shelf over the sink, leaned out the window and blew it, producing a cawing noise: "Gaak gaak." The bird looked around and listened intently as John continued to make crow calls, watching him until it must have decided he was some kind of a crow too, responded with a firm "Gaak" of its own and flew off. John put the crow call away and said, "I have to stay here to move the boat, in case our turn comes. Will you run the mail up to the main office while we're waiting here? One of the pilots from the small airline that services Namu will be coming in on his regular schedule and can take it with him."

"How do I get up there?" I asked nervously. But I knew the answer. I had already counted the rungs on that ghastly ladder between me and the top of the dock. There were eight.

When I lived with John, the first attempt at anything unfamiliar was like stepping off a high diving board. I usually improved with repetition — except with swinging ladders. My trusty new ladder had three steps and lay firmly against anyplace to which it could be attached. The long ladders at the fish-plant docks at low tide were dangling, shivery structures; as I looked up at them from below, they disappeared into the sky. Fish docks on concrete pediments or creosoted pilings seemed to be especially high above the water and were weighted down with ponderous derricks, winches and heavy ice-making machines. All this weight probably required the reinforcement of the heavy beam edgings that stuck out. When I climbed up or down their ladders, I had to swing out in space around these beams at the very top and scramble over them without being able to look at my feet. All I could do was pray that they would land on the next rung.

I can still recite the list of B.C. dock ladders that scared me out of my mind: at the government floats in Port Hardy, on Texada Island and at Namu. The worst one, which plagued me all our life together, was below the ice chute at the Campbell Avenue fish dock in Vancouver. In the spring and fall, when John fished near home and made a 6-to-10-hour trip (depending on the weather) in the boat to Vancouver to sell his fish, we would go to Campbell Avenue dock, unload our fish below the headquarters of John's favourite fish buyer, Norman Johncox of Billingsgate & Co., and then move under the ice chute to be first boat to take on ice when it opened at 5:00 the next morning. We would set off for home as the sun rose, gliding in the quiet of the early morning under the graceful span of the Lions Gate suspension bridge, which connects the municipalities of West Vancouver and North Vancouver to the business centre of the city of Vancouver, and on into the open water of Georgia Strait, crossing Howe Sound, with its rim of snowcapped mountains off the starboard bow.

The first time we went to the Campbell Avenue dock together, after we had finished selling our fish, John wanted to take me out for dinner to his favourite restaurant, the On-On, in Vancouver's Chinatown. I stood on the deck of the *MoreKelp* facing the black oily pilings, looked up the 30 or 40 feet — it might as well have been 100 — of ladder swinging from the overhanging ledge of the dock above, looked down at the garbage floating in the water below and said to John, "No. You go out to dinner and tell me about it. Or bring me some."

"Nonsense!" John said, disappearing into the pilothouse and coming back with a coil of heavy rope in his hand. He tied one end around me under my arms. Then he ran up the ladder, paying out rope along the way. At the top, he stood on the pier, holding his end, and instructed me to start climbing. "I'm right here holding on to you," he called down. "Nothing can happen to you, with me at the other end." I felt like a dog on a leash, but up I went. When we returned home that night, he tied my leash around me again, stood at the top, helped me get on the ladder over the terrible edge and slowly paid out the rope as I descended, so that if I fell, as I told him later, we would both go into the water. If anyone else was awake when we returned to our boat late at night after a social evening in Vancouver, we must have made quite an impression: me descending on my leash, John standing at the top, paying out rope and encouragement.

At the Namu dock, John ran me up the ladder on my leash, and I delivered our mail, wrapped in the usual plastic vegetable bag, to B.C. Packers' front office. I stopped on my way back at the company store to buy some groceries: a weary head of lettuce, two bananas, eggs and milk — as little as possible when I saw the food prices.

As I came out on the dock, a handsome young woman with red hair in braids wrapped around her head ran up the ladder — how I envied her! — and stepped out on the top of the dock not far from me. I had noticed her earlier on the deck of the troller called *The Venture*, just ahead of us in the lineup, which was now unloading its fish. Her husband was standing below beside their open hatch, whose huge cover was laid back on the deck, guiding the pails that swung down on the winch into his hold, where a young boy was loading them up with fish. She ran over to the sorting table as the fish were brought up and dumped there from the pails and then followed them to the weighing platform, making notations on a small pad she was carrying. I was impressed. I thought: If I am going to be of any use to John, I had better do this too. John, in his oilskin rain gear — waterproof overalls, coat and hip boots — was busy down in the hold throwing out the fish blankets on the deck. "If she can climb up to this dock, I can go down from it," I muttered. With my heart beating right up in my throat, I moved slowly down the ladder, without my leash, my grocery bag swinging from my arm. Hand over hand, gripping the wire sides of the ladder so tightly that my knuckles were white, I descended, feet groping from space to space, until they set down, as if they were independent of my head, on the solid planking of the float beside our boats. I climbed into our boat, dropped my groceries into the sink and ran over to the open hatch. "I'm going up to watch over your fish," I yelled down to John. I climbed up the ladder and learned something about myself: If I absolutely had to go up or down a ladder without John and the rope, I could. Exception: Campbell Avenue.

When our turn came to unload, I looked over the side of the dock at John, who had stopped scrubbing pen boards to move the boat forward. The young boy came aboard and began loading the descending buckets with fish from our hold. When the first bucket was hoisted up, overflowing with our salmon, which hung over the edges haphazardly, a youth at my level above grabbed it, opened a latch at the bottom of the bucket and slid the fish out onto a wooden-slatted platform, sorting the salmon into species and dumping them into square metal wagons big enough to hold 700 pounds.

The rain was coming down in such a torrent that I could barely see through it, dripping down my face and off the end of my nose. To escape the downpour, I walked into the shed behind the wagons holding our fish and stayed while they were being graded. A young man with a red beard was standing against the wall observing, so I went over beside him. He was a biologist from the University of British Columbia, working for the summer as a fish sampler in a hatchery recovery programme. "As the salmon are brought up, I watch for salmon tags, either an internal nose or adipose-fin clip. If the salmon has that tag, we want that information for federal Fisheries," he explained. "It's part of a 10-year study that takes in the area from Prince Rupert to California, to show the intertwining of American and Canadian fish: who catches the fish and the distribution. We can tell the number of fish Canada is catching, and vice versa. The tags give the brood year, whether it was a fall or spring run, where the fish was let go, how old it was and its size. All five Pacific salmon species are a little different: they spawn in fresh water but live in salt later, and some spend a year in a stream, some in lakes, some in the ocean. You can even tell the rate of growth from the scale samples we take: they are like the rings on a tree."

When I went outside again, the rain had stopped. I looked over the edge of the dock. John was just pulling away to let in another troller. I saw the *MoreKelp* go out of the unloading area, and then I watched the distinctive diamond-shaped metal piece at the top of our port trolling pole travel around through the thicket of stationary poles until it stopped moving. I had come back too late to go down the ladder; thank God. I set out on land in the general direction the boat had taken, over to the float area, where all the fishing vessels were tied up, and walked up and down the maze of floats until I saw John. He was leaning over the chain rail of our boat, which was on the outside, talking to a shorter man whose vessel was between us and the float. The other man looked so much like John Chambers — except that he didn't wear glasses, he had less hair and what he had was whiter — that I wasn't surprised when John introduced me to Chambers' younger brother, Jimmy.

"We're just leaving for the union meeting. Come along," John said, so I followed them from the float along a path to a marine ways. Men and women of all ages, sober-faced and quiet, were sitting on top of and beside a gill-netter, up on the ways for repairs, and on the rails used to pull up boats. The dampness of our surroundings, the greyness of the day, where only a thread of yellow peeping out from the dark clouds across the sky hinted at the existence of a sun, accentuated the gloom of the occasion; all present would lose a sizable part of their year's income in a strike of any length at the height of the fishing season. I sat in a kind of daze at this twist in our fishing life — unexpected by me but apparently a relatively common occurrence. A steering committee for Namu was elected, and contract terms were discussed. "No one-year contracts; let's make it good enough to last two years," someone said, and there was a buzz of approval. I was barely listening, recalling something I had heard on the float, on my way to find John. I had passed two young fishermen, and one was saying, "If the strike goes on, I don't know what I'll do about the payments I owe on my boat. I can't get any unemployment insurance, I have a wife and kids, and there won't be any jobs. God, I stopped drinking, and now this!"

At the end of the meeting, on the way back to our boats, I listened to John and Jimmy talking about exhaust pipes. I was surprised again and again at the intricacies of fishing revealed in ordinary conversation; and exhaust pipes, which I had never thought about at all, were no exception.

"My exhaust pipe used to rattle so that I could never catch any fish," Jimmy said.

John replied, "I've always had mine hanging from the inside with big springs."

"Well, that's what I'm doing now, and I'm fishing real well," Jimmy said.

When we arrived back at Jimmy's boat, to which we were tied, John said, "We call these floats the Toonerville Docks. Probably the name came from a newspaper comic strip in which everyone sat around and did a lot of talking." Jimmy's troller, the *Kitty D.*, had a small wheelhouse abovedeck — big enough for one person to sit down in and from which Jimmy steered. The wheelhouse contained the VHF and Mickey Mouse radios and a sounder, switches for all the wiring behind the seat, including a light for the engine room below, and an instrument panel that showed all the engine gauges. His living quarters were in a trunk cabin underneath. "All the fish boats used to have sleeping and eating quarters below like this," John explained. "The *MoreKelp* was the first fishing boat in our harbour with a big pilothouse containing all that you needed abovedeck, and everyone came around to see it. I find it much better when I'm fishing alone — especially when I have to get up suddenly to move the boat or in any kind of bad weather. When I slept below, I could never get proper rest. I was always worrying about what I couldn't see that might be happening outside."

"I've never known anything else but this, so I'm quite comfortable with it," Jimmy said as he went ahead of me down three small carpeted steps into his cabin. It had simulated-brick linoleum on the floor, a little wooden table that folded flat against the wall and, behind it, eating utensils, glasses, jelly, spices and other staples. The bench I sat down on had storage lockers underneath, and I faced a small stove whose oven had an indicator that I envied, since I had to guess at the heat of ours. Jimmy's stove was under the wheelhouse close enough to where he steered for him to reach down to it from his seat. There was a little sink with a tiny pump, and towels and dishrags hung from green-and-white-painted racks attached to the ceiling. Jimmy's pocket watch was fastened around another rack on the wall.

At the bow were two bunks, one coming from either side; whoever slept in the lower one would have his feet right under the other bunk, with only inches to spare. I thought, I would stub a toe every time I kicked off the covers, and appreciated my own bunk as I never had before. I heard music and discovered a radio on the far side of the stove, toward the stern, along with batteries, fuel tanks and the engine, which was below the wheelhouse. I knew there was a small closet with a toilet, or head, tucked away somewhere, although I didn't see it. Portholes along the sides, a skylight in addition to a ceiling light, a tiny electric fan and the curved shape of the cabin, which occupied the whole forward area below, somehow blended with the other furnishings to make a snug atmosphere. Our pilothouse seemed to lack that homeyness, perhaps due to its long, skinny shape — more probably because there was no truly comfortable place to sit down.

Fishermen in Namu could have their meals at the cookhouse for a small fee during the short thrice-daily period when it was open. John said the meals were excellent, and it would be a change from cooking on the boat. We invited Jimmy to join us, and we all climbed over into the *MoreKelp* to have a drink outside while we waited for the supper hour. John unfolded the deck chair and sat down in it, Jimmy settled on the hatch cover and I on my foam-rubber cushion to enjoy the late-afternoon sun, which had unexpectedly come out. The men talked about the strike, and I listened.

When we came back from dinner, John untied our lines from the *Kitty D.*, and we left. "I can't stand the noise and all those other boats," he said. "We're going to Boom Bay."

It was like hopping in a car to go around the corner. John had barely started the motor and moved out into open water when we were going through a narrow opening between rocks and trees into a small inlet — Boom Bay.

While John tied up to a decaying, half-sunken dock, I looked around. We were parked in a graveyard of old floats and fish-camp buildings that John said B.C. Packers was storing along the beach around the bay. The background, trees high enough to melt mistily into the lowering clouds, was a deep blue-green, and the water around us was very black. Fallen logs littered the shore and floated around in the murky water. The greying light vanished without giving us a glimpse of anything so cheerful as sun or even a few of its rays.

John came in, and I was about to tell him this was one of the most depressing places I had ever been, when he said, "Namu is not really a harbour. It's too open. The word 'Namu' means 'whirlwind' in the language of the neighbouring Bella Bella Indians. It blows so in winter in Namu and there is so much wave action that B.C. Packers moves almost all the floats from there to here and doesn't put them back where you saw them until spring. I've been coming to Boom Bay to anchor for years. Our own name for it was Bachelors' Bay because of the number of bachelors, before the days of unemployment insurance, who lived here in float houses — regular houses, built on floats, that can be towed from place to place. They would fish in summer, go to Vancouver in the fall, and around Christmastime, they would come back and do their spring overhaul of their boats. In those days, it was a cheap place to live. There were always from two to five float houses here and lots of crabs to eat."

John poured himself the customary shot of Scotch that marked the shift from his preoccupation with the day's work to his preparation for dinner and bedtime. "Oh, this place brings back memories," he said, sitting down on the steering seat. "Very few people know about Boom Bay now, but in the late '30s, they were all here: Bob Merkle, Alec Gow, Walter Wright. If you needed to do last-minute rigging up and work on your poles, they always had a planing bench; one had a drill press, another had a band saw, and among the three of them, they had a wonderful collection of old pieces of pipe, hose and generally useful junk that all fishermen need. As a youth, Bob Merkle had drifted down the Mississippi River with another kid, and they used to steal chickens that a black woman would cook for them. He used to say, 'Boy, oh, boy, *that* was chicken! I'm talking about *chicken*, not these goddamn frozen seagullies we get now that are not fit to eat,' and he'd roll his eyes back so far, the pupils would disappear. He also had trapped all through the Northwest Territories, and once, he told me, he had gotten a thousand dollars' worth of furs from an Indian on condition that he come back and marry his daughter." John pulled the stool down and stretched his legs across it. "Bob said, 'I never did get back, but I always wondered what she was like.' Then there was Walter Wright, who had a little gill-netter. That was probably not his real name, because he was French. I *loved* his French accent. He had huge eyebrows, always wore a woolly tuque, smoked a huge meerschaum pipe and was a wonderful cook. On harbour days, he would call to me, and I would row over. There would be a marvellous smell of cooking, and he would be drinking gin and making pies. And Alec Gow. He was an extremely kind and cheerful man. Two old people, Joe and Agnes, lived in a float house near here; they were a real love story. Joe was Irish, and Agnes was a Rivers Inlet Indian. They fished, and she taught Joe to trap. Alec was always taking their mail to them and their old-age pension cheques. When Agnes became very ill and Joe was exhausted from taking care of her, Alec took them to hospital. He brought them home again, and they toughed it out on the float another four months, until Agnes died. Then someone towed Joe and his float house down here. His son flew up and tried to get Joe to leave with him, but he wouldn't. The manager of the cannery used to pop in, but he was busy, and Alec looked in on him, but he'd have to go again. Joe lasted only two weeks after Agnes; he died of grief and exhaustion."

"And Alec?" I asked.

"All, all gone," John said. "Alec was fishing and lay over at Goose Island for a week in a sou'easter one August and had a very bad stroke. He had a friend with him who got on his phone to the other boats at Spider Island camp nearby, and they sent an airplane for him, but it was very rough, and Alec was so heavy, they couldn't get him into the plane or even on the pontoon. They put him in his bunk on his boat and towed him back to Spider, where they did manage to get him on a plane. He lasted only three days, fortunately. Lack of exercise on the boat, I think, did it."

Robin Skelton

Cat Creek

I wasn't so much wandering that summer as drifting. I had it in mind to explore the interior of British Columbia and, while doing so, take a few photographs and maybe write something or other. I told myself it was research, but it was, in reality, a holiday, and I was enjoying it very much indeed, moving from place to place whenever I felt like it or the weather changed or a faint stirring of conscience told me that exploration consisted of more than spending the day driving around back roads and the evenings sitting in beer parlours. The beer parlours were, in fact, the most interesting part of my experience. After all, 20 ruined cabins add little more to the stock of human knowledge than two or three, while in the beer parlour, there was usually some old-timer willing to tell improbable and garbled tales and to hint of lost gold mines, hidden caches and sometimes even undiscovered murders.

It was in one such beer parlour that I met an old-timer who particularly interested me. He was, or had been, a Yorkshireman and was about as old as the century. He had come over from England in the lean years of the late '20s, drawn by stories of gold, and had indeed worked as a placer miner and in the Bullion and other mines before settling down to being a ranch hand. Like many Yorkshiremen — and Irishmen and Scots too, for that matter — he had retained his original accent, though it was somewhat flavoured with Canadian terms and expressions. One such expression caught my attention particularly. We were sitting together in a corner of the beer parlour, watching a large young man, rather loud in the voice and even louder in his shirting, buying drinks for a party of friends and acquaintances and talking of his plans to go back to university in the fall and how great it would be. He played some sort of game, I gathered, and hinted, if comments made at the top of one's voice can ever be called hints, that he had received offers to "go professional." The old-timer looked him over sardonically. "Ah," he said, "he's taking gold from Cat Creek, that one is!"

It was an expression new to me. I said, "What do you mean?" "It's a thing they used to say," he told me, "in the old days up Likely way. Taking gold from Cat Creek! Aye!" and he chuckled. "There's a story about Cat Creek?" I hazarded, waving a finger to get more beer, and he said slowly, "You could call it a story, I reckon." I knew by now that there was no use putting the question direct, so I took a pull at my beer and waited, and he took a pull at his. "It was around '31 or maybe '32," he said at last. "This chap had a little place a bit from the lake, a good-sized cabin, and he was well suited with it. He'd been placer mining, had done well with it and then retired, you might say. He wasn't old, though. About 40. Young, really. Maybe that was the trouble." I sat in my chair, and gradually, with many small digressions, he told the story.

He explained that the man, who was known generally as Black Joe, though his actual name was James Weatherby, had got his nickname not only because of his black hair but also because of his disposition. He was one of those saturnine creatures who could not bear to give any-one a civil word, and he was inordinately proud of the cabin he had built, of the small garden he had made beside the little creek and of the neatness of everything in his establishment. He had been, like many miners in those days and earlier, a merchant seaman, and the obsessive neatness that seems to become part of the character of many sailors used to living in small cabins, where everything must have its proper place, had become part of his character also. He was a proud man (turkey-proud, the old-timer said) and the more so because his cabin was unlike any other in the country, in its spit and polish and in its garden. The garden was indeed very attractive. Unlike the majority, he had chosen to make a flower garden rather than one for vegetables, and in order to defeat the long winter, he had even constructed a small glasshouse (a greenhouse, the old-timer called it), which he kept heated with a stove. He'd planted a lot of bulbs on both banks of the little creek that ran through his property. The creek had a name, an Indian name, which meant something like "hurrying water that runs shallow" — it was a very small creek — but naturally, it was generally known as Black Joe Crick, though he called it Weatherby Creek and tried without success to get the name on the maps. Though Black Joe's cabin was set back a good way from the lake and fairly isolated, there were a good many people wandering the area in those days, most of them either prospecting or looking for work, so he sometimes had visitors, whom he invariably made totally unwelcome. He was the kind of man that keeps a dog to chase visitors away, but he didn't have a dog, because dogs dig in gardens and bury bones and generally cause untidiness. He was a very tidy man.

One day in the summer of '31 or '32, another man moved into the country and took up a place on the same little creek, only higher up, and built a cabin there. He was an Irishman, and he was working in Bullion. He had a good job there, but he didn't like living near the mine, so he built this place for his wife and himself. He was called Red Connolly because he had bright ginger hair, and what is more, his wife had ginger hair too, of that vivid kind that you see sometimes in Ireland among the travelling people. As if two lots of ginger hair in the house were not enough, they had a big ginger cat, a huge thing. It must have been almost the only cat in the district. People didn't go in for cats much round there in those days, at least not outside the larger settlements and the ranches. Anyway, this great cat was a wanderer and spent a lot of time roaming the bush and even more in sitting by the creek. It used to take a drink by dipping its paw into the water and then licking it. It had huge green eyes and the sort of tail you'd see on a fox, big, bright and bushy.

Black Joe and Red Connolly didn't get on at all well. For one thing, when Red Connolly was building, all sorts of debris would come floating down and often beach on Black Joe's land where there was a bend in the creek, and for another thing, Red Connolly's wife played the harmonium, and the two cabins weren't so far apart that Black Joe couldn't hear *The Wearing of the Green* and *Finnegan's Wake* coming at him through the trees, which irritated him to the point of frenzy. He'd been in the Black and Tans after World War I and had no love of the Irish. He himself came from Ilkley in the West Riding of Yorkshire (the old-timer pronounced it Ilkla), where there was little singing in the pubs except on Saturday nights and those devoted to music took it out on Handel's *Messiah* once a year around Christmas. All this, however, was as nothing to the irritation caused by the cat. In the early morning and evening, when it felt a natural urge coming on, it would sneak down along the bank of the creek to the softest and most accommodating piece of earth for its purpose, which was Black Joe's garden, and there, after performing its functions with healthy thoroughness, it would scrabble the earth over the deposit with such zeal and energy as to uproot bulbs and smother new shoots. Occasionally, it would thoughtfully urinate over one of the most promising spikes of green. Its attraction to green may perhaps have been due to the Irish in it; who can tell?

Black Joe cursed, threw things and generally tried to make life difficult for it, but that ginger cat was the match for any man, and Black Joe found himself spending more time than he liked not only tidying up after the cat but also picking up the things he had thrown which, in truth, often did more damage than the cat had done.

This could not go on forever, obviously. One morning, Black Joe rigged up a snare near one of the most promising of his plants and sat in the cabin waiting for the evening visitation. It all occurred just as he had hoped. Just as the dusk was deepening into dark, he heard a great yowl and ran out and found the cat snared by the back leg. He didn't want to make a mess by clubbing the beast, so he got a sack out of the glasshouse and a few stones, tied the cat in the sack, along with the stones, and dumped the thing into the creek, just at the bend where there was a deep bit. Then he went to bed. He had a restless night, it seems. That yowl kept on coming back to him in his dreams, but as it gave him more satisfaction than anything else to recall his victory, he wasn't too disturbed.

The next morning, he went down to the creek, reclaimed the bundle and took out the dead cat and buried it in his compost heap. Then he laid the sack out to dry in the sun and put the stones back on the rockery he was making under the cabin window. He was a very neat man indeed.

It wasn't long before Red Connolly's wife came down by the creek to enquire after her cat. Black Joe was unusually polite. He said he hadn't seen the cat, and he'd keep an eye open for it. He said it might have got caught in a trap. He wasn't a good liar. The woman looked him over and told him that if that cat didn't turn up, she'd know who to thank for it and that he'd come to regret what he'd done. She was a tall woman, big-boned and with one of those white, freckled faces that go with red hair, and that morning, her face was so white, the freckles stood out like little spots of brown fire. Red Connolly himself did and said nothing. It looked as if the incident was over, though the tunes the woman chose for her harmonium that day and the following days were more mournful than usual, even a little eerie. They reminded Black Joe of bagpipe music, he said. They wailed a good deal.

It's hard to say what put it into Black Joe's head to straighten the course of the creek that summer. It may have been that the bend in it was still causing debris to land on his property, or it may be just that being a tidy man, he liked the idea of a creek that ran straight rather than crooked. Anyway, he decided to try and take the kink out of it just at the point where he had drowned the cat. He started by cutting into what you might call the inside of the elbow and putting what he took out over onto the other side. It was slow work because of the rocks, but he went at it with energy, and by noon, he had got a good deal done. He took a little time off, then, and would probably have taken longer had not the harmonium started up in the woods behind him, wailing quite indescribably. It was probably some of that Irish music they call traditional, which usually means half tuneless and half tangled. He decided that he would do well to work out his irritation with the pick-axe and shovel and so started work again, and by the time evening had come and the music suddenly stopped, he was feeling quite cheerful. It was just as the light was beginning to go that he made his discovery. He had decided to take another shovelful out at the bottom of the bank, when he saw a gleam. He bent down and scrabbled for it and found he had a nugget about the size of a small broad bean. He left his shovel and pickaxe where they were, a most uncharacteristic thing for him to do, and went back to the cabin and looked at it under the lamp. It was a funny shape, like most nuggets are, I expect, and an imaginative man might have seen something odd about it. Black Joe wasn't an imaginative man. He'd made his small fortune by mining, and nuggets meant money to him more than they meant romance. If he'd shown it to anybody then, it's likely that someone would have spotted what it was, or at least what it looked like, but naturally, he kept his discovery dark, and the following day, he was very busy attending to all the things necessary to ensuring that he had absolute title to whatever gold he could get out of his creek and the land around it.

Nobody can keep a gold strike quiet, however, and in no time at all, there were prospectors all up and down that creek, except on Black Joe's land and Red Connolly's property above it. Red Connolly said he wasn't interested in working his own claim, he got enough pay for working in Bullion. But he made sure nobody else could move in on him, nevertheless.

Black Joe worked hard for the next few days, but he got very little for it. He got more than anyone else on the creek, however, for he found several very small nuggets — worth practically nothing, admittedly, but promising a good deal, and nobody else found anything. He dug back from the creek into his garden and then took down the glasshouse and dug there. Every day, he found something but never much. It was not like anything he'd come across before. The gold seemed to be scattered at random; there were no big or even medium-sized pockets of it, just occasional tiny nuggets and, once in a while, one as big as a dried pea. He'd got a good sluice box working by now, using the waters of the creek from higher up, diverting it by way of a flume he'd built. Before long, however, he reached the upper end of his land, and it looked to him as if it was Red Connolly's property that had the real stuff in it. The nuggets seemed to be more frequent farther up the creek, certainly. He found it hard to approach Connolly, but at last, he did so. He asked him first if he could stake out a claim or two on his land. Connolly told him no. Then he suggested a partnership, since Connolly wasn't willing to work the property himself. Connolly said no. By this time, Black Joe was in a state that bordered on fury, but he managed to restrain himself long enough to ask if Connolly had any mind to sell out. Connolly said he'd ask his wife and they'd think about it.

That night, Black Joe counted up what he had got so far and found that he'd taken out roughly $200 in three weeks' hard work and that he'd spent maybe half of that on equipment and on paying the two Chinese he'd got in to help him after the first few days. A sensible man might have stopped there, but Black Joe was lost to sense by that time. He

went to the bank and drew out his money, and he went up to Red Connolly and slapped it all down on the table and said, "Will this buy you
out?" Red Connolly looked at him. The wife looked at him. The wife
said, in a voice curiously gentle for her, "We might as well, Sean. I've
never liked it much here since the cat went." So that was it. Black
Joe got the Connolly property. The Connollys moved down nearer Bullion mine, and the very next day, Black Joe and his two Chinese set
to work.

They found nothing, of course. Not a speck of gold was anywhere
to be found, and after a couple of weeks, Black Joe let the Chinese go
and went on himself. The rest of it you can guess. Black Joe ran out
of money and time and sold first Connolly's cabin and then his own
and finally abandoned the whole operation. He hung on to the first nugget he found until the very end. Then he sold it in a beer parlour and
went on down to Victoria.

At this point, the old-timer paused. I guessed he was expecting a
question, and I thought I knew what it was. "So they called the creek
after the cat?" I hazarded. "Not exactly," he said slowly, "more like after the nugget. Do you want to see it?" and he put his hand in his vest
pocket and brought out a little washleather bag and spilled a nugget
onto his palm. "See!" he said. "That's the cat nugget. That's why they
call it Cat Creek. And why they say when anyone blathers a lot, like
that chap ower theer, or when folks spend a deal of time on something
useless, they're taking gold out of Cat Creek. Here. Take a look." I took
it in my hand. I turned it this way and that. It was a nugget all right.
There was no doubt about that. But try as I might, I couldn't see that
it looked like a cat at all.

Mary Burns

Suburbs of the Arctic Circle

I have to laugh at people who think it's different up North, cleaner and freer. Oh, it's freer, I suppose. You don't find yourself running into barbed wire when you're out for a stroll, and the Mounties are generally willing to ignore minor infractions of the law. There is only one Mountie in our town anyway, Frank McCloud, and Frank is new and doesn't yet know where to look for trouble. Andy Hanson was transferred to Labrador after Raven's Roost hit the national news last year. Andy knew where to look for trouble, but he also knew that if he didn't look, he wouldn't see, and for official purposes, there would be no trouble.

I don't believe it is cleaner up here, but then, I haven't been Outside for close to 10 years. Still, most places have their undersides, and R.R. is no different in that respect. Undersides are where you find the dust devils, the dirty socks and underwear shoved there in the heat of some moment you had forgotten until everything was turned upside down. The death of Esau Isaac had that effect on Raven's Roost, but to understand why, you'd have to know the place.

First of all, no one who lives here calls the town by its full name. It is embarrassing even to write it on the mail orders we send to Simpson-Sears. I picture the catalogue girls in Edmonton or Vancouver opening our letters and wondering who would ever live in a place called Raven's Roost. The trader who christened the settlement could have named it after himself, as so many have done, but no, he supplied his own interpretation of the words the Indians used.

R.R. lies south of the junction of the Yukon and White Fish rivers. At the north end of town, just past Peter Groenen's Esso station, is the big silver bridge you see pictured on postcards. The highway and the river form the main boundaries of R.R. The Catholics built their church on the east side of the highway, thinking they would encourage settlement there, but the Commissioner of the Territory, an Anglican, put a development freeze on the land surrounding the church, and now it sits alone, directly beneath the cemetery and about half a mile south of the dump. Churchgoers load their pickups with the week's garbage on Sundays to save themselves a trip.

The town proper stretches along the riverbanks on the west side of the highway. The main town road cuts through the centre of it, leaving the Indians on one side, on the river flats, and the white people, the nursing station, the RCMP, the school, the teacherage, the stores and the Anglican church on the higher ground. We get tourists coming through who say we ought to do something about the appearance of the town. They say it's a shame to have such a ramshackle collection of buildings in the middle of this stunning natural setting. I imagine they would sooner see us living in neat little log cabins or maybe Swiss chalets hung with flower-filled window boxes. Well, we don't pay much attention to the tourists; they're gone as soon as the blackflies hatch.

They do have a point about the scenery, though. I felt the same way when I first saw it, before I got distracted by the business of daily life here. We have pines and spruces marching up the hill behind the Catholic church, halfway up Blue Mountain; and on the riverbanks, we have the leafy trees, aspen, some birch, low willow and alder. For a week or so in early June, the new leaves are that cool, popsicle-green colour that makes you wish you could open your eyes wider to take more of it in. And right around that time, as well as for weeks after, we have the lupins — dark blue thickets of them surprising you, even though you know they were there last year. Later comes the fireweed, its colour explaining its name. The river changes with the seasons: in summer, it is green as the trees on its banks; in fall and winter, before it freezes, it turns a colder and colder blue and reflects the low sun in coppery patches. In spring, the river runs brown as the mud outside the RRX tavern at that time of year.

The RRX, which stands for Raven's Roost Crossroads, is located on the east side of the highway too, but south of the main town road, whereas the Catholic church is north of it. You have to pass the RRX to get to town from anywhere south, and south is where people usually come from. South is the airport, the fastest link to the Outside; south is the only real city in the Territory. My husband Jack was one of the few who made regular trips north, but that is because it was his job to do so.

The setting is particularly important to this story, because if the RRX had been anywhere else, the incident would never have grown as it did. Think of the river as the bar of a T and the main town road as the stem. The teacherage sits about a quarter-mile down the stem, toward the river. You'll see that anyone coming into town from the RRX has to pass the teacherage on the way in.

Nat and Bonnie Hemple told the reporters from the CBC that six cars passed the teacherage the night Esau Isaac died. That means at least six people had driven past the spot where Esau was sitting, at the junction of the highway and the main town road. We all heard Nat's voice on the radio, toward the end of *The World at Six*: "I can't believe it, but it's true. That road is the only way into town. We were sitting up late, grading papers, and we could hear the cars clearly because engine sounds are brittle in that kind of cold. It was 50 below; I know because I checked the thermometer right before we went to bed. If only we'd known that poor Esau . . ."

Poor Esau! Nat didn't say that he and his wife were unlikely to know about Esau or anyone else in the town. They had applied for a transfer at Christmas, the whole town knew, and it didn't make them any more popular than when they'd arrived in September, all bright-eyed and itching to change things. The Department of Education did not accept their request for transfer; they were being forced to stay until the school year was finished. But they didn't have any friends by then, so they kept to themselves, except when they were at the school. I don't think they ever drank at the RRX. I doubt they drank at all.

Say what you like about us, no one was happy to hear about Esau's death. He was a harmless old drunk who had been a fine trapper in his day. He was over 70 when he died and had been living alone in a cabin near the south end of the Indian village. The cabin had run down some since May, his wife, had drowned two summers earlier as they were coming downriver with their moose. But Esau kept his traps in good condition, they say, and spoke of going out on his line again one day. Esau might have wanted to die. Some said he sat out there on purpose, like the old Eskimo people who plant themselves on an ice floe and wait to freeze to death because they know they are no longer useful. But the Hemples would have none of this theory or any other the townspeople cooked up.

They told the news reporters that R.R. was "a hotbed of racial injustice." Those were their exact words. They said the North was not the friendly place Outsiders believed it to be, a place where people could depend on one another, but was just like that New York suburb where 37 people watched a woman being stabbed to death without once attempting to help her. It was just the sort of shock story they use to finish the national news. We've all heard similar, and I, for one, have felt satisfied that I didn't live in a place where people casually murdered each other and abandoned their babies. I have never written in, but I have felt smug.

I guess the story was printed in papers all over the country, because our post office was clogged with letters from righteous citizens for weeks afterward. It was Judgement Day in Raven's Roost, and we were all sentenced to shame on account of six people, five of whom probably hadn't even seen Esau. Knowing us to be isolated there on the highway and to consist of only 300 souls, more or less, depending on the season, you will understand that Esau's death, or Nat Hemple's story of it, hit our town harder than a fuel shortage in January. We had to depend on ourselves, and this is how I learned something about what is generally called human nature. As I already said, I don't think our sins were any more original than those you would find in Vancouver or Toronto. It's just that cold contracts, and you get in the habit of looking at things extra closely, as if through a magnifying glass.

Take Esau's funeral. Under ordinary circumstances, there would not have been much of a turnout. The Indians would have held their potlatch and shared their grief; a few whites would have attended, the

RCMP and the priests. The mixed-bloods, like my neighbour Jo Bouchard, might have gone, depending on which way they were leaning at the time. But it would not have amounted to a town affair. The reporters were responsible for that. Despite the weather being almost as bad as the night Esau died, people flocked to the graveyard like fruit flies to browning bananas. There were TV cameras and a lot of indignant-looking young people from the Indian organization in Whitehorse. Predictably, the Indians stood on one side of the grave and the whites on the other. I stood with Jo Bouchard — Jack was out driving that day — close to the exact middle of those two groups, between the currents that passed from one to the other, and when it was finished, I wanted a stiff drink. You had to suspect those who were crying hardest; it seemed they were doing it only to show they were better than the ones who stood there dry-eyed. Jo, for instance, was related to Esau; Esau had been her mother's half-brother, but Jo didn't cry. Her brown cheeks stayed smooth as the bronze on Esau's casket. And that's another thing. The townspeople contributed money to the Band for Esau's funeral, something that never would have happened if it hadn't been for the publicity. Then, on the way down the road from the Indian graveyard to the community hall, where coffee was to be served, everyone told Esau stories: about the snowshoes he had made for them or the time they went hunting with him or brought him and May a hamper at Christmas. It was as if people wanted to connect with the dead Esau in a way they hadn't when he was alive.

We should have been stronger. We should not have let the accusations of Hemple and the Outsiders chafe us as they did. But fame has a momentum that can carry you away. I think of movie stars who complain about their privacy being invaded but keep giving interviews all the same. Fame is a teaser, and we fell for it.

Travellers who drive through R.R. no doubt wonder why there is a town here at all. While the filling stations serve a useful purpose, there is no need for an entire community around them. Well, the community began on the flats, which was the site of one of the largest Indian fishing camps on the river. You can find the old drying racks cartwheeled in the weeds behind the Indian village, and dogs will dig up years-old fish skeletons. Two or three of the Indian families still set out nets in late summer, when the salmon are running upriver, but most rely on the stores for food and on government cheques to pay for it.

Art Neary keeps an outfitter's camp at the back of Blue Mountain, and some of the younger native boys who haven't left R.R. — or who have returned — guide for Art in the fall. Then there are those like Jo Bouchard, who fit themselves into the regular white life of the town. Jo was born in the village just after the highway was built, in '43. Her father, one of the army men who constructed it, didn't stick around for long, and her mother died of smallpox before Jo was 6, so Jo was sent to live with a foster family, the Bouchards, in Whitehorse. When the Bouchards moved south a few years later, Jo went right along with them. She was educated to grade 13 in Vancouver and eventually came back to R.R. with a welder, Noel Rien, and they set up a trailer on the lot next to ours.

Jo and I could see the Indian village clearly from the cliffside where our trailers sat, and aside from visiting relatives down there now and then, that seemed to be enough of a connection for Jo.

Sometimes, I could hear the guitar-accompanied hymns from their gospel services and the barks of their husky dogs, but usually, the villagers were quiet, and the flats appeared a sleepy gathering — much different from the time when everyone must have been astir, catching and drying fish. That's the Indian side of town.

The white side is like Noah's Ark: we have two of practically everything. Bill Luksic started it all with the service station he opened when the highway was smooth enough for regular vehicles to travel over. He soon saw he ought to have a café and a few rooms for overnighters, and once these were finished, he applied for a licence to serve liquor. Edna Farrone, who runs the General Store with her husband Ted, says it was Bill who gave them the idea of moving down from the triangle of mining towns north of here and opening a store. Then the government got into the act, putting in a highway-maintenance camp and a post office. The highway crews set up trailers and built houses, and the population began to grow, which meant the government had to supply a nursing station and an RCMP post. We have two cafés now, Bill's and the diner the Groenens operate near the bridge, two stores, two churches and two graveyards.

Bill Luksic was the unofficial mayor of R.R., the man who pressured the territorial government into grading our streets in the spring and thawing our pipes in the winter. The summer before Esau died, Bill had circulated a petition asking the Commissioner to grant us local government status. He didn't need to try too hard to convince us we should have some kind of say over our affairs, and since all of us ended up signing, we figured we would be declared a Local Government District before the year was up. We also figured Bill would be appointed chairman, which would make his unofficial position official. Bill had the confidence of a born leader, and he knew how to settle an argument. He didn't look like the politicians you see pictured in magazines and newspapers. He was not a glad-hander, and he dressed the way the other men do here, in work greens and quilted down vests. If Bill had stayed in Edmonton, his natural qualities might never have surfaced, but a town like this one demands all a person has. Those who cannot cope with the demands either leave or are diminished in mind by the truth they have discovered about themselves. Naturally, there were some who, out of jealousy, resented Bill, but even they had to admit that if it hadn't been for Bill, there would be no R.R. as we knew it.

Bill's wife Naomi was chairman of the school committee and had been for years. There was talk of replacing her long before Esau's death, because her own daughter was grown and gone and Naomi was out of touch with the times, but she was always reelected, probably because most of us thought so much of Bill.

When there was an accident on the highway or a drowning in the river, Bill was the man the newspapers contacted for details, so of course it was him they called to get the other side of Nat Hemple's story. Bill wasn't very cooperative this time, though, and that was because it was Bill who knew, if anyone did, the six people who left Esau to freeze to death on the road. The six would have been coming from Bill's tavern, or most of them would have. You won't find many pleasure drivers out on a night like that. My husband Jack was out, but that was business. Bill told the reporters that he had not kept track of the time people left his place that night. And when they asked him if he agreed that there was racial tension in our town, Bill just said that the young teacher didn't know what he was talking about. He was uncharacteristically quiet on the subject, and that didn't make life any easier in R.R.

Bill was over 55, but he never looked his age until things started going bad. He was bald since before I met him but wiry and always on the move, and we never thought of him as one of the oldest men in town, apart from some of the Indians. The night he stopped by our trailer to talk to Jack was the first time I noticed the depth of his forehead creases and how his spotted hands were never still but fiddled with the salt and pepper shakers on the table or spun the can of milk. His voice was weary; it had the rasp a person with a cold gets, only Bill did not have a cold. As far as I knew, he had never been sick a day in his life.

"We've got a hell of a mess on our hands," he said.

Jack was at the fridge, opening beers for us. "I don't see why, Bill. This thing has got out of hand, is all, just because of that radio report. You know yourself that every town in the Territory has had something like it happen. Look at Whitehorse: wasn't it just last year a bartender threw an old drunk out of his place, just as he's supposed to do? But the bloody fellow up and died on him. Nobody planned it that way."

Bill didn't answer immediately but took a long drink of his beer, set the bottle down and then snapped and unsnapped the bottom of his vest several times.

"I had a visit from Groenen today."

"Oh?"

"He came by to remind me, as if he had to, about our petition sitting down in Whitehorse. Then he got around to what happened in White Fish Crossing last year, how the Indians wouldn't sign the petition, so the government wouldn't give the rest of the community their local government. 'Mind you, Bill,' he said, 'we've always had a tighter town than they got up at White Fish. I'm not saying the same thing will happen here. But after all that publicity we got, we have to watch ourselves.' "

"What was he getting at?"

"Same thing Andy Hanson was getting at the day after he found Esau. Same thing the whole town thinks, that I know damn well who was in the tavern that night and that I ought to be the one who nails them so the rest of us can clear our names."

Bill looked at me and then at Jack, and he raised his eyebrows as if to say, What do you make of that? He wasn't asking what we thought of Peter Groenen, because he already knew. Groenen is a sour man, a Dutchman who feels that World War II was a plot directly aimed at his family. The war ruined them, and this had given Groenen a grudge against life in general and against Bill Luksic in particular, because Bill had settled here first and in the best location. No, it wasn't Groenen Bill was worried about, it was the burden circumstance had laid on him, and it wasn't me he wanted to hear from so much as Jack. Bill trusted him more than any man in town, for he knew Jack's worth.

Bill had taken a chance on us when we were first married and arrived in R.R. with a nearly broken-down truck and all we owned in it. He put us up at the RRX and loaned Jack the money to repair the truck and start his hauling business. Another man might have run off with Bill's money or forgotten him when he wasn't needed anymore, but not Jack. Jack still trucked Bill's liquor up from Whitehorse once a month for only the cost of the gas. Now, Bill needed something more from Jack, but I wasn't sure exactly what.

"You know, Bill, there could have been 10 cars pass the teacherage that night — or two. I don't care if those Hemples are schoolteachers, I don't think they can count. I drove past that corner myself that night, coming from the triangle, didn't I, Shirl? I didn't see Esau. Hell, I've given him and the other old buggers plenty of free rides. Nobody's gonna make me feel like Judas just because I drove into town that night."

"Well, you got home early anyway, Jack," I reminded him.

The coroner had put Esau's time of death at approximately 11:30, which meant he might have been sitting out on the road from 10:30 or so. Jack had arrived home at 10:00; I was sure of it because the radio was on. I had to ask this next question because, like everyone else in town, I was curious. I couldn't help it.

"Do you know and are you just not saying, Bill?"

Jack looked mad enough to slap me. "It's his business. Either you're a friend, or you're not. Now give it up, Shirl."

Bill didn't want to give it up, though. He had to tell someone, and he probably thought Naomi would blab it all over town if he told her. That's what I thought then. Her change of life was hard on her, is how Bill explained it. Ever since, she hadn't been too sure of herself but needed to prop herself up with positions, such as being chairman of the school committee and R.R. representative on the territorial tourism board. She liked to flaunt the Hawaii vacations she and Bill could afford to take every year, to be on top of a pile of people she considered inferior. She didn't fool anyone, though, especially not Bill.

"It's all right, Jack. Shirley doesn't mean anything. Fact is, I probably could say. The place was slow that night. You know how it is when it gets that cold."

He was aching to tell us. His hand was white from gripping his bottle so hard, and his foot was tapping a nervous beat on the lino floor. But Jack didn't want him to say, and that had me worried.

"Give it a miss, Bill. It won't do anyone any good to know those people now. Esau isn't going to rise from the dead. Besides, who's to say any of them actually saw the old guy? You know how exhaust freezes up in this weather. Each one of those cars was probably hid in its own cloud."

"Would you say that at the inquest?"

"I didn't know there was going to be one."

"There is. Hanson told me today. The coroner's coming up a week from Friday, and they're going to hold it at the school."

So that's why Bill had been acting so squirmy. It was one thing to have to answer reporters, who were going to write what they wanted no matter what you said, another to have to testify before an official inquiry.

"I'll sleep on it, Bill," Jack said.

"Yeah, me too. If I can, eh?"

"Just remember who your friends are," Jack called as Bill stepped over the snow to his truck. We stood at the door and watched him drive away, and I noticed that Jo Bouchard's lights were on and that she — or someone — had just slid the curtains shut.

Jo was not only my neighbour, she was my best friend aside from Jack. She had more formal schooling than me, and she'd seen more of the world. It was Jo who persuaded me to join the library and to send for correspondence courses. Noel and Jack laughed at us for pursuing something as useless in R.R. as education, but I know that in his heart, Jack was happy to see me doing it. Besides keeping me busy while he was out on the road, the schoolwork was making me more my own person. Jo and I planned to study until we earned enough credits for our teaching certificates. We wanted to teach at the R.R. school. Before the Hemples came, we had both worked as aides, but the Hemples didn't like having amateurs around, and they got Naomi Luksic to support their point of view. Noel was glad. I think he understood that Jo was smarter than he was anyway and that it would be hard not to face that if she actually became a certified teacher. He got her pregnant every year, until they had five kids and she finally put her foot down and got some birth control.

The morning after Bill's visit, I stopped by Jo's to get her to walk to the post office with me so I could tell her about the inquest.

"Bill was over last night and told us," I said, to give her a chance to say she knew because she had seen him leaving. But she didn't admit she'd been watching. She acted surprised to hear he was there.

"I thought old Luksic was lying low. I haven't seen him since the funeral, and good thing too."

"What do you mean by that?"

"Come on, Shirley. You know damn well he's just trying to protect himself and some of his buddies. I bet I could name the guys who left Esau to die that night, and one of them would be the same who turned in Billy Jim last summer for peddling whitefish to tourists. You know I don't have any love for Nat Hemple, but he wasn't all wrong about the prejudice part. It was pretty clear why Naomi didn't want me in that school, and it wasn't because of a tight budget, like she said. I would have worked for nothing; they knew that."

"That doesn't make sense, Jo. She didn't want me either, and my mother wasn't an Indian."

Jo's face was getting redder as we walked and not just from the cold. Her eyes were burning, and her lips were turned down so that the lower one squeezed the mole at the corner of her mouth.

"Think what you want, Shirley."

"I'll tell you what I think. I think a few of us ought to try and keep some sense in our heads. Don't you know that getting us riled and setting us against each other was just what the Hemples wanted? Why should we play right into their hands?"

Jo didn't answer me. She was into what I called her Indian princess snit, the silent treatment, which is how she got whenever she was pushed too far. She had responded like this when we got the notice from the school committee that we'd no longer be allowed to work as aides. She'd argued about it just so long, then let it drop completely and kept to herself for the better part of a month, which is a long time to go without visiting your next-door neighbour and your closest friend.

I have to think, now, of the timetable. Esau was found on a Tuesday. The radio and the newspaper reports filled in the days before the funeral, which was Saturday. Bill paid his visit to us on the Tuesday after and told us the inquest would be a week from that Friday. The government didn't know what it was doing, letting us all simmer that long. They shouldn't have stretched it out for another week. Anyway, the Hemples left on the Sunday after the funeral. They simply packed their car and drove off. So there was no school for 10 days, until the Department of Education could find replacements.

Meantime, life had to go on. We couldn't just stop cold and wait until we were cleared or condemned. We had to go on eating and sleeping and working and filling in the evenings just as though nothing had happened, but it was hard, because people were even jumpier than they usually are in February, and the kids' being home just made it worse. The wives were getting irritable because of having to deal all day with bored and noisy kids and were taking it out on their husbands when they got home at night. Ted Farrone, who managed the curling rink at the community hall, decided to close for a week, and that was another bad decision. Curling was the only thing we had to do in winter besides snowmobiling. But Ted said nobody had been out for several days and he wasn't going to waste heat and electricity just to keep the place open.

I could see why nobody was interested in curling. Curling brought people together and forced them to look at one another, and it was getting so none of us could bear to do that. Even though I knew everything was going to turn out all right, that in a year or so we'd probably laugh at ourselves, I got caught up too.

Instead of going to the store on Wednesday, when the fresh produce was delivered, I waited until Thursday and found that half the other women in town had decided to do the same thing. We were all a little embarrassed too, and though we said hello and how's Johnny's cold, because we had to say something to each other, we didn't linger in the hardware section to see if there were any new kitchen goods there, and nobody invited anyone home for coffee.

Edna Farrone was one of the few who dared to look people straight in the eye.

"That'll be $37.24. Want it on your tab?" she asked. And through her dusty spectacles, I saw her peering at me so intensely, she must have thought she could read my mind. She probably wanted to come right out and ask me if I knew, but so far, nobody had had the guts to do that. I tried to pretend it was an ordinary shopping day. "No, I'll pay, and say, Edna, did you ever get that arrowroot starch I ordered last month?"

"I asked for it. Don't blame me if it never got here." She was unnecessarily sharp about it.

Another thing that happened was that everyone started to group off. As I've said, there were two stores in town, Farrone's General, where just about every family did their big shopping, and the R.R. Market, which was run by a Danish man and his Indian wife. The Market carried much of what Farrone's had but in smaller amounts and didn't get a shipment of fresh meat and vegetables once a week but sold only frozen meat. The Market was closer to the Indian village than Farrone's and so did a big business in canned milk, sugar and tea, things like that, and sold chips and pop to the Indian kids. Well, through the week following Esau's funeral, I noticed a gradual slackening of activity at Farrone's and an increase in the Market's business, and the difference in clientele was the difference in skin colour and eye shape.

What surprised me most, though, was seeing Jo Bouchard pulling a sled up the hill on Friday morning. Two bags of groceries sat on the sled, and they had obviously come from the R.R. Market. I slipped on my parka and ran out to meet her.

"Just thought you should know that little Noel and Chrissie are playing at my place. Sure will be a relief when we get the new teachers, eh?"

"Sure will."

It was cold enough that our breaths made a fog between us as we stood there. "Well, I better get this stuff inside," Jo said.

"Come for coffee when you're finished."

She said she would, but she didn't. She called at 5:00 to say she'd got held up by some tax forms she was working on and asked me to send the kids home.

Peter Groenen's business picked up, and he put a help-wanted sign in the window of the café. I think this was going too far. He couldn't have needed more help in the winter. The sign was just his way of thumbing his nose at Bill Luksic, for business at the RRX had fallen off drastically. Instead of stopping at Bill's place for their morning coffee, the highway crews switched to Groenen's. And as though the presence of graders outside Groenen's was a signal, the truckers started stopping there too. Not all of them, of course, but enough to make a difference. Some people are like sheep, they will follow the tail they see directly in front of them. Bill kept the tavern open as usual, but business was down there too. This is not to say that drinking came to a stop. People took their boxes of beer home to drink, and Jack and me were no exception.

Of course, when Jack had goods to haul up to the mining triangle, he'd be gone the whole day and a good part of the evening. By the time he got home, it was usually too late to invite friends over, so we were used to spending our evenings alone. That was nothing new. We would have a few beers or tea, and I would read a book or catch up on mending, while Jack sat nearby filing his tools or sharpening his knives or simply looking through the *Geographic*. When you've been married to someone for over 10 years, there isn't much need to talk, and Jack was never much for it anyway. But during that hard time in town, I needed to talk. My skin felt itchy, as if I'd rubbed it with that angel hair the kids drag home from school after decorating for Christmas. My stomach felt jittery too. I was only feeling the same as everyone else in town, but it was no comfort to know that. An itch is an individual thing with an individual cause and can only be relieved by an individual scratch. Jack seemed calm enough, but I thought I saw a private, worried look in his eye.

What I had told Bill Luksic about Jack's coming home at 10:00 the night Esau died was not exactly true. I thought he came in about then, because it seemed to me I had just heard the 10 o'clock news and dozed off for a minute when I heard his truck outside. But I didn't get up to look at the clock in the kitchen. So part of my reason for feeling itchy was not knowing for sure about Jack.

You see, the feelings in town had got so bad that even we who knew we had nothing to do with Esau's death had developed guilt about one aspect or another of the case. Jo had said, right after hearing of it, that she'd planned on driving up to the RRX that night but didn't because it was too cold. So Jo felt guilty for *not* going out. Somebody else said he wished he hadn't given Esau any money for the hunting knife he wanted to sell, because if Esau hadn't had any money, he couldn't have gone to the RRX. I believe some person might have taken responsibility for the weather if he honestly could have.

"You know," I said to Jack when I could no longer stop myself, "we haven't had Noel and Jo over for cards in a long time."

Jack was flipping through the newest *Geographic*, and he just grunted a reply.

"It's still early; I could ask them, but I bet they wouldn't come."

Jack did not look up or ask me why I thought that, so I kept going while my nerve was up. "Jo has been acting peculiar lately. I think she's avoiding me. I know that's been happening with some other people in town, but Jo and I have been friends for so long. . . . You know, Jack," I said, "I bet you there are plenty of couples sitting together like we are here tonight, feeling a little uneasy but not knowing what to do about it. If you think about it, if there were six, then six wives or husbands have something to feel ashamed about. I'm surprised nobody has told on anybody else yet."

"It's not so surprising. The only way a person would know who was out that night is if he was out too or if he was married to someone who came home about that time. Wives wouldn't tell, and you can be sure a guilty person wouldn't tell on a guilty person. I'll be glad when this damn thing is over. It isn't the same town anymore."

I took out another sock and dropped the darning egg into it. "I have an idea why Jo is acting so cold. She must have heard you come in that night. She probably thinks you were one of those who passed Esau."

Jack slapped his magazine down hard on the coffee table. "Goddamn it, Shirley. Do you suspect your own husband?"

"It isn't that I suspect you, honey, it's just that I want to be absolutely sure so I can say so without thinking someone might trip me up. I was asleep, remember?"

"All I can say is, it's bloody lucky those Hemples left when they did. Otherwise, there might have been a couple more cases for the coroner."

"Well?"

"Well what?"

"Are you pretty sure you got in just after 10:00?"

"You just won't give it up, will you? Well, I don't know what the hell the time was. I was more worried about keeping on the road than looking at my watch. If Esau Isaac was sitting out on the highway when I came by, I sure as hell didn't see him. He didn't try to flag me down, that's for sure. Is that good enough? Do you think you can clear me with your half-breed buddy on the basis of that?"

His blue eyes were glinting like the bridge steel in the brightest winter sun. I was about to tell him it wasn't Jo I was concerned about so much as myself, but Jack wasn't finished having his say.

"You think knowing is going to solve everything? Jesus, Shirley, you're a smart woman, you ought to know better. Just how do you think you'd feel about testifying at some neighbour's trial, about buying groceries or curling with somebody half the country had accused of manslaughter? Eh? Did you ever think of that?"

He got up and headed for the bedroom then, without even saying good night. I couldn't blame him, really. It is terrible to think that the person who is closest to you in the world doesn't trust you, and it wasn't much easier being the one who doubted. I waited until Jack was asleep before I turned in, and I lay awake a long time wondering about how the town would survive the inquest. For what Jack had said was true.

Once we knew who had been purposely neglectful, our attitudes toward them would change. Friends could be set against each other, marriages could be affected. Some marriages already had been affected. I knew for a fact that Jo and Noel had been fighting more than ever since Esau died. Jo hadn't said as much, but when you live next door to someone for that long, you get to noticing certain things about their habits, and when the habits change, you can tell something is up. I'd heard them yelling at each other more too: sounds carry sharply through the cold nights and reverberate on the metal of our trailer. I didn't hear anything from there the night Jack and I had our set-to, but that's because Noel had stamped out of their place that morning and gone to Whitehorse. The kids told me.

When I knocked on her door the next morning, she was still in her bathrobe, the shocking pink velour I had helped her pick out of the catalogue. The kids were at the kitchen table playing with cereal, but Jo had been working at her desk. The desk lamp was on, and there was a cigarette burning in the ashtray beside a pile of papers.

"Morning, Josephine, busy?" I asked, as brightly as I could, to break the ice.

"Matter of fact, I am, Shirl. There's these books . . ."

"I thought you did those last week. Noel couldn't be doing that much business, 'specially not from Whitehorse."

She didn't say anything to this but scraped a pile of sugar off the table into her hand.

"Is the coffee still hot?"

She couldn't refuse me. She poured two cups, handed me one, and we carried them into the sitting room, out of earshot of the kids.

"I was thinking we might get together and set up a little tutoring programme for the kids, while we're waiting for the new teachers. But if you'd rather tell me about Noel instead . . ."

"There's not much to say. He may be gone for good this time, and I can't say I care. It was bound to happen someday."

"Anything to do with Esau?"

"Aw . . ." She leaned her head back against the chesterfield and closed her eyes.

"Look, Jo. I don't mean to pry. It's just that it was never considered prying before. You've been keeping your distance lately, and I can't figure out why."

"You can't? Oh, come on, Shirley. The whole town's dividing up.

You're either with me or against me, eh? You saw me walking up from the Market the other day, so I guess you can figure which way I'm gonna go. Noel saw it too. That's why he left."

"Because of the Market? But that's silly."

"Not only the Market. I've been doing the Band's bookkeeping. So far, I've been doing it at home, but Charlie wants me to work at the Band office down in the village. I told Noel, and he blew his stack and walked out. That was part of it, anyway."

"But you can't really work down there, Jo. You've got the kids to consider. Noel was probably just thinking of them."

"Yeah, them and the fact that his woman might be going back to where she came from, where she really belongs. Aunt Lizzie said she'd look after the little ones. Her cabin is just down the road from the Band office, you know. It would work. We could even move down there."

"What about me, though? You can't think it's come to me being against you, not after all these years. I haven't had a better friend, Jo."

"I didn't say I thought that. We can still be friends. I'll only be down the hill. You talk like it's the other side of the moon. And Shirley, I don't want you to think I've come to this decision just because of Esau. I've been thinking about it a long time. Maybe it's why I came back here in the first place. It was me more than Noel who wanted to come, you know. I've had advantages most of my people haven't had, Shirl. I have something to offer, and they can use it. Esau's death and that radio report just pointed up what a lot of people have known for a long time. In a crunch, you can't count on white people to come through."

"Oh, Jo. You can't believe that stuff Hemple said."

"You look around, Shirley Grant. Just open your eyes and see what there is to see. How many Indians do you see working on the highway crew, eh? It's the only decent work in town, and it goes to Outsiders, people who weren't born here. As for Luksic, did you ever see him throw a white out of his tavern?"

"Bill said Esau left on his own."

"Sure, Bill *said* that."

"Well, I believe him. He's a good man."

"Uh huh. Just like those six who left Esau to die. It could have been Aunt Lizzie or me or anyone, as long as they had brown skin."

I didn't believe it. Things just weren't that way in R.R. Jo was overreacting, and I think the fact that she was related to Esau had more to do with it than she wanted to admit. But I wasn't going to argue with her. I could only hope she would change her mind when things cooled off. Of course, there was something I didn't know at that point.

Bill Luksic paid us one more visit before the inquest. He called first, to see if Jack had got home. I said he had, and Bill said he'd be right over. When the pink from the cold had left his face, Bill looked unnaturally white. We offered him a beer, but he said he'd rather have some of the brandy he'd given us at Christmas, if we had any left.

"Maybe I ought to turn in," I said, seeing how shaken he was. I knew it was Jack he wanted to talk to more than me.

"No, you stay, Shirley. You'll find out eventually anyway. Wives always do. I'd just as soon you hear it from me."

He drained the glass of brandy in one swallow, and when Jack reached for the bottle to give him a refill, he shook his head no. "Thanks anyway. I just wanted a little. My insides feel like I've been leaning on a riveter all day." He took a deep breath. "Last time I was here, I asked you if you'd tell the coroner what you thought about the Hemples, about them not being able to tell how many cars there were, I mean. I just said it then, now I'm asking you seriously if you'll say that."

"Sure I will. It's what I honestly think. But it's not going to prove anything."

Bill dropped his head onto his arms, and for a moment, I thought he was crying. Except for the low murmur of the oil heater and the drip from a kitchen tap, there wasn't a sound in the trailer. Bill raised his head after a few long minutes, and his eyes were wet, sparkling anyway, with a combination of anger and shame.

"I know who passed Esau that night and left him to die. I don't know if every one of them saw him, but I know who drove past, and it wasn't six people, it was five. I'm going to tell you who they are because . . ."

He paused for another long breath, and I felt so scared, my heart was beating like crazy. Jack was right: when it came right down to it, I didn't want to know.

"Two of them were Indians. They were sitting with Esau earlier in the night, and he had asked them to drive him home. But they were drunk and kept telling Esau how soft he was getting. How they heard he used to walk clear into Whitehorse in the old days. I don't know why Esau felt he had to leave just then. They would have taken him if he waited. Anyway, those two were the Jim boys, Rufus and Billy, and they were driving Billy's old car, so you were right when you said the

Hemples couldn't count. There were only four cars.

"One of the others was Ted Farrone's. Ted hadn't been in long, only about a half-hour or so. He came to ask me about arrangements for the bonspiel, had one beer and left. Now, Ted doesn't have much love to spare for Indians, but I can't think he would knowingly have left old Esau out there in the cold. Maybe he would have. Anyway, the third vehicle was Noel Bouchard's. He was pretty drunk that night. He'd been fighting with Jo and just sat there all night, drinking steadily and not talking to anyone. I hear he's left town. Maybe that's why. I think I will take another shot of that, Jack, if you don't mind."

"Jo! Well, she said she almost went up there; maybe she was going to try and make it up with him. And for sure that's why she's been acting so funny. My God! Esau was her mother's half-brother."

"Yeah, well, he might not have seen Esau either. We'll never know, I guess."

"So who was driving the fourth car, Bill?" Jack asked.

Bill drank his brandy down before he spoke and kept his eyes on the table all the while. "That's really what I came to see you about. You see, the fourth car was Naomi's. You know how it's been. She gets these notions into her head. Well, the school is one of them notions. I'm not saying she shouldn't have been reelected chairman; it's been good for her in a way, and I'm real thankful because I know, and you don't have to spare my feelings, that you would have preferred to have someone else.

"Well, Naomi talks about the school in a real possessive way. She says things like, I have to go down and check my building today and such, as though she owns it or something, and she talks of calling up the minister about every little thing that goes wrong. That night, she was worried that the file cabinet doesn't have a lock. I tried to get her not to go, but she insisted. So she drove past the teacherage twice, see, and I know she saw Esau because she told me she did. She pulled out shortly after he left. She said he was standing at the crossroads, trying to flag her down, but she didn't want him smelling up the car with vomit, and she didn't want to drive into the village at night."

"And she saw him on the way back too?"

"Yep, and that's the worst of it, because she could tell he was freezing. She said she'd been right not to stop the first time because he obviously had vomited, and she could see in the car lights that it had frozen to his mouth and the front of his parka. He was sitting then, but he was still conscious, because he raised an arm to hail her. She drove right by."

"Did she tell you right then?"

"She told me the next day, after Andy had found him. I knew she would have had to pass him. She admitted it right away, but she said a cruel thing. She said it served him right. I made her promise not to tell anyone, but it wasn't easy. She was proud of herself. And that was only the start. She won't come to bed at night, hardly sleeps at all. She sits in the bar writing letters to the government, the Commissioner, the Education Minister. Anybody. She says she knows people are stealing from the school, and she knows it's the Indians who are doing it. She wants Indian kids barred from the school and a few of them put in jail. She was raving so bad this morning, I had to take her into Whitehorse. They put her in hospital right away."

"Aw, Bill . . ."

It's funny how a man and woman go along with daily life, the colds, the money troubles, the sick kids, the bad feelings you wake up with some days and can't put a name to, shuffling the burden of those things back and forth between each other, so looking back, none of them seem to have amounted to much. Then suddenly, you're hit with something that reminds you you're two separate people after all.

Jack was too good a man to rub it in. After we had done our best to comfort Bill and he'd gone home, surely colder and lonelier than he'd ever be, Jack didn't say, "Well, are you happy now, Shirl?" He sat on the chesterfield quietly, his long legs stretched out and his arms crossed on his chest, thinking, while I tidied the kitchen. When I was finished, I sat down at the other end of the chesterfield, for I had some thinking to do too.

Oh, I pitied Bill and I pitied Jo, but at the same time, I was relieved that the trouble hadn't come any closer to me; as close as Jack, say. I was about to tell him this when Jack stood and stretched and headed for the bedroom. I followed him right in, and we lay down on our favourite sides, and we stayed that way, not touching, for the rest of the night. I wondered what Jack was turning over in his mind but was reluctant to ask him. As for me, I guess I mainly pondered how it was that two people—Noel and Jo or Bill and Naomi, for two good examples—could live with each other as long as they did and still not know what each other had in them.

The next day, I learned how that was true of me too, for to my surprise, Jack decided to take charge of the town. He went so far as to cancel his route for that day, dress in his second-best clothes and go from house to house, on the flats and on the hill, talking to every R.R. citizen he could.

My 8-year-old, Tommy, is a lot like his dad. He can spend hours quietly entertaining himself with a game or a book. One thing he especially likes is building tall houses out of playing cards. He'll get one almost finished, a marvel of a delicate thing four cards high or so, when his little sister or me or Jack will come into the room, stirring the air just enough to throw the whole thing off balance, and down it will come. Tommy might yell at us to watch what we're doing, but I can see he isn't really mad, because he'll clear the table and just start all over again.

Well, a card house is a lot like what we had going in R.R., and you can imagine how nervous everyone felt at the prospect that the inquest would collapse it, same as the radio report had done. The day before it, the Thursday, I practically tiptoed everywhere, and by night, it felt as if I'd been holding my breath all day. Anything *could* have happened. Charlie Benjamin, the Band Chief, could have used the inquest as a platform from which to state all his complaints about being Indian. And since Jo had got so chummy with him, she might have chimed in. Peter Groenen could have accused Bill and Naomi, because he surely knew what had happened to Naomi by then, and it would have been a good opportunity for him to get rid of the Luksics. But then, Bill could have said in public that Groenen had a policy against hiring Indians at his place. That's how it is in R.R. The corner of one life touches the corner of another, so that if we had been really determined to do it, we could have found ways to embarrass or destroy just about everyone.

What did happen was this. Nearly the whole town showed up at the school first thing Friday morning. The coroner from Whitehorse, a court recorder and a bunch of reporters were already there. The coroner called Andy Hanson first, and Andy described when and where he had found Esau. Then the nurse testified as to how he looked when Andy carried him into the nursing station. Then Bill was called. He said Esau had been drinking at the RRX since about 7:00 that night and had left after 10:00 by himself.

Did Bill know Esau didn't have a car? He did. Did Bill know what the temperature was that night? He did. Wasn't Bill concerned about the old man's ability to make it home in that weather? Bill hesitated here, knowing he should have been concerned. But he couldn't explain that he was more concerned with Naomi at the time and had actually been in his private quarters, arguing with her, at the time Esau left.

"I wouldn't have let him go if I didn't think he could make it."

A couple of reporters sniggered at this.

The coroner then tried to get Bill to say who else had been in the bar that night. Bill said he couldn't remember, that people had come and gone as usual, and he had not taken much notice of who had come in and who had left. The coroner didn't go for the story, but he couldn't get Bill to change it.

I pitied him, having to sit there and lie in public, but wouldn't it have been worse for him to incriminate his poor, sick wife?

The coroner asked if anyone else wanted to testify. Jack stood up and asked to be sworn in, and once he was, he told the inquest about how he'd driven into town that night about 10:00 and didn't see Esau or notice whose cars were parked at the RRX. He also said he believed the Hemples must have been mistaken and that even if they had heard that many cars, it was likely that none of the drivers saw Esau, because the ice-fog would have hidden him from them, particularly if he were lying down in the snow.

"Thank you, Mr. Grant," the coroner said. I could tell he wasn't impressed. "Anyone else wish to testify?" he asked.

The room was perfectly quiet. None of the townspeople even so much as shifted in their seats. After a few minutes, I heard one of the reporters say, "Oh, my God," and I was mad at the disgust I heard in his voice, because he had no idea what was going on in that room. Esau was dead, there was nothing we could do about that. But we could spare each other and save our town: that was *all* we could do, and it was something *only* we could do. It did not concern any of the Outsiders. I was so proud of my Jack, for he was the one who had convinced everyone to stick together.

As it ended up, Bill took the blame, for the coroner wrote in his report that Bill should never have let Esau leave the tavern alone in his condition in that severe cold. One of the newspaper articles said there was some talk of charging Bill with criminal negligence, but that never happened.

It has been over a year since the death of Esau Isaac turned R.R. upside down. We've got ourselves back to normal, but there have been the changes you'd expect, and for some of us, definitely me, life is different here now. I don't call Jo Bouchard my best friend anymore. You see, I discovered that Jo had been keeping a lot from me, mainly that she had more going with Charlie Benjamin than bookkeeping.

The thing that caused Noel to leave, and who could blame him, was Jo telling him she'd been having an affair with Charlie. She was pregnant, in fact, during that whole mess. She has her baby now, and she says she has her pride back too: she says she's not ashamed she's Indian anymore. Well, who would have thought she ever was?

Jo and Charlie came in the other night after the big bonspiel. Since the tavern was extra busy, I was helping Jack serve. Jo was in her cups or had her nerve up for some other reason. She followed me to the bar and started telling me all this while I was pouring drinks, never thinking I might not want to hear it.

I didn't want to hear it because it seemed that when Jack took over the RRX and we moved up here, and Jo married Charlie and moved down there, we were forced into acting more like representatives of the two sides than pure people. So now there is that between us, a kind of fence in a place where no one even has a proper yard.

Rudy Wiebe

On Being Motionless

The Inuit understanding of visible phenomena is expressed by their language as two-dimensional: the very grammar of Inuktitut requires that you express all phenomena as either roughly equal in size — things are as broad as they are long, that is, *areal* — or as unequal — they are longer than they are broad, that is, *linear*. This understanding explains why it is really impossible for a living being to be ultimately lost on the vast expanses of the Arctic landscape, either tundra or ice.

Two corollaries expand this linguistic structural understanding and further explain what I mean: first, an areal thing changes dimension and becomes linear when it moves; second, any area without easily observable limits (a field of ice, the sea, an expanse of tundra) is automatically classified as long and narrow, that is, as linear also. In order to live, a human being must move; to live in the Arctic, a human being must, generally speaking, move quite a lot to acquire enough food.

Therefore, in order to live, he/she must become a linear dimension in a linear space. That means that another moving person (also linear) will certainly find them, because even in the largest space, their moving lines must at some point intersect, and the very rarity of those lines in the "empty" Arctic makes them all the more conspicuous.

All this changes radically, of course, when the human being's dimension changes back to areal, that is, the person becomes motionless. To locate a body may take very long: to find even a few of Franklin's 130 dead sailors took 13 years, and Andrée, the Swedish lighter-than-air balloonist, and his two assistants, who began their misconceived drift for the North Pole on July 11, 1897, were not found until July 9, 1930, and that by accident. A body may truly be lost forever, even if it quickly freezes and lasts for years. But on the so-called empty barrens of the Arctic, it is actually impossible for a living person to stay lost; or by the same token, it is impossible to hide.

Aklavik (an Inuktitut word which means the "place of the brown bear") is today a cluster of 750 people almost invisible in the enormous Mackenzie Delta. All Saints (Anglican) Church Cemetery there contains the grave of a man who tried to hide in the Arctic. Albert Johnson, as he is called, should have known better. He never saw Aklavik alive; he was brought there only to be buried, and since he had killed one policeman and almost killed two others, he was buried, on March 9, 1932, as far away from the tiny log church as possible, on the edge of church property in unhallowed ground, as they say. However, since 1932, the town has grown; the brown log church has become a museum, and a new prefab structure stands there bluer than the sky. The town is today so large that Main Street, with its two stores, hamlet offices and fire station, runs along the back of the cemetery. As a result, Albert Johnson's grave now borders on Main Street: the entrance to the cemetery is right there, beside two broken tree stumps, trees once planted on the grave itself and now dead, that stick like symbolic rotten columns out of the picket fence outlining his grave site. One stump has a large white A painted on it, the other an even larger J. Beside the grave stands a square sign with crudely painted scenes from Johnson's life. It bears the following legend:

THE MADTRAPPER
ALBERT JOHNSON
ARRIVED IN ROSS

RIVER AUG. 21, 1927
COMPLAINTS OF
LOCAL TRAPPERS
BROUGHT THE RCMP
ON HIM HE SHOT TWO
OFFICERS AND BE-
CAME A FUGITIVE OF
THE LAW WITH HOWL-
ING HUSKIES, DANGER-
OUS TRAILS, FROZEN
NIGHTS. THE POSSE
FINALLY CAUGHT UP
WITH HIM. HE WAS
KILLED UP THE
EAGLE RIVER
FEB. 17, 1932

The slender white crosses, the picket fences of the graves of the good Aklavik citizens crowd about, spreading to the distant corners of the large graveyard, but only this once ostracized "fugitive of the law," who according to the sign was apparently hunted for 4 ½ years, receives so much attention. Every tourist goes there to take a picture. Why are murderers so much remembered?

I will not tell this man's well-known story here; at the moment, I wish to use him as the most obvious example of a person in the North with a secret, and in contemplating Albert Johnson's secret, I believe some of the wider secrets of the Arctic landscape will become clearer. At least, I trust their outlines will.

In one of the most beautiful short stories ever written, "The Lady With the Pet Dog," Anton Chekhov has his protagonist recognize: "The personal life of every individual is based on secrecy, and perhaps it is for that reason that civilized people insist so strongly that personal privacy be respected."

Chekhov's protagonist, Gurov, is thinking of the double life he personally leads. Gurov recognizes that "he had two lives, an open one," which is the conventional public one that everyone knows, "and another life that went on in secret . . . that no living soul knew of . . . . Everything of importance . . . everything about which [he] . . . did not deceive himself" is in that second, secret life.

Now, despite a massive manhunt and 55 years of sporadic search by police and private persons, we still know nothing whatever of Albert Johnson's secret life. In fact, his public life is known for certain only from July 7, 1931, when he appears south of Aklavik in Fort McPherson, until he is killed "up the Eagle River" on February 17, 1932, and he becomes a motionless dot on the river ice. His most elementary secret, that of his name, still defies discovery. The legend (I use the word in both of its possible meanings) on the grave board on Aklavik's Main Street, which states that Johnson "arrived in Ross River Aug. 21, 1927," is fact only if we identify him with a man who in Ross River called himself Arthur Nelson. Ross River, Yukon Territory, is, as the raven flies, over 600 kilometres from Fort McPherson, Northwest Territories; it is almost twice that far by mountainous river, which is how Albert Johnson arrived there. Historian Dick North of Whitehorse has identified Johnson with Nelson, but Nelson's past, his story, seemed untraceable before Ross River. However, after 20 years of "obsession" (North himself uses that word) with Johnson/Nelson, the historian is at last positive he has found the man's real name and, with it, all that vast revelation of human activity and personality, of family and past and birth and place which a public name must expose, that immense factual story which every human being in the retrospect of memory has lived. Strange to say in this strange enough matter, North believes that the fugitive's name really was Johnson; only his given name was different. Instead of the relatively distinctive "Albert," North says it was, of all things, "John." John Johnson — surely one of the most ordinary, common names possible in North America.

This John Johnson was born in Norway and, from the age of 1, grew up in North Dakota; he was a convicted bank robber and horse thief by age 17 (1915) and spent several years in various United States prisons before apparently disappearing into Canada in 1923. After years of following every shred of evidence to build his case, all North lacked to make the last, indisputable identification between the two Johnsons was Albert's fingerprints. However, the prints taken from Albert Johnson after his death have disappeared from the Royal Canadian Mounted Police files.

How it has come about that one of the most famous police forces in the world has not kept the ultimate record of an unidentified criminal I will not try to explain here (that's a complicated story also). North writes, "This left only one recourse for me, and that was to dig up Albert's body . . . he was buried in permafrost, and consequently, his skin probably would be in good enough shape to 'lift' the prints." On April 27, 1987, the news went round the Yukon by radio and newspaper that the hamlet of Aklavik had given Dick North permission to exhume Johnson's body.

Oddly enough, on that Monday, April 27, I was in Old Crow, the most northerly settlement in the Yukon. That evening, I met some 20 Loucheux people of the Old Crow community who came to talk with me about my writing and particularly what I knew about Albert Johnson. We are talking quietly, slowly comparing bits of information, when the one man who has remained standing against the wall on my left suddenly asks, "Do you know who shot him first, that Albert Johnson?"

His tone is incredibly loud in the — until then — friendly room. Everyone is peering at me intently.

"I'm not sure," I say. "Do you?"

"Sure I know," he declares. "Anybody here knows that; it was Johnny Moses right from here, Old Crow; he was a special constable for the police, and he had permission to shoot; he was the best shot, and he fired and hit him first in the foot so he couldn't run to the bank and get away; he'd have got away, they'd of never got him, that's why he was stuck there in the middle of the Eagle River. It was Johnny Moses." And then the man is shouting, "What they say is all bullshit in all them books. Bullshit! When they got him there on the Eagle River, the police shot him so full of lead, they couldn't lift him into the plane; 10 men couldn't lift him, he was so full of lead."

Some of the people are smiling a little. The school principal, who is my host and apologizes later for not warning me about a possible outburst from this very man, looks most uncomfortable. What this Old Crow man says is obviously impossible, but it is not ridiculous. Once, years before in Victoria, British Columbia, when I read from *The Temptations of Big Bear* the scene of the police attack in 1885 on the Big Bear's sleeping camp at Loon Lake Crossing, a Cree Indian asked me after the reading whether I knew that the North West Mounted Police had killed over 300 of his people there and buried them so their bodies could never be found. I knew that if such had been the case, the entire band would have had to be annihilated; as it was, I knew of only two men actually shot and killed there, while an old woman on the retreat hanged herself in terror. But it seemed to me then, and it seems to me also in Old Crow, that the story I am hearing is far from ridiculous. Something beyond mere facts is being told, a truth only words, not facts, can create. But before I have to say anything, the man continues even louder:

"It was Christmas, Jesus Christ Christmas, when the goddamn police bang on his door, so why didn't they bring him a turkey and 'Merry Christmas' and leave him alone? Eh?"

My mind is stumbling, but I try to turn his rage a little: "Well, even if the police come banging on your house at Christmas and disturb you, you're *still* not supposed to shoot them through your door."

Some of the people chuckle with me, but for a few more moments, he rants almost wildly. I am stunned; I cannot quite believe what is happening.

But it is certainly in keeping with the whole extraordinarily beautiful day. It began by flying from Dawson City, the brilliant spring sun on the snow of the Ogilvie Mountains, the sinuous bends of the Porcupine River and the tiny village set against the airstrip at the foot of Old Crow Mountain, its green spruce and streets packed in the solid snow of all-Skidoo traffic. That afternoon, I had given a long reading and told stories at the school, and then I was taken back to the airport, where the band had arranged that its plane fly me to the Richardson Mountains and the Eagle River. "We're gonna show you where Albert Johnson got shot," the pilot told me. I had never been there. With us came two Old Crow high school students who had read my novel *The Mad Trapper* and two band elders. One of them, the venerable old woman seated beside me in the Cessna, introduced herself as the sister of Johnny Moses, the RCMP special constable who had been at that shoot-out 55 years before, though she did not then tell me her brother had shot Albert Johnson first. So we flew east over the widely scattered, still deserted summer fish camps and hunting camps in the snow at the caribou crossings, along the frozen river, farther east until the Richardson Mountains appeared, abruptly, like enormous unglaciated pyramids folded irregularly into each other, like a random scattering of scrawled, conical shapes, and all so deadly white with their creeks outlined by black spruce. Clouds covered the Barrier River Pass, which Johnson crossed in an impossible blizzard after killing Constable Edgar Millen, so we could not fly there but over the twisting loops of the Bell River, the deserted roofless walls of the three buildings of La Pierre House, the beautiful circular sweep of the Bell west around a mountain to join the Porcupine and there, just like a map, the Eagle

River entering the broader Bell from the south.

We eased lower, the air as calm and solid as a rock. We saw a moose feeding among willows, and the pilot laughed, "Oh, what the hell," and went down to 150 feet, and I saw tracks, mink and marten trails looping out from the riverbanks, even the tiny spoor of weasel, everything so icy sharp in the incredible air, I had no need to breathe, only look. And then the plane made a wide turn, and I saw what I had imagined, tried again and again to imagine years before: I saw the tight reversed-S turn of the narrow river outlined by the straggling black spruce, the tight reversed S where Johnson, deceived at last by the twists of the river, ran backwards in his tracks because he thought the posse was already ahead of him and, rounding the tight bend of that betrayal, suddenly met the dogs, the men, the rifles racing after him head-on.

It was so exactly as I had imagined it, in the plane I knew I was dreaming. It seemed I saw through that window, past the strut and the motionless wheel, under the shadow of that wing, the actualization of what I had dreamt 16 years before and then dreamt over and over again, tried to snare in the words of a short story, of a film script, of an essay, of a novel. There, on exactly such ice, between those precise tiny bristled trees, 55 years ago. Although, of course, the river under that ice could not be the same. But perhaps it was. Precisely every particle how many diurnal cycles later?

The man in the community centre at Old Crow, standing in the steady 10:30 p.m. daylight of April 27, has stopped shouting. He is talking quietly now but with very great intensity.

"Men go crazy, you know," he says. "I've seen men, anybody here has seen men go really crazy. You can't help that, and you should just get out of the way, leave them alone, they'll be okay, just leave them alone. Why do you have to bother a man when he goes really crazy, eh?"

Such words do not seem to expect words in reply. After a while, I ask them all, "What do you think, should they dig him up now to get his fingerprints?"

Nobody says anything. "They'd probably find out for sure who he was then," I say.

A woman at the back says, "They should leave him alone."

Next morning, a Skidoo stops beside me as I walk down the street; it is driven by a lean, handsome man about my age in a wolverine-trim parka. We met at the hall the night before, and now, in the sunlight, he wears dark glasses so I can't see his eyes.

"I was gonna say something," he says, "but then that guy got going . . ." He shrugs.

"Oh, yeah," I say. "We talked after. He told me his father was a Danish whaler who came to Herschel Island on a whaling ship, so I asked him where were his blue eyes and blond hair."

But the Skidoo driver refuses to laugh. He says instead, "Johnny Moses was my uncle. My mom lives over there. She was with you on the plane."

"Did your uncle ever talk about that manhunt?"

"Not to me."

"How come?"

He says thoughtfully, "I guess he didn't want to. He talked to my mom a lot, I know, but that's all."

"Would she talk to me about that?"

"I don't know." He is silent for a time but makes no move to go. The morning sun is almost stunning on the snow. "Once, a few years before he died, he was working with a construction crew near the Eagle River. They got close to that place on the river, and one of the workers made a joke about it, said something like, 'Hey, Johnnie, isn't this the famous place you shot Albert Johnson?' and he just put down his tools and walked away from there. Just disappeared. The foreman got worried and radioed my mom, and I went out to look for him. It took me two weeks. He was camped in the bush way up the Porcupine, just his rifle and knife. Not even a tent. He knew how to live in the bush like that."

"He came back with you?"

"Yeah. I stayed with him a few days, and then we came back."

I don't know how I can ask what I want so badly to ask, and finally, I say something unnecessary, totally obvious. "He wasn't working for the police anymore?"

"No. He never did after that," and it is clear from his tone what "that" is. "There was something about that Johnson . . . something strange."

That was the same word a Hareskin man from Fort Good Hope used to describe the Mackenzie River. He said it twice, very thoughtfully, remembering, perhaps, his lifetime beside its heavy brown darkness and all the people that had vanished into it: "The river is strange . . . strange. It will roll a body along the bottom for six days before it lifts it up so you can see it, 40 miles away." That had happened to his best friend, who, with his girlfriend, disappeared late one spring night following him in a riverboat headed for Fort Good Hope. In the morning, they found the boat, its kicker still idling slowly, turning circles on the river, and the girl asleep huddled in the bow, still unaware that she was alone. "His body was way past Good Hope; six days later, it come up. We only recognized him from the bits of clothes left on him. Sometimes, they won't come up at all if the water's too cold. Maybe in the spring, somewhere. But then you don't know them anyway."

The novel *But We Are Exiles* by Robert Kroetsch, the best novel yet written set on the Mackenzie River, opens with just such a scene. Peter Guy, pilot on the riverboat *Nahanni Jane*, is in a canoe dragging the opaque depths of the Mackenzie with grappling hooks:

. . . The line in Peter's hands came taut just then; a chill shuddered up into his arms and aching neck. He heard himself yell, and the skipper . . . cut off the outboard motor with a turn of a thick wrist; the canoe began to swing downstream, bow first, anchored by the quarter-inch line in Peter's hands. "Pull him in!" the skipper shouted in the sudden silence, the motor popping and then dead.

Peter gave a jerk, another, to set the hooks, his stomach going queasy, and now the grappling hooks and line and whatever it was they had snagged began to come up, heavy, still too far down to be seen in the sun-filtering green and then dark of the water; the line curled, dripping around his high-topped boots as if to entangle him; the wet, cold line stiffened his fingers.

And bent over, he could feel the stillness strike the back of his bare head, half knocking life into him, half knocking it out. His breath came in lumps. He glanced up at the breath-tripping hush; at the broad river, mirror-smooth in the afternoon sun; at the old riverboat where she lay tied up beside her two black steel barges. No one had seen the canoe stop. The lifting bow bobbed gently. He looked down again at the water and this time saw his own face watching him; the prematurely balding blond head, the full lips and squinting deep-set eyes suggesting a moodiness that didn't belong with his tall and hard body. He studied the reflection as if not sure whom he might see.

The image mimicked his hesitation, mocked his doubt by repeating it. The deep-set eyes worried against the slant of light. The mouth, pursed and offering a kiss, in its subtle retreat, threatened now to open and drown. Peter shook his head to be sure it was himself he saw. A drop of water from the rising line scarred the face, exploding its frail composure.

The grappling hooks swam into view. They did not bring up from the darkness Michael Hornyak, burned and dead and already a little soggy. "Goddamnit," the skipper said. . . .

You look into the moving, dark, strange Mackenzie River, and you will see nothing but yourself; though you will not appear the same as you always imagine yourself. You follow a moving, dark, strange man in linear (like the river) pursuit for six weeks along Arctic mountains and rivers and an endless recrossing of tracks, and what else can you expect to see?

Some of the men who took part in that Albert Johnson pursuit cannot bear ever to talk about it; some can talk a little, but none of them will *do* it again; they refuse to repeat that story. There were three Loucheux Indians in that posse on the Eagle River on February 17, 1932: Johnny Moses, Peter Alexis and Lazarus Sittichinli. Only Sittichinli is still alive; in fact, in 1987, he is the last man left of the entire hunt. The last white man, airplane mechanic Jack Owen, died in St. Albert outside Edmonton in 1985; he was flying Wop May's Bellanca, circling over the Eagle River while the great pilot himself was taking pictures of the shoot-out like a regular tourist.

Lazarus Sittichinli lives with his wife in a small red house in Aklavik, two blocks from Albert Johnson's grave and across the street from the Anglican hospital and the Anglican church. He opens the door to me whom he has never seen or heard of: a tiny, dark, shrunken man, a few hairs bristle on his face, oddly powerful hands still with heavy, hornlike nails. He walks to the kitchen table supporting himself on a four-point walker; he gestures for me to sit down. He is 97 years old, and he says it was he who lifted Johnson up out of the hole he had dug in the snow on the Eagle River and turned him over so they could look at him. Peter Alexis and Karl Gardlund, who had been shooting from the same side of the river as Sittichinli, had advanced with him. Behind them came trader Frank Jackson and the police inspector.

"You know this man?" the inspector asked.

Alexis said, "I never know him."

In the warm house, Mrs. Sittichinli sits dozing in a soft chair while the old man tells me that whole story again. Without prompting, as easily as if it had happened yesterday and acting out all the parts, changing voices, his brown hands shape the story in air, and I know it so well,

I see and hear only the details that no one else can ever give me, the particularities which will disappear when this amazing Lazarus dies a year later: "Johnson, he had a bullet cut all across his belly. He had no grub, he was eating spruce gum and whisky-jack. He had a string with a rag tied on it in the barrel of his .30-.30 to keep out the snow so it wouldn't clog up and explode, and he would jerk the string out and clean the barrel and shoot like that just about all the same motion. He was down there behind his big pack, and I got down and lifted him up and turned him over. He didn't weigh nothing for a man, not as much as a big dog."

I mostly watch Lazarus' high-boned face move, shift in his slightly offbeat English; or his ancient wife, a soft mound breathing, her moose-hide moccasins crisscrossed by thongs under her long cotton dress. They have been married for 76 years, and 12 of their 14 children have already died. But there are plenty of grandchildren and great- and great-great-grandchildren around; one of them comes in to start supper. "My one son, he marry a Husky," he laughs, and it takes me a moment to realize he means "Inuit," or "Inuvialuit," as the Mackenzie Inuit call themselves. Aklavik was the place of meeting between the Loucheux (or Kutchin) Indians and the Inuvialuit — they were always nervous, suspicious of each other, they were traditional enemies — and I ask him, "Do you Indians hunt beluga whales now?" But he says no, they never did. He never liked muktuk (whale blubber), he liked hunting caribou at the river crossings and sheep, lots of Dall's sheep in the mountains. "I'm always lucky hunting," he says. "All the men from town here always follow me hunting in the Richardson Mountains, sheep. All my life, we live on hunting and trapping, we always live in the bush. Living like that."

"Could you do it, working as special constable for the police and live in the bush?"

"I never did after that," he says. "I quit, then."

So then I can ask him why. He is tired now and clearing his throat of phlegm, his toothless jaws moving sometimes as if he were eating Loucheux words that my Canadian ear could not understand anyway, though I should be able to see them in his hands and eyes. The story is long, but he wants to tell it long, how he drove his dog team back then from the Eagle River through fog over the mountains after four days, and the inspector, whom May had flown in with the badly wounded Hersey and Johnson's body, told him to take a holiday after so much hard work on the two-month patrol. He was earning only $75 a month. But next morning, the inspector (Lazarus never calls him Eames or Alex; he names him only by function) was at his door as usual, telling him to haul in four tall trees for flagpoles. Several other things happened then, but now Lazarus shifts erect at the table, his black eyes suddenly fierce, bright. "I was mad," he says. "I tell him I'm not working no more. I quit now; you break your word, I break my word. I go home. A little later, the inspector, he come to my house. 'Why you quit?' 'You're asking too much.' 'No, no, you stay with us.' 'No.' 'Well, be the town police then.' 'No,' I say, 'I won't police my own people, that's no good.' So I go home, and I stay quit."

Like every storyteller in the North, he has acted all the parts as he speaks them, his voice changing to suit authority or obedience or anger. But at times, there was something else in his tone; something like the man in Old Crow remembering his uncle Johnny Moses who had followed the twisting, spiralling river of Johnson's self-mocking flight almost as far as Lazarus Sittichinli and who had been there when Lazarus lifted that frost-mutilated, starved body out of the snow. "I said I have a good place on the Husky River," this ancient man tells me in his strange, abstracted tone. "Good trapping. And I work sometimes in the hospital. But not the police."

William Nerysoo speaks the same way. He is 94 years old, living alone in a one-room house surrounded by Fort McPherson. He took no part in the six-week hunt; he was the man who originally reported to the police that he believed Johnson was disturbing his traps, and that report started it all. When I visit him in 1983, the first thing he says to me is, "I won't tell you anything about that. Everybody comes here and asks me. I go to the store, and the little boys yell after me, 'Hey, Mad Trapper! Mad Trapper!' I don't tell you anything." "Okay," I say. "Okay." What else can I say? His neighbour William Snowshoe comes into the little house then. We talk about the caribou of the Porcupine River herd moving north beyond the Richardson Mountains to their spring calving grounds, and suddenly, Nerysoo says, "Maybe I'll tell you one thing." So he does that, and then we talk about the caribou some more, and suddenly, he says again, "Maybe I'll tell you one thing." After an afternoon, he has told me his whole story, and though I will not repeat it, his tone and his rectangular, gaunt face and his gentle, insistent return to that trapline are telling me more than his words about that trap and the fatal report he once made because it was his place and his living. What is it about these strong, fierce-eyed old men? They are, in Chekhovian terms, "insisting so strongly on preserving someone's personal secret." It seems they are, for that insistence, the most civilized of people. I asked Lazarus Sittichinli about digging up that famous grave down his street.

"I don't like that," he says. "There are people who do all kinds of things to themselves—if you want some fingerprints, take theirs. But no digging. Johnson, he had enough suffering. Leave him alone."

Alone with his locked, his unlockable secret. His told and untold, his trackable and untrackable story. The long river of his flight is as obvious and as opaque as the Peel on which he first appeared, the gigantic Mackenzie whose opaqueness it somewhere, indecipherably, enters. Or as Peter Guy would have it in *But We Are Exiles*, the Mackenzie riverboat pilot with "1,100 miles of river in his head," on that river, "a man is defined free from the terrors of human relationship . . . an order maintained as precariously as that maintained by the hands on the wheel. The chaos held in check . . . ." In check, perhaps; but it, of course, remains there, lurking.

These Indian men remember their roles in the hunt for that man who defended his aloneness with such single-minded and truly horrifying intensity, with no joy, with no recalled heroism. At the same time, they are themselves the furthest thing from being loners. White people like Albert Johnson or Peter Guy appearing from somewhere in southern Canada may be that—leave them alone—but a Loucheux or Inuit loner seems merely incredible. It is a contradiction by very concept. All Indians and Inuit have extended families that stretch far beyond children in all possible directions of cousins and nieces and parents and multiple adoptions and in-laws. No native of the Arctic seems to live as a solitary; everyone lives in a community, and in any one community, everyone, except for the few resident whites, is related to everyone else. Further, when any community has an occasion or festival, all those extended relations from all the other communities within a day's flying will arrive by chartered plane to help in the celebration. When they do that, they tell each other their continuing stories even as they live any number of new ones: stories here are a construct of actions and spoken words by means of which humanity remembers.

And this oral storytelling, so refined and perfected by millennia of practice, is the very affirmation of their nonaloneness: the storyteller and the poet/singer presuppose a community of listeners, otherwise nothing can be told. One may read a book alone (in fact, most of us prefer that), but one cannot tell a story alone, which is why any language changes so drastically when it moves from oral to written form. Now, the most minimal and therefore most powerful word, spoken or written, about any human being is *name*, and anyone who can hide that goes beyond secret into enigma, that is, into intentional and impenetrable obscurity. There is, then, no story to tell, and the original people of the Canadian Arctic, living in tiny communities on the immense polar landscape, find such a refusal of story especially strange, disturbing, puzzling as only an oral, communal people can. But they respect it. Leave him alone. The story is there, but there is no story to tell. Or as William Nerysoo tells me, under most conditions, I won't tell you the part of the story I know. Yet he is too much a person of his people and his landscape ultimately to refuse it; all I have to do is be there and wait long enough.

When I visit William Nerysoo again four years later, I do not talk to him about Johnson at all, and that very fact helps me comprehend a further dimension of the landscape of story in his life. Because Nerysoo *is* a great storyteller; he tells me a collection of his stories translated into English is with an editor, and they will, hopefully soon, be well and properly published. From behind the curtain of his bedroom, he brings out the manuscript and lets me glance through it. There are many brief stories: one called "Rat and Beaver — Changing Tails" begins, "This story started over a hundred years ago when beaver was a man. Families of beaver . . . ." Now, somewhere before 1800, David Thompheard and recorded the ancient Cree stories of the beaver's being an ancient people that lived on dry land, though the Cree remembered them as being always beaver, not humans, so of course I want to read this Loucheux story. The old man laughs aloud:

"How much will you pay me, to read it?"

"How much do you want?" I ask.

"Two thousand dollars!"

Then we both laugh and talk of other things. It is exactly the same experience the Danish explorer Knud Rasmussen had in 1921, when he asked a Netsilik Inuit shaman to sing him his song so he could record it; the shaman wanted a rifle in exchange, or he would not sing it.

Songs, stories are beyond value; they are the memory and wisdom of a people, the particular individual rivers of the sea of life that constitutes us all. And when you hide that, when you insist the river of your life is as opaque as the Mackenzie or Peel, you are defying the ancient assertion of that sea; you still do have a story (you cannot *not* have a story, because you had a mother, you had a place and time when you were born, you have moved because you are alive), but if you persist so absolutely with silence, motionless silence even unto death, then we will respect your refusal of your own story. We will leave you alone. Though we will continue to tell what little we do know, because that is the only way human life continues.

Death continues to hide Albert Johnson. Experts disagree about whether the permafrost at Aklavik is strong enough to preserve his body so well that fingerprints could still be taken. "Hell," one Aklavik resident tells me, "I've lived here for 12 years, and I've seen the Mackenzie flood the graveyard so bad, there were bones floating around. There's nothing left of him." A moving graveyard? The river aiding and abetting a secret again? Besides, the territorial governor explained to me, in 1932-33, three suicides had been buried around Johnson, and now, even if the bodies were well preserved, no one would know exactly which body was whose. Ironically, the iconoclast Johnson, who in life refused to live near anyone, in death is protected by what he would have considered a crowd. In any case, soon after the April 27 announcement, a petition against the disinterment was signed by more people than actually live in Aklavik. It seems that historian Dick North, with his implacable white man's obsession to know, is not going to get his clinching evidence. Johnson remains an enigmatic secret. Perhaps 55 years is enough to leave him there; to leave him motionless and *alone*.

Permissions

Matt Cohen, "Country Music," from *Columbus and the Fat Lady*, Anansi, 1972. Reprinted by arrangement with Bella Pomer Agency Inc.

Maurice Henrie, excerpts from *La chambre à mourir*, L'Instant Même, 1988

Wayne Grady, "Tobacco Road," from *Saturday Night*, July 1982

Wallace Stegner, "The Question Mark in the Circle," from *Wolf Willow* by Wallace Stegner, first published by Viking Press. Copyright ©1961 by Wallace Stegner. Copyright renewed ©1990 by Wallace Stegner. Reprinted by permission of Brandt & Brandt Literary Agents, Inc.

Don Gayton, "Deeper Into Prairie," from *The Wheatgrass Mechanism: Science and Imagination in the Western Canadian Landscape* by Don Gayton, 1990. Published by Fifth House Publishers

George Galt, "The Wheat Farm," from *Whistlestop*, published by Random House of Canada, 1990

Heather Robertson, "Miami," from *Grass Roots*, James Lorimer and Co., 1973

Edward Hoagland, "The Old Men of Telegraph Creek: The McPhees and Others," excerpt from *Notes From the Century Before*, copyright ©1969 by Edward Hoagland. Published by North Point Press and reprinted by permission

Edith Iglauer, excerpt from *Fishing with John*, reprinted by permission of Sterling Lord Literistic, Inc. Copyright ©1988 by Edith Iglauer

Robin Skelton, "Cat Creek," from *Telling the Tale*, Porcupine's Quill, 1987

Mary Burns, "Suburbs of the Arctic Circle," from *Suburbs of the Arctic Circle*, Penumbra Press, 1986

Rudy Wiebe, "On Being Motionless," from *Playing Dead*, NeWest Publishers Ltd., 1989